RETHINKING THE
HISTORY OF WALES

MEDIEVAL
WALES
c.1050–1332

RETHINKING THE HISTORY OF WALES SERIES

Series Editors:
Professor Paul O'Leary, Aberystwyth University
and Professor Huw Pryce, Bangor University

This series aims to stimulate fresh thinking about the history of Wales by introducing particular periods and themes in ways that challenge established interpretations. Whether by offering new perspectives on familiar landmarks in the historiographical landscape or by venturing into previously uncharted terrain, the volumes, each written by a specialist in the field, will provide concise and selective surveys that highlight areas of debate rather than attempting to achieve comprehensive coverage. The series will thus encourage an engagement with diverse understandings of the Welsh past and with its continuing – and sometimes contested – significance in the present day.

RETHINKING THE
HISTORY OF WALES

MEDIEVAL WALES
*c.*1050–1332

CENTURIES OF AMBIGUITY

David Stephenson

UNIVERSITY OF WALES PRESS
2019

www.uwp.co.uk

British Library Cataloguing-in-Publication Data
A catalogue record for this book is available from the British Library.

ISBN   978-1-78683-386-0
eISBN   978-1-78683-387-7

MIX
Paper from
responsible sources
FSC® C013604

Typeset by Marie Doherty
Printed by CPI Antony Rowe, Melksham, UK.

For Jan

TABLE OF CONTENTS

ACKNOWLEDGEMENTS

I should like to thank Huw Pryce both for the invitation to write this book, and also for the time and effort which he put in to comment, with typical perceptiveness, on a draft of it. I owe a great debt of gratitude to fellow historians of medieval Wales, past and present, for the stimulus which their works have provided. The extent of that debt will be apparent throughout this book. Conversations with Hugh Brodie, whose work promises to shed much light on this period, have proved consistently stimulating and enlightening. I am particularly grateful to Emma Cavell for allowing me to read important papers prior to their publication, and for her careful scrutiny of, and illuminating comments on, a draft of the book. Cath D'Alton has drawn the maps with her customary skill and forbearance. I am grateful to Llion Wigley and all his colleagues at the University of Wales Press for their guidance and support. Particular thanks are due to Elin Nesta Lewis for her careful and very helpful copy-editing. In the course of the volume's preparation I have received notable help from Bethan Phillips and Dafydd Jones. The biennial Bangor Colloquia on medieval Wales and the meetings of the Welsh Chronicles Research Group have been important sources of ideas. Not for the first time I want to thank the members of the medieval history groups at Llanidloes, Newtown and Berriew. They have heard much of this book. Their good humour and their comments are invaluable. The Powysland Club remains a great source of learned companionship and of resources, not least in its splendid library. As always, my greatest thanks are due to my wife Jan, who has contributed to this book in so many ways: she has borne with remarkable tolerance my frequent disappearances into the medieval centuries and has offered crucial support when it has been most needed.

ABBREVIATIONS

AC	John Williams ab Ithel (ed.), *Annales Cambriae* (London: Rolls Series, 1860). Note that all references in this source should be checked against Henry Gough-Cooper's online edition, for which see the select bibliography
AWR	Huw Pryce (ed.), *The Acts of Welsh Rulers, 1120–1283* (Cardiff: University of Wales Press, 2005)
BBCS	*Bulletin of the Board of Celtic Studies*
Bartrum, *Welsh Genealogies*	P. C. Bartrum (ed.), *Welsh Genealogies AD 300–1400*, 8 vols (Cardiff: University of Wales Press, 1974)
ByT Pen. 20 Trans.	Thomas Jones (ed. and trans.), *Brut y Tywysogyon, Peniarth MS 20 Version* (Cardiff: University of Wales Press, 1952)
ByT, RBH	Thomas Jones (ed. and trans.), *Brut y Tywysogyon, Red Book of Hergest Version* (Cardiff: University of Wales Press, 1955)
CACW	J. G. Edwards (ed.), *Calendar of Ancient Correspondence Concerning Wales* (Cardiff: University of Wales Press, 1935).
CAP	William Rees (ed.), *Calendar of Ancient Petitions Relating to Wales* (Cardiff: University of Wales Press, 1976).
CChR	*Calendar of Charter Rolls, 1226–1516*, 6 vols (London: HMSO, 1903–27)
CCR	*Calendar of Close Rolls, 1272–1500*, 46 vols (London: HMSO, 1900–55)
Close Rolls	*Close Rolls, 1227–1272*, 4 vols (London: HMSO, 1902–38)

CPR	*Calendar of Patent Rolls, 1232–1509*, 53 vols (London: HMSO, 1891–1916)
Davies, *Age of Conquest*	R. R. Davies, *The Age of Conquest: Wales 1063–1415* (Oxford: Oxford University Press, 2000) [Originally published as *Conquest Coexistence and Change; Wales 1063–1415* (Oxford: Oxford University Press 1987)]
Davies, *Lordship and Society*	R. R. Davies, *Lordship and Society in the March of Wales, 1282–1400* (Oxford: Oxford University Press, 1978)
GBF	Rhian M. Andrews et al. (eds), *Gwaith Bleddyn Fardd a Beirdd Eraill Ail Hanner y Drydedd Ganrif ar Ddeg* (Cardiff: University of Wales Press, 1996)
GDB	N. G. Costigan et al. (eds), *Gwaith Dafydd Benfras Fardd ac Eraill o Feirdd Hanner Cyntaf y Drydedd Ganrif ar Ddeg* (Cardiff: University of Wales Press, 1995)
GLlF	K. A. Bramley et al. (eds), *Gwaith Llywelyn Fardd I ac Eraill o Feirdd y Ddeuddegfed Ganrif* (Cardiff: University of Wales Press, 1994)
GLlLl	Elin M. Jones (ed.), *Gwaith Llywarch ap Llywelyn 'Prydydd y Moch'* (Cardiff: University of Wales Press, 1991)
GMB	J. E. Caerwyn Williams et al. (eds), *Gwaith Meilir Brydydd a'i Ddisgynyddion* (Cardiff: University of Wales Press, 1994)
Littere Wallie	J. G. Edwards (ed.), *Littere Wallie* (Cardiff: University of Wales Press, 1940)
Lloyd, *A History*	J. E. Lloyd, *A History of Wales from the Earliest Times to the Edwardian Conquest*, 2 vols with continuous pagination (3rd edn; London: Longman: 1939)
LTMW	Dafydd Jenkins (ed.), *The Law of Hywel Dda: Law Texts from Medieval Wales* (Llandysul: Gomer Press, 1986)

Patent Rolls	*Patent Rolls, 1216–32*, 2 vols (London: HMSO, 1901–3)
Smith, *Llywelyn ap Gruffudd*	J. Beverley Smith, *Llywelyn ap Gruffudd, Prince of Wales* (2nd edn; Cardiff: University of Wales Press, 2014)
Stephenson, 'Empires in Wales'	David Stephenson, 'Empires in Wales: from Gruffudd ap Llywelyn to Llywelyn ap Gruffudd', *Welsh History Review*, 28, 1 (2016), 26–54
Stephenson, *Medieval Powys*	David Stephenson, *Medieval Powys: Kingdom, Principality and Lordships, 1132–1293* (Woodbridge: Boydell Press, 2016)
Stephenson, *Political Power*	David Stephenson, *Political Power in Medieval Gwynedd: Governance and the Welsh Princes* (Cardiff: University of Wales Press, 2014)
WAR	James Conway Davies (ed.), *The Welsh Assize Roll, 1277–84* (Cardiff: University of Wales Press, 1940)
WHR	*The Welsh History Review*
WKC	T. M. Charles-Edwards, Morfydd E. Owen and Paul Russell (eds), *The Welsh King and his Court* (Cardiff: University of Wales Press, 2000)

MAPS

MAP 1: *Uplands and principal rivers*

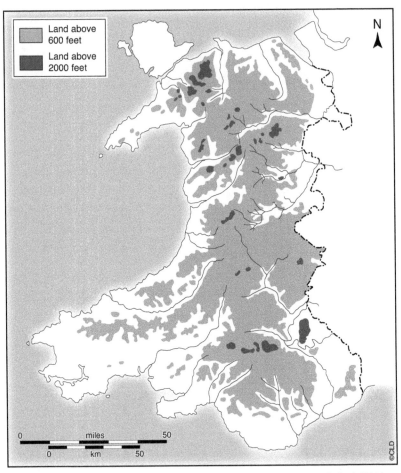

© Cath D'Alton

MAP 2: *Principal medieval political divisions: realms and lordships*

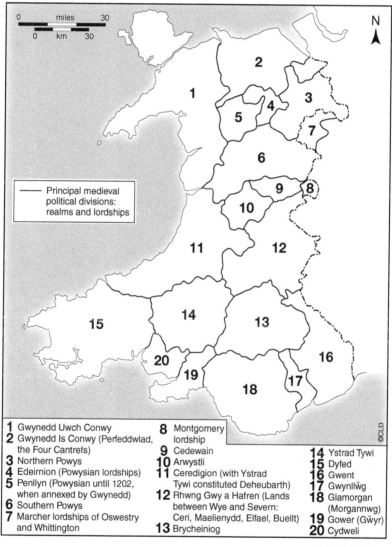

1 Gwynedd Uwch Conwy
2 Gwynedd Is Conwy (Perfeddwlad, the Four Cantrefs)
3 Northern Powys
4 Edeirnion (Powysian lordships)
5 Penllyn (Powysian until 1202, when annexed by Gwynedd)
6 Southern Powys
7 Marcher lordships of Oswestry and Whittington
8 Montgomery lordship
9 Cedewain
10 Arwystli
11 Ceredigion (with Ystrad Tywi constituted Deheubarth)
12 Rhwng Gwy a Hafren (Lands between Wye and Severn: Ceri, Maelienydd, Elfael, Buellt)
13 Brycheiniog
14 Ystrad Tywi
15 Dyfed
16 Gwent
17 Gwynllŵg
18 Glamorgan (Morgannwg)
19 Gower (Gŵyr)
20 Cydweli

© Cath D'Alton

MAP 3: *Cistercian lands in Welsh polities*

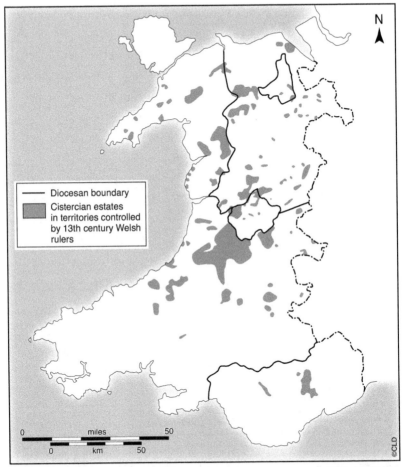

© Cath D'Alton

MAP 4: *The regional ascendancy of Cadwallon ap Madog in the lands between Wye and Severn, 1175–9*

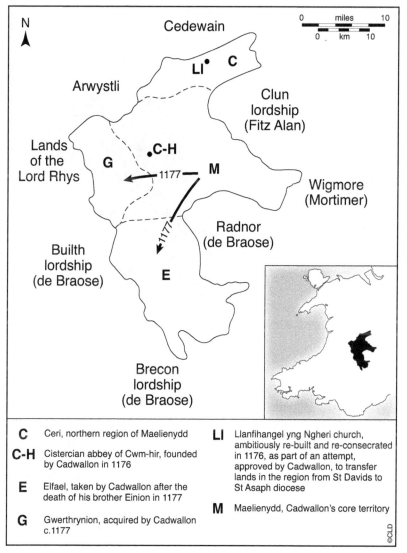

C	Ceri, northern region of Maelienydd	**Ll**	Llanfihangel yng Ngheri church, ambitiously re-built and re-consecrated in 1176, as part of an attempt, approved by Cadwallon, to transfer lands in the region from St Davids to St Asaph diocese
C-H	Cistercian abbey of Cwm-hir, founded by Cadwallon in 1176		
E	Elfael, taken by Cadwallon after the death of his brother Einion in 1177		
		M	Maelienydd, Cadwallon's core territory
G	Gwerthrynion, acquired by Cadwallon c.1177		

© Cath D'Alton

MAP 5: *The principality of Wales at the time of the Treaty of Montgomery, 1267*

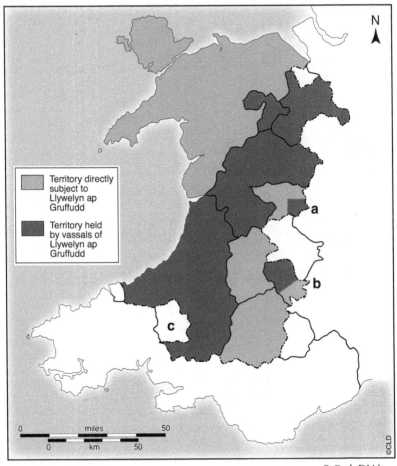

N

Territory directly subject to Llywelyn ap Gruffudd

Territory held by vassals of Llywelyn ap Gruffudd

a

b

c

0　　miles　　50

0　　km　　50

©CLD

© Cath D'Alton

MAP 6: *Edward I's Wales*

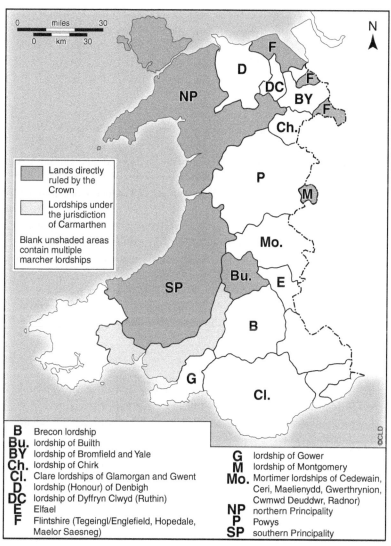

B	Brecon lordship	**G**	lordship of Gower
Bu.	lordship of Builth	**M**	lordship of Montgomery
BY	lordship of Bromfield and Yale	**Mo.**	Mortimer lordships of Cedewain,
Ch.	lordship of Chirk		Ceri, Maelienydd, Gwerthrynion,
Cl.	Clare lordships of Glamorgan and Gwent		Cwmwd Deuddwr, Radnor)
D	lordship (Honour) of Denbigh	**NP**	northern Principality
DC	lordship of Dyffryn Clwyd (Ruthin)	**P**	Powys
E	Elfael	**SP**	southern Principality
F	Flintshire (Tegeingl/Englefield, Hopedale,		
	Maelor Saesneg)		

© Cath D'Alton

NOTES TO MAPS

Map 1

The predominantly upland nature of most of Wales, and the landscape marked by alternation between high ground and often deeply incised river valleys are at once clear. These phenomena were sometimes obstacles to communication and political control, and helped to promote distinct regional and even local identities and loyalties.

Map 3

Only the Cistercian lands which lay within territories subject to Welsh rulers for significant periods in the thirteenth century are shown here. The extent of the Cistercian territories, generally subject to wide immunities from exaction and service, is impressive. Areas devoid of Cistercian holdings sometimes suggest the continuing power and influence of traditional *monasteria*.

For a map of all Cistercian lands in Wales see David H. Williams, *An Atlas of Cistercian Lands in Wales* (Cardiff: University of Wales Press, 1990), p. 91; for the large number of non-Cistercian religious houses in Wales see Janet Burton and Karen Stöber (eds), *Abbeys and Priories of Medieval Wales* (Cardiff: University of Wales Press, 2015), map 1 (Benedictines and Cluniacs), map 2 (the solitary Premonstratensian house at Talley, as well as Cistercian houses), map 3 (Regular Canons and Knights Hospitaller).

Map 5

a. Ceri, in the southern part of the shaded area, was divided between lands held directly by Llywelyn ap Gruffudd, and those held by members of the local native dynasty: see D. Stephenson, 'The lordship of Ceri in the thirteenth century', *Mont. Colls.*, 95 (2007), 23–31, at 26.

b. The lordship of Elfael Is Mynydd (southern Elfael) was held directly by Llywelyn ap Gruffudd, while Elfael Uwch Mynydd (northern Elfael) was held by members of the local native dynasty. Elfael was not explicitly included in the lands of the principality in the Treaty of Montgomery, but it was in Llywelyn's hands.

c. The lordship of Maredudd ap Rhys, excluded from the principality in 1267, but acquired by Llywelyn in 1270.

GENEALOGICAL TABLES

TABLE 1: *The Dynasty of Deheubarth*

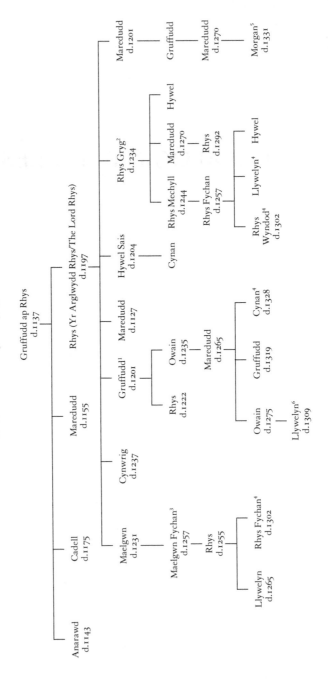

TABLE 2: *The dynasty of Gwynedd*

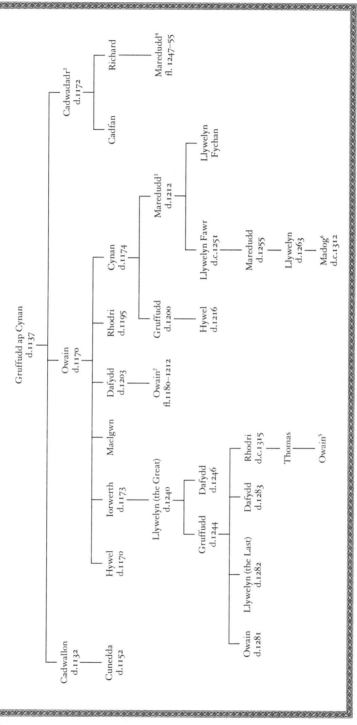

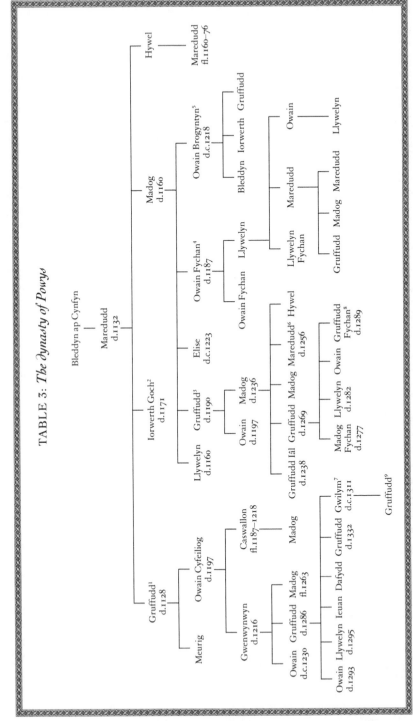

TABLE 3: *The Dynasty of Powys*

TABLE 4: *The family of Ednyfed Fychan*

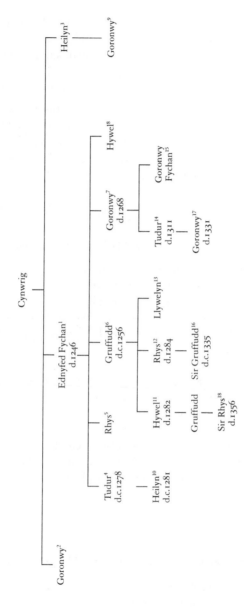

NOTES TO GENEALOGICAL TABLES

Tables 1–3 are simplified depictions of the ramifications of the three major royal houses of the twelfth and thirteenth centuries, and are included principally to help to identify members of princely or lordly dynasties discussed in the text. Tables 1 and 3 illustrate the tendency to fragmentation which characterized many Welsh polities, table 4 presents a selective genealogy of the family of Ednyfed Fychan, whose careers symbolize the rise of the administrative elite in both *pura Wallia* and the March in the thirteenth and fourteenth centuries. The family also illustrates the capacity of elite families to adapt to, and to contribute to, political change.

Table 1

A succinct account of the dynasty of Deheubarth is given in *AWR*, pp. 7–14.

1. Progenitor of lords of part of Ceredigion.
2. Progenitor of the dynasty of Ystrad Tywi.
3. Progenitor of lords of part of Ceredigion.
4. Lords who survived the war of 1282–3, but were taken as prisoners, and experienced periods of captivity, and in some cases periods of employment in royal armies beyond Wales.
5. Dispossessed of Hirfryn by Llywelyn ap Gruffudd in 1270; subsequently involved (possibly as an *agent provocateur*) in support for Dafydd ap Gruffudd, 1283, the Glamorgan rising of 1294–5 and Sir Thomas Turberville's plot of 1295; emerged as a prominent supporter of the Crown, 1297–1316. Knighted in 1306 (at the Feast of the Swans).
6. Survived the war of 1282–3 unscathed, probably because he was a minor. He held lands in Ceredigion: half of the commote of Is Coed, half of the commote of Gwynionydd and a *Gwestfa* (estate or estates, probably in Mebwynion).

Table 2

A succinct account of the dynasty of Gwynedd is given in *AWR*, pp. 21–34.

1. Effectively co-ruler of Gwynedd with Owain, 1157–70.
2. Exiled in England from *c.*1197.
3. Progenitor of a lineage which periodically exercised rule in Meirionnydd.

[4] Exercised lordship in Llŷn, *c.*1147–55

[5] Owain Lawgoch was active in French service in the 1360s and 1370s; planned invasions of Wales where he claimed the principality. He was assassinated on the orders of the English government, 1378.

[6] Rebel leader, claiming to be prince of Wales, in 1294–5; surrendered to Edward I, and subsequently held in honourable confinement in the Tower of London; his son Maredudd was an esquire to Edward II.

Table 3

A succinct account of the dynasty of Powys is given in *AWR*, pp. 37–45.

[1] Progenitor of the dynasty of southern Powys – the principality of Powys in the early thirteenth century, and the barony of Powys in the late thirteenth century and the fourteenth centuries.

[2] Ancestor of the lords of Kinnerley and Sutton Maddock, Shropshire.

[3] Progenitor of the dynasty of northern Powys (Bromfield).

[4] Progenitor of the lords of Mechain.

[5] Progenitor of the lords/barons of Edeirnion, many of whom (not shown in this chart) held important offices, as in the cases of Gruffudd ap Dafydd of Hendwr who was sheriff of Merioneth in 1300, and *rhaglaw* of Penllyn and Ardudwy for life by 1304, or Madog ap Gruffudd of Hendwr who claimed successfully the office of *penteulu* in Powys in 1322.

[6] Married Catrin, sister of Llywelyn ap Gruffudd, prince of Wales; their daughter Angharad was the mother of Madog ap Llywelyn, prominent in the lordship of Bromfield and Yale until his death in 1331.

[7] Progenitor of the lords of Mawddwy in the fourteenth and fifteenth centuries.

[8] Ancestor of Owain Glyn Dŵr.

[9] Sheriff of Merioneth, 1330–1.

Table 4

For the family of Ednyfed Fychan in the thirteenth century see Stephenson, *Political Power*, pp. 102–6, and appendix II. For the subsequent history of one branch of the family see Glyn Roberts, *Aspects of Welsh History: Selected papers of the late Glyn Roberts* (Cardiff: University of Wales Press, 1969), chapter VI. For important analysis see A. D. Carr, *The Gentry of North Wales in the Later Middle Ages* (Cardiff: University of Wales Press, 2017), 30ff.

[1] *Distain* to Llywelyn ab Iorwerth and to Dafydd ap Llywelyn. Married Gwenllian, daughter of the Lord Rhys.

[2] Carried out diplomatic missions for Llywelyn ab Iorwerth and Dafydd ap Llywelyn, 1221–41; held as a hostage (for Dafydd), 1241–5; latterly engaged in attracting Dafydd's men to the king.

[3] Served Llywelyn ab Iorwerth and Dafydd ap Llywelyn; acted as an envoy, and as *rhaglaw* of Dinorben.

[4] *Distain* to Llywelyn ap Gruffudd.

[5] Demanded by Henry III as a hostage for Dafydd ap Llywelyn, 1241; served Llywelyn ap Gruffudd, and was *rhaglaw* of Dinorben in the 1260s, but by 1269 had to provide sureties for his fidelity to the prince.

[6] *Distain* to Llywelyn ap Gruffudd.

[7] *Distain* to Llywelyn ap Gruffudd.

[8] Bishop of St Asaph, 1240–7.

[9] Prominent as an official of Edward I after 1277; served as royal bailiff in Gwynedd Is Conwy and as a member of judicial commissions; opposed Edward I in the war of 1282–3; presented a statement of grievances to Archbishop Peckham in 1282; died against the king's peace in 1283.

[10] Hostage for his father in England until 1263; received lands from Prince Llywelyn at a later date.

[11] Died leading forces against Llywelyn ap Gruffudd at Menai.

[12] Married to Margaret Lestrange; an opponent of Llywelyn ap Gruffudd in the later 1270s and 1280s; imprisoned by Llywelyn by 1277, released under the terms of the Treaty of Aberconwy.

[13] Prior of the Dominican friary of Bangor; in the war of 1277 he arranged for three of his kinsmen, including his brother Rhys (see n. 12) to leave Prince Llywelyn and do homage to Edward I. He was engaged in making extents of Anglesey for Edward I, 1283.

[14] Probably served Llywelyn ap Gruffudd, 1274–8; *distain* to Madog ap Llywelyn, 1294 × 95; one of the deputation to Edward I from north Wales, 1296; swore fealty to Edward of Caernarfon in 1301; *rhaglaw* of Dindaethwy, 1302–3; benefactor to the Dominican friary, Bangor.

[15] A member of the entourage of Madog ap Llywelyn, 1294 × 95.

[16] The mainstay of royal governance in north Wales in the reign of Edward II.

[17] One of deputation of four men from north Wales to Edward I in 1296 expressing concerns at the king's suspicions of the community. Led Welsh troops, for example in Edward II's Scottish expedition of 1316.

[18] The mainstay of royal governance in the southern principality in the reign of Edward II and much of that of Edward III.

INTRODUCTION

This investigation of the development of Wales in the high Middle Ages adopts some perspectives which are perhaps unorthodox and at times controversial. The period from the mid-eleventh century until 1282 is usually discussed in terms of the growth of the power of native rulers, from Gruffudd ap Llywelyn (d.1064) to Llywelyn ap Gruffudd (d.1282) and the development of a native polity of Wales, a process pictured as brutally cut short by the conquests of Edward I of England. That discussion tends to be centred on the rulers of Gwynedd, and their rise to be princes of a wider Welsh polity, though the similarly ambitious and successful Lord Rhys of Deheubarth is also accorded much attention.[1] The half-century which followed the war of 1282–3 is usually depicted as a period in which a conquered Welsh population suffered at the hands of ruthless English royal government and from the tyranny of the English marcher lords.

Both of these approaches contain significant elements of truth, but it would be wrong to assume that they represent anything like a comprehensive portrayal of the multifaceted political dynamics of Wales during these centuries. It is certainly the case that the growth of the power of the most prominent Welsh rulers, the developing sophistication of the governance which they exercised, and the increasing extent of the territories which they controlled, all left clear traces in the surviving sources. Similarly, the momentous nature of the Edwardian conquest of the 1270s and 1280s is a central feature of the history of Wales. But all of those phenomena were complex, and were accompanied and often opposed by other, less well-understood, forces.

It is my intention in this book not only to set out the more generally accepted narratives and analyses of Wales in these centuries, but to advance alternative constructions of the shifting patterns of Welsh social and political development. Many of those alternative constructions have already been glimpsed and pondered by some of the leading historians of the past half-century, such as R. R. Davies, J. Beverley

Smith and A. D. Carr.[2] Of great significance in this process was Glyn Roberts, a scholar prominent in the middle decades of the twentieth century. Professor of Welsh history at Bangor from 1949 until his death in 1962, Roberts focused on medieval history only in the later years of his life, and the work which he produced in that period consisted mainly of very detailed, often groundbreaking, accounts of some of the leading northern Welsh families of the Middle Ages, together with a handful of much briefer studies of wider importance.[3] These last, which included essays derived from radio broadcasts in the late 1950s and a crucial paper on the period 1282–1485, unfinished at the time of his death, established that there was evidence that opposition to the efforts of hegemonic Welsh rulers was widespread within Wales, and that the post-Conquest decades were marked by the prominence, not only in the Crown territories but also in the March, of Welsh magnates characterized by both wealth and power.

In reviewing the book of collected essays by Roberts which was produced in 1969, Rees Davies noted that Roberts had 'begun an important re-orientation in our approach to the study of post-Conquest Wales', and emphasized that 'the full measure of that re-orientation, as of so much in these later essays, yet remains to be worked out'.[4] As noted above, much work was subsequently done in which the influence of Glyn Roberts was apparent. But the importance of his perceptions will not be fully realized until the attitudes and actions of regional Welsh rulers and magnates in the twelfth and thirteenth centuries have been fully explored, and detailed studies such as that by Ralph Griffiths of the officials of the southern principality after 1277 and that of A. D. Carr on the development of the gentry of north Wales have been broadened to trace the development, in the pre-Edwardian period and in the post-Conquest decades, of Welsh administrative and military elites both in the March and in the Crown lands.[5]

The contribution offered in this book is founded in significant measure on the work of the major figures noticed above, on the numerous important studies that have appeared since the start of the present century and on my own recent work on the rulers and communities – lay and ecclesiastical – of medieval Powys and the March.[6] It is hoped that it may prove a step towards a sustained treatment of Welsh history in the central medieval period which breaks free from the fixation with princes, particularly princes of Gwynedd, at the expense of other Welsh rulers, magnates and communities, and from a reading of Welsh history in the twelfth and thirteenth centuries which is dominated by notions of progress towards a principality of Wales as a process of liberation and unification, and from a perception of the post-1282 period as one marked primarily, and often virtually exclusively, by colonial repression and subjugation.

In my own case, the influence of Glyn Roberts goes beyond his published work. Though he died several years before I began research on medieval Welsh history, I have gained an insight into his thinking by a somewhat unusual route. My copy of J. E. Lloyd's seminal *History of Wales from the Earliest Times to the Edwardian Conquest* was formerly owned by Roberts, and contains a small number of marginal notes and marks made by him. Though far from explicit, these marks are a significant guide to things that Roberts thought were significant or worth further consideration. A good example is provided by Lloyd's reference, almost in passing, to the fact that in the 1240s Henry III held significant territory in northern Ceredigion 'which he administered through a Welsh bailiff, one Gwilym ap Gwrwared of Cemais'.[7] Roberts had heavily underscored Gwilym ap Gwrwared's name. That name does not appear in the index to Roberts's selected essays, but the fact that his attention had been drawn to it is interesting. Gwilym ap Gwrwared's family was of great moment in the story of medieval Welsh poetry, for he was descended from poets, and was the ancestor of Dafydd ap Gwilym.[8] But his real importance in social and political terms was that he exemplified the emergence in the thirteenth century of a class of Welsh administrators and landholders who became eminent through service to the marcher lords and the Crown. His career is examined more thoroughly below, along with those of many more like him.[9]

Like all historical works, therefore, this one has its intellectual antecedents. Each of the scholars whose names are mentioned above has provided stimulus and inspiration. Nevertheless this book seeks to break free of some of the assumptions and approaches that have dominated work on medieval Wales. One of the characteristics of the historiography of medieval Wales is the tendency for the subject to be dominated by relatively few great figures – most of whom have been noticed in the preceding pages. It is true that we have come a long way from the situation described in 1972 by Ian Jack, who reported the comment of a university lecturer that 'he had perforce to treat the thirteenth century as a dialogue between himself and Sir John Lloyd'.[10] Even so, the influence of the great practitioners, while it has had the effect of maintaining a very high standard in the writing of Welsh medieval history, has also tended to restrict the opportunities for constructive debate. One very perceptive survey notes that

> the study of the medieval history of Wales has not, on the whole, engendered major controversies nor incited the development of revisionist debates among their modern successors. On the contrary, historians writing on Wales have approached their subject from a number of distinctive, but by no means mutually exclusive, let alone overtly confrontational, perspectives.[11]

This reinforces a point made by A. D. Carr, that 'there has been little scope for the kind of debates which have developed in other fields. The only real historiographical debate has been over the causes of the breakdown in Anglo-Welsh political relations in the late thirteenth century and the conquest of 1282–3.'[12] Even Rees Davies, who emphasized the importance of the March and gave due weight to social, economic and ecclesiastical changes, and who set events in Wales firmly within the context of wider British and European history, tended to discuss Welsh political development within a traditional framework which owed much to the guidelines established by Sir John Lloyd.

With the advantage of being able to draw on the considerable amount of fresh work that has appeared in the present century, often based on recently published definitive editions of crucial source material, embracing the *acta* of Welsh rulers of the twelfth and thirteenth centuries, the poetry addressed to rulers in the same period and to the *uchelwyr* of the fourteenth and subsequent centuries, it is perhaps time to open up new areas for investigation and, perhaps, subsequent debate. We need to ask questions about how meaningful the very concept of Wales was at different times and in different places in the high Middle Ages: of course there was a geographic notion of Wales, and of course poets and storytellers, as well as Gerald of Wales, could point to its extent – from Porth Wygyr in Anglesey to Portskewett (Porth Ysgewin) in Gwent.[13] But there were other political entities, such as Gwynedd, so often the expansionist 'imperial' power within Wales, and the polities of Powys, of Deheubarth and the lordships of the March, in which, as we shall see, a Welsh administrative class had become prominent in the thirteenth century. We need to investigate whether these should be seen merely as lesser, subordinate entities, or whether they, rather than 'Wales', constituted the units on which the political allegiance of their communities were focused.[14]

We need to probe the Age of the Princes from the standpoints not only of the princes and those who aspired to princely status but from those of the other rulers of parts of Wales on whose support the princes often relied, or whose opposition they strove to overcome. We need to take account of the outlook of the subjects of the princes and of other Welsh rulers. We must not assume that they all took part in the princes' wars and schemes of expansion with enthusiasm. That point has real political significance when we consider the attitudes of the ministerial elite who provided much of the backbone of princely and lordly governance; as officials of this type become more and more visible as the period progresses, we can see that not all were convinced of the rightness of the princes' policies, and that some of them became redoubtable opponents of princely ambitions.

We need too to ask questions about how we identify the crucial milestones in the development of the Welsh polity, or polities, in these medieval centuries. How important, in particular, was 1282 in that development? J. Beverley Smith and Llinos Beverley Smith have indeed noted 'the dominance, indeed, in some important respects, the tyranny of 1282 as the critical caesura of Welsh political history'.[15] While it is clear that the wars of Edward I saw 'a dynastic holocaust' we should remember that the power and prestige of most of the Welsh ruling houses had been the targets of the policies of the princes of the twelfth and particularly the thirteenth centuries.[16] In that sense Edward I merely continued a process that was already under way long before he was born. We can also see that the importance of the ministerial aristocracy was not ended with the events of 1282–3: the royal and marcher lands of the early decades of the fourteenth century were just as reliant on the support of the ministerial elite as the Welsh and marcher lords of the thirteenth century had been.

It is my hope that however modest this contribution may be, it may inspire or annoy others to improve still further our understanding of the complex and sometimes tortuous development of Wales in these centuries. A book of limited length such as this one is not the place to present a comprehensive study of the development of Wales over nearly three centuries. I have tried instead to pursue some of the themes that I consider to be particularly important and interesting, and to suggest what seem to me to be profitable avenues for further research and consideration. The principal focus of the book will be on Welsh political and socio-political development. Economic, ecclesiastical and cultural themes will be noticed, but will be discussed primarily in so far as they relate to the core focus of the volume. Wherever possible I have tried to look at individuals whose careers and experiences test our sometimes rather casual assumptions and generalizations, and to give readers an opportunity to meet some of the people, high and low, who made this story.

1

An outline survey of
Welsh political history, *c.*1050–1332

This chapter will be devoted to outlining a fairly conventional narrative of developments in the political history of Wales between the high point of the career of Gruffudd ap Llywelyn in the 1050s and early 1060s, and the years that followed the tumultuous reign of Edward II, who had been the first of the English princes of Wales. It will therefore sketch the story of what is known as the Age of the Princes, covering much of the twelfth and thirteenth centuries, and then the half century that followed the conquest of large parts of Wales by Edward I in the wars of 1277 and 1282–3. This is intended principally both as an introduction to the subject and as a point of departure for the following chapters, which will cover the ground in rather less familiar ways.

The record of events in the Welsh chronicles for the tenth and eleventh centuries depicts a period of considerable chaos. It has been well said that the chronicle entry for 1043 that 'Hywel ab Owain, king of Morgannwg, died in his old age' is quite exceptional in describing the death of a king who had reached old age and is not explicitly described as having been killed.[1] For a century and more before Hywel's death the chronicle of events in Wales had been a record of killing and maiming, the devastation of whole regions, now by Vikings, now by Welsh, less frequently by English. It is clear from this record that chroniclers had been impressed by the prevalence of violence.

But already in 1043 the career of a new force in Wales was under way. Emerging as the victor in a battle with English forces at Rhyd y Groes (possibly near Buttington in mid Wales) in 1039, Gruffudd ap Llywelyn of Gwynedd, son of a former ruler of that region, had made himself by degrees the master of most of Wales by the mid-1050s.[2] There are many indications that Gruffudd's progress to dominance in Wales was accomplished with considerable brutality: stories that circulated long after his death credited him with bitter jokes about his killing of rivals, and something of the character of his ascendancy may be judged from the chronicler's comment that when he encountered the southern ruler Hywel ab Edwin at the battle of Pencadair in 1041 'there Gruffudd defeated Hywel, and he seized his wife and took her for his own'.[3] But for all his savagery here was a man who for a time might be called without exaggeration the king of Wales, a man who quite possibly did adopt that title, and who commanded respect even from his English neighbours until he was brought down by a great assault led by Harold Godwinson in 1063, and was finally killed by his own men.[4]

Gruffudd's importance has been debated: some have seen him as a statesman of considerable stature, whose rule within Wales prefigured the ascendancies of the great leaders of the twelfth and thirteenth centuries. Others have seen his career as simply an interlude in a general pattern of dynastic strife and confusion, and indeed, Gruffudd's rule was far from tranquil: his ascendancy occupied only some seven years before his fall and death, while after his demise the pattern of instability soon reasserted itself across Wales. His successors, in the northern half of Wales at least, were his half-brothers Bleddyn and Rhiwallon the sons of Cynfyn, but they were challenged in 1069 by the sons of Gruffudd ap Llywelyn, Maredudd and Ithel. At a major battle in Mechain, Ithel was killed, and Maredudd died of exposure while fleeing; but Rhiwallon was also killed, leaving Bleddyn as the only surviving credible claimant to rule in the north.[5]

Bleddyn ap Cynfyn's reign was not an ignoble one for he left a reputation as a just ruler who had made significant improvements to the Welsh law.[6] But he was killed by the leading men of Ystrad Tywi in 1075, probably attempting to secure control of at least part of the south. The Welsh chronicles for that year record the multiple conflicts and deaths that then took place as others scrambled to seize or to maintain regional power. An adventurous and aggressive lord, Trahaearn ap Caradog, apparently from the land of Arwystli in mid Wales, established himself as ruler of the combined polity of Gwynedd and Powys, and for a time managed to fend off the efforts of a rival, Gruffudd ap

Cynan, to remove him until Gruffudd killed Trahaearn and his ally
Caradog ap Gruffudd of Morgannwg at the battle of Mynydd Carn
in south-west Wales in 1081.[7] But any hopes that Gruffudd ap Cynan
may have entertained of establishing himself as the dominant force in
Wales were dashed when, shortly after Mynydd Carn, he was captured
by the earls of Chester and Shrewsbury and imprisoned in Chester
for some thirteen years. Gruffudd's abrupt departure from active participation in the scramble for territories allowed a son of Bleddyn ap
Cynfyn, Cadwgan, to become powerful enough to make his presence
felt in regions as diverse as Gwynedd, Ceredigion, Powys, Dyfed and
the Anglo-Welsh borderland.[8]

THE ARRIVAL OF THE NORMANS AND
THE CREATION OF THE MARCH

Gruffudd ap Cynan's confinement in Chester is a reminder that since
the 1060s a new element had entered into the politico-military situation in Wales with the arrival of the Normans. Bleddyn ap Cynfyn
and his brother Rhiwallon had joined forces with an English rebel,
Eadric Silvaticus, in opposing the Normans for a time in the 1060s
as the newcomers consolidated their hold on the border region adjacent to Wales, and later Bleddyn had suffered a defeat at the hands
of Robert of Rhuddlan, a henchman of the newly installed earl of
Chester.[9] In the aftermath of Mynydd Carn, King William himself
had made a journey – certainly a military progress – through Wales
to St David's. The claim of one Welsh chronicle that his purpose was
to offer prayers to the saint cannot disguise the near certainty that
William had decided to assert his control over southern Wales, while
his barons began the occupation of much territory in the central and
northern parts of the land.

By the time of the Domesday Book in 1086 Norman lords operating from the earldom of Chester had claimed much of the north,
and others, led by the Montgomery family, earls of Shrewsbury, had
made significant inroads into mid Wales, from where they were able
to raid into Ceredigion, and Arnulf of Montgomery even established
himself at Pembroke, while parts of the south-east were coming under
Norman control.[10] Thereafter the limits of Norman dominion fluctu-
ated. Much of north Wales, particularly Gwynedd west of the Conwy,

was re-taken by native forces by the end of the century, by which time Gruffudd ap Cynan had escaped from his prison in Chester and had begun the process of consolidating his hold on Gwynedd.[11]

In mid Wales, following the fall of the house of Montgomery in the aftermath of Robert of Bellême's revolt against Henry I in 1102, the earldom of Shrewsbury was allowed to lapse, thus creating a patchwork of lesser lordships in its place, while sons and grandsons of Bleddyn ap Cynfyn fought among themselves until one, Maredudd ap Bleddyn, was able to secure primacy in a re-constituted polity of Powys, and was not dislodged even by an attack led by Henry I himself.[12] But in the south Norman lords seized control of Brycheiniog and lowland Glamorgan, as well as much of Gwent, while others encroached on the lands between Wye and Severn, and in the early decades of the twelfth century Norman control was established in Ceredigion and even more securely in Dyfed.[13] There would be further developments: thus Ceredigion would be recovered from the Normans in the mid-1130s, lost again in 1158 and finally regained in 1165, and the Norman hold on eastern Gwynedd was ended in 1167.[14] By the mid-twelfth century a division of Wales had begun to appear which would be long-lasting, between a *pura Wallia* marked by native polities in the north and west, and the March (regions of Norman, or what was increasingly described as English, lordship) in the east and the south.

The development of the March was perhaps the single most significant element in the history of Wales in this period. There may be a sort of pre-history of the March in the Anglo-Saxon period, but it first emerges as a named region, a March of Wales, in the late eleventh century in the Domesday Book. But the *Marcha de Wali[i]s* found there apparently comprised only a small tract of territory lying both east and west of Offa's Dyke on the Welsh/Herefordshire border. It did not constitute a separate lordship, or even part of a single lordship, as part of it was held by Osbern fitz Richard and part by Ralph de Mortimer. Here nine hides lay waste *in marcha de Wales*, and here eleven manors were said to exist *in marcha de Walis*.[15] It is entirely possible that other areas were considered to lie in such a marchland, but the Domesday clerks did not trouble to make the point. Thereafter explicit references to the March are few, until we encounter the Pipe Rolls, the records of the audit of the accounts of English county government. Apart from some stray early survivals, a copy of a fragment of a roll of 1124, and the original roll from 1130, the Pipe Rolls run with very few gaps from 1155 onwards throughout the medieval period and beyond.

In the mid-1160s references in the Pipe Rolls to *Marchia Wallie* suddenly become quite frequent: and it is clear that this at first refers to the Shropshire/Powys borderland.[16] Subsequent references imply that by the 1180s the March of Wales was thought by some in the English administration to embrace areas much further south than Shropshire. Thus Hywel ab Iorwerth, lord of Caerleon, was paid 20 marks to maintain himself in the king's service in the March of Wales in 1183–4. This development clearly relates to the Welsh offensive of that year in Glamorgan and its eastern neighbour Gwynllŵg.[17] In terms of the thinking of the English royal administration it begins to appear as though the twelfth-century concept of the March of Wales was closely associated with military tension or crisis.

As we advance through the thirteenth century we begin a new period in the evolution of the March. Whether because of a changing mentality, or because of a growing richness in our primary sources, or a combination of both, we begin to see the March, when it is explicitly so designated, less in terms of military geography and more in terms of the articulation of lordship. The lords are mainly though not entirely Norman or, as we increasingly have to call them once again, English. The population of the marcher lordships is partially English, particularly in the towns developed by the lords, but principally Welsh. The lords characteristically claimed and exercised wide-ranging rights or liberties, amounting to quasi-regal powers.[18] These liberties may have existed since the earliest days of Norman encroachment into Wales, but it is in the thirteenth century that they are clearly expressed – often in the face of English governmental attempts to limit or to challenge them.

By the final quarter of the thirteenth century the March was moving ever further into lands previously regarded as purely Welsh polities. It was thus possible for the lord of southern Powys, Gruffudd ap Gwenwynwyn, the great enemy of Prince Llywelyn of Wales, to declare forthrightly that he, Gruffudd, was the king's baron of the March, even – and particularly – in respect of his claim to the *cantref* of Arwystli in the very heart of Wales.[19] In response to the prince's contention that Arwystli could not be said to have marcher status, as the

March signified a zone adjacent to 'pure' Welsh territory, Gruffudd could respond that barons of the March held a great number of territories that were not simply on the Anglo-Welsh borderland but were in what he described as 'the remote parts of Wales'.[20]

By the 1280s this view of the March and its extent was given royal endorsement when Edward I created as marcher lordships, and gave out as rewards to several of his greater barons, territories that had formerly been secure parts of the principality of Llywelyn ap Gruffudd. So were formed the marcher lordships of Denbigh, Dyffryn Clwyd, Bromfield and Yale and Chirkland in the north, Cedewain and Ceri in mid Wales, and Iscennen and Cantref Bychan in the south, many of them regions that had hardly been regarded previously as part of the March. In the post-Conquest era the March rapidly came to denote any Welsh territory that lay outside the direct principality lands of north and west Wales, and the county of Flintshire; its one-time military nature as a zone of containment of, and confrontation with, Welsh polities had clearly become largely redundant.

THE AGE OF THE PRINCES

Within the shrinking confines of *pura Wallia* political development is often depicted by reference to a series of great rulers from the second quarter of the twelfth century onwards. The rulers who have received most attention from modern historians have been those drawn from the dynasty of Gwynedd: Gruffudd ap Cynan (d.1137), his son Owain ap Gruffudd, known as Owain Gwynedd (d.1170), Owain's grandson Llywelyn ab Iorwerth (d.1240), and his grandson in turn, Llywelyn ap Gruffudd (d.1282).[21] Members of other ruling houses have been less prominent in the historiography, but Rhys ap Gruffudd of Deheubarth (Yr Arglwydd Rhys, 'the Lord Rhys') was well served by a biography and a collection of studies in the 1990s.[22] Members of the dynasty of Powys, descendants of Maredudd ap Bleddyn (d.1132), such as Madog ap Maredudd (d.1160) and Gwenwynwyn ab Owain Cyfeiliog (d.1216) have had to wait until the past decade for full assessment.[23] With the exceptions of Madog ap Maredudd and Gruffudd ap Cynan, who were essentially regional rulers, the characteristic common to these major figures was pursuit of a political dominance within *pura Wallia*, and at times the re-establishment of Welsh ascendancy in much of the March.

There were certainly aspirants to that kingship of Wales fleetingly held and almost certainly enunciated by Gruffudd ap Llywelyn. This, as we have seen, may be glimpsed in the chronicle accounts of rulers of the later eleventh and early twelfth centuries, such as Bleddyn ap Cynfyn – 'he who eminently held the kingdom of all the Britons after Gruffudd' and Cadwgan ap Bleddyn.[24] And when Rhys ap Tewdwr of Deheubarth was killed by Norman forces in Brycheiniog in 1093, the Welsh chronicler lamented the death of a man 'with whom fell the kingdom of the Britons'.[25] The chronicler was surely writing in Llanbadarn Fawr on the west coast of Ceredigion, and probably very close in time to the events in the 1090s which he was recording, but even if his vision was geographically and temporally limited, his words convey the idea that there was, ideally, a single Welsh kingdom. The same idea can be seen clearly in the letter addressed by Owain Gwynedd and his brother Cadwaladr to Bishop Bernard of St David's in 1140, accepting his claim to an archbishopric over Wales and asking for his help in replacing Meurig, the bishop of Bangor. The attempt to ally with a would-be archbishop suggests that Owain was intent on consolidating a united realm of Wales. This is also suggested by the title which he adopted on that occasion, that of *rex Wallie*, 'king of Wales'.[26]

This was an opportune time for such a move: Henry I, the fearsome king of England, had died in 1135, and the rule of his successor, Stephen, was soon crippled by civil war. Within Wales Madog ab Idnerth, ruler of the lands between Wye and Severn, died in 1140; the claimant to rule in the south, Gruffudd ap Rhys, had died in 1137, and his sons were as yet largely untried, while Owain and Cadwaladr had been active in clearing Norman forces from Ceredigion. It is possible that in the years around 1140 his adversary Madog ap Maredudd of Powys was distracted by intra-dynastic feuding.[27] But Owain Gwynedd enjoyed only a fitful ascendancy. He had to share his heartland of western Gwynedd with his brother Cadwaladr for many years, and though Owain intervened in the territory of Ceredigion on several occasions in the early stages of his career, it was his son Hywel who was most active there, and neither Owain nor Hywel appears to have exercised any control there after the late 1150s.[28] He had also to face intervention in eastern Gwynedd from English royal and baronial forces in league with those of Powys in the 1150s, and suffered significant loss of territory there in 1157, though he drove the English from their strongholds of Rhuddlan and Prestatyn in 1167, a year in which he had also seized for a brief period a measure of control over southern Powys.[29] But in spite of having been restricted to only limited territorial expansion Owain Gwynedd clearly saw himself as the leading ruler of *pura Wallia* for much of his later career, and this is reflected in his assumption of the expansive titles of *Walliarum rex* and *Walliarum princeps* titles which might be rendered as 'king/prince of Wales'; they may also be translated literally 'king/prince of the Waleses', so perhaps may suggest rule over the regions of Wales.[30] The ambitions which surely underlay those titles were encouraged and nurtured by the court poets, who accorded Owain titles such as 'chief of kings', and even 'emperor', and who pictured him receiving tribute from lesser rulers, and as exercising power across the length of Wales from Anglesey to Gwent.[31]

It was perhaps with greater justification that in the years which followed Owain Gwynedd's death the Lord Rhys of Deheubarth was able to claim the title of *princeps Wallie*, though in 1184 he appears with what was perhaps a more realistic expression of his dignity, when his description in a charter as *Walliarum princeps*, was balanced by his use of the title *Sudwallie proprietarius princeps* (proprietary prince of south Wales) in the same document.[32] The latter designation is perhaps picked up and reflected in Rhys's description in the chronicle *Brut y Tywysogion* as 'prince of Deheubarth and the unconquered head of all Wales'.[33] The implication of these two titles may be that Rhys claimed an overlordship throughout Wales but direct lordship only in Deheubarth. His position in the latter region was surely confirmed and strengthened in 1172 when, according to the *Brut*, he was recognized by Henry II as 'justice on his behalf in all Deheubarth'. And writing in the early 1190s the author of the Anglo-Norman verse account of the arrival in Ireland of forces from south Wales in the later 1160s was able to recall Rhys as the 'king of Wales'.[34] Rhys's ambitions may well have been at their height in the 1170s and 1180s. In the earlier decade he intervened, not for the first time, in the land of southern Powys. He had invaded this last territory as early as the 1150s, and joined Owain Gwynedd in an invasion of the same land in 1167. He fought yet another war against its ruler, Owain Cyfeiliog, in 1171, but this seems to mark the end of his ambitions in that region.[35] He had however claimed lordship in the *cantref* of Meirionnydd in 1177, when his claim was accepted by Henry II. The royal endorsement seems not to have been of much account however as Rhys's claim was strongly opposed by Gruffudd and Maredudd, the sons of the former lord of Meirionnydd, Cynan ab Owain Gwynedd.[36] There is no evidence that Rhys's ambition in this region ever became a reality. But in the 1180s he emerged as the protector of Rhodri ab Owain Gwynedd, lord of Anglesey, who had married Rhys's daughter precisely to secure the southern lord's support against rival members of Owain Gwynedd's family.[37]

Rhys had asserted his supremacy in the land between Wye and Severn, and in much of south-east Wales in 1175, when he had brought the lesser rulers of those regions before Henry II at Gloucester, for a meeting designed to discuss Welsh affairs.[38] The eminence enjoyed by Rhys was confirmed in 1176 when he held a great festival, at the newly re-built castle of Cardigan, which featured contests in poetry and in music for prizes offered by Rhys. The festival, which may have been held to mark Rhys's succession to sole rule in the south after the death of his brother Cadell in the previous year, had been announced throughout the British Isles.[39] And in 1179, the foundation of the Cistercian abbey of Llantarnam, or Caerleon, may mark another aspect of Rhys's dominance, for it was created as a daughter house of Strata Florida, the great abbey in Ceredigion which lay under Rhys's patronage and had been effectively re-founded by him in 1165.[40]

An important affirmation of Rhys's dominance in eastern Wales south of the Severn valley is perhaps provided by the entry into Welsh territory of Archbishop Baldwin and his party in 1188 to preach the third Crusade. The archbishop arrived in the March at Radnor, where he was met by Rhys, clearly acting as the overlord of the region, with several lesser rulers.[41] We can thus picture the Lord Rhys as pre-eminent in the 1170s and 1180s throughout the whole of southern Wales, territories which included his core land of Deheubarth, the land between Wye and Severn, and much of Gwent and the uplands of Glamorgan, while also extending into the south-western march-land of Dyfed. Like Owain Gwynedd, Rhys was hailed by the poet Cynddelw as an 'emperor'.[42]

The power of the Lord Rhys declined in the 1190s, and the eminence of the realm of Deheubarth was only fitfully and partially restored in the generations after his death in 1197. For a time the ascendancy in Wales passed to the south Powysian ruler Gwenwynwyn. Like Owain Gwynedd and the Lord Rhys, Gwenwynwyn employed the title *princeps* – though he claimed no more than to be prince of Powys.[43] But in practical terms, we can see him as the overlord for several years of Maelgwn ap Rhys, who emerged towards the close of the century as the dominant force amongst the sons and grandsons of the Lord Rhys. Gwenwynwyn also acted as the patron of one of the claimants to rule in western Gwynedd, Maredudd ap Cynan ab Owain Gwynedd. Within central and eastern Wales Gwenwynwyn extended his authority by absorbing into southern Powys in 1187 the territory of Mechain, formerly ruled by another branch of the Powysian royal house, and by annexing in 1197 the south-western cantref and kingdom of Arwystli.[44] That he exercised some influence over northern Powys around the turn of the century is suggested by the foundation of the north Powysian abbey of Valle Crucis as a daughter-house of Strata Marcella, founded in southern Powys by his father, Owain Cyfeiliog, and to which Gwenwynwyn was a substantial benefactor.[45] The latter's importance appears from a grant made to him by King John in 1199 confirming his lands and castles in north Wales, south Wales and Powys, and all rights acquired or to be acquired in those regions from the king's enemies.[46] This grant, made at a time when John appears to have resolved to treat Gwenwynwyn much as his father had treated the Lord Rhys, amounted to a licence to the Powysian lord to extend his power over much of Wales.

In the event, Gwenwynwyn was unable to sustain his ascendancy. His apparently treacherous detention by John at Shrewsbury in 1208, though it hardly reduced him to the broken reed pictured by Rees Davies, does mark a point after which he could hope to be no more than a central figure in a confederation of Welsh rulers.[47] And when he refused to accept the evident intention of the dynamic and younger ruler of much of Gwynedd to make himself far more than a member of such a confederation, Gwenwynwyn was driven into an exile in 1216 that proved final, for he died in the same year.[48] His land of southern Powys was occupied by Llywelyn ab Iorwerth, to whose stellar career we must now turn.

Llywelyn was the son of Iorwerth ab Owain Gwynedd. Iorwerth does not feature in the account in the *Brut* of the struggles amongst the members of the ruling dynasty to take control of Gwynedd which marked the generation after Owain Gwynedd's death in 1170. But it appears from an elegy composed by Seisyll Bryffwrch that Iorwerth was lord of Arfon, and he was it seems also lord of Nantconwy until his death, which probably occurred in 1173.[49] His only son Llywelyn was born in that year, and was almost certainly removed from Gwynedd – and from mortal danger – by his mother Mared/Margaret, daughter of Madog ap Maredudd of Powys. The young Llywelyn was apparently brought up in the north Powysian March, but had appeared in Gwynedd, seeking to pursue a claim to lands and rule, as early as 1188.[50]

By 1202 he had established control over most of Gwynedd, and by 1204 had negotiated a hugely prestigious marriage to Joan, natural daughter (subsequently legitimized) of King John.[51] In 1208 Llywelyn had begun to exert power beyond Gwynedd, when he launched a campaign in Ceredigion against Maelgwn ap Rhys, and annexed southern Powys when its ruler, Gwenwynwyn, was detained by King John. Though he lost control of southern Powys in 1210, when it was regained by Gwenwynwyn, and then fell disastrously foul of his father-in-law in 1211, suffering a military defeat which resulted in the loss of Gwynedd below the Conwy, Llywelyn was able to take advantage of John's political difficulties in England to recover his position in 1212, and became the central element in a confederation which included both Gwenwynwyn and Maelgwn ap Rhys.[52] By the close of the second decade of the thirteenth century Llywelyn had emerged as the dominant force in *pura Wallia*, consequent on the fall and death of Gwenwynwyn in 1216 and the reduction in Maelgwn's power in the wake of the rise of other members of the family of the Lord Rhys. The lords of the south all owed their lands and their position to Llywelyn, for in 1216, at an assembly held at Aberdyfi, he had presided over a distribution of lands in which each was allotted a specific territory.[53] In the following year he took Swansea, which he handed to Rhys Gryg, one of the sons of the Lord Rhys, while he also granted newly won territory to Morgan Gam, lord of Afan.[54]

Llywelyn was thus the direct lord of all of Gwynedd, and of southern Powys, as well as being the overlord of northern Powys and of Deheubarth. His power even extended into the Middle March, where he was lord of Montgomery and the protector of the Welsh lords of

Maelienydd. Though he suffered reverses in a war against English royal and marcher forces in 1223, after which he had to relinquish his hold on the lordship of Montgomery and also on Cardigan and Carmarthen, Llywelyn remained strong enough to repulse an invasion of Ceri by Henry III in 1228.[55] He was able to negotiate a marriage for his son Dafydd with Isabella, a member of the de Braose family, which brought him in 1230 the lordship of Builth, and he was able to demonstrate his power in the borderland by terrorizing the whole of the eastern March in several campaigns in the early 1230s.[56]

Llywelyn's activities were not confined to warfare however. He was far removed from the lords focused on war and booty who had roamed Wales in the eleventh and early twelfth centuries. Like Owain Gwynedd and the Lord Rhys he devoted much effort to the public presentation of his power and status. His rule saw a development of his formal title: for most of his principate his documents presented him as *Princeps Norwallie* (prince of Gwynedd/north Wales), but by 1230 this had been replaced by the title *Dominus Snowdoniae et Princeps de Aberffraw* (lord of Snowdon[ia] and prince of Aberffraw).[57] Aberffraw, the name of his principal court in south-west Anglesey, was being promoted at this period by the jurists of Gwynedd as the chief court of Wales, to which the rulers of lesser courts, Dinefwr in Deheubarth and Mathrafal in Powys, owed allegiance, and so to claim to be prince of Aberffraw came very close to claiming to rule a principality of Wales.[58] A step closer to such a claim was taken by Llywelyn's wife, Joan, who entitled herself *domina Wallie* (lady of Wales), while one of Llywelyn's closest advisers, Maredudd ap Rhobert of Cedewain, referred to him in a document of *c*.1216 as *Dominus Wallie* (lord of Wales).[59] And in a passage that we can probably date close to the events recorded, the compiler of *Annales Cambriae*, writing almost certainly at Whitland, described Llywelyn in an entry for 1219 as prince of all Wales.[60] That concept was more fully articulated by Llywelyn's court poets, who could express with vigour concepts that might have been impolitic in formal diplomatic documents. So for Dafydd Benfras Llywelyn was 'king of Wales', to Einion Wan he was 'true king of Wales' and to Einion ap Gwgon and to Llywarch ap Llywelyn he was an 'emperor'.[61]

After his various triumphs in 1216, Llywelyn's policy also embraced plans to manipulate the succession to his growing principality.

Llywelyn was determined that his younger son Dafydd, the product of his marriage to Joan, should succeed to the principality that he was establishing. This would mean depriving his elder son Gruffudd, born from an earlier relationship with a Welsh woman of distinguished ancestry, Tangwystl Goch, of any hope of becoming prince of Gwynedd or of any wider polity. Llywelyn secured the support for this plan of the English government in 1220, of the pope in 1222 and of the lesser Welsh rulers in 1226. In 1229 Dafydd did homage to Henry III.[62] It seems that Llywelyn, who suffered an apparently debilitating stroke in 1237, attempted once more to strengthen Dafydd's position by instructing the magnates of Wales to meet at Strata Florida in 1238 and swear fealty and perform homage to Dafydd. Against a background of furious English protests, the swearing of fealty went ahead, but Llywelyn seems to have backed down on the question of the more significant issue of homage.[63] Attempts to conciliate the talented but turbulent Gruffudd seem to have failed, and Llywelyn also failed to reach a lasting peace with Henry III, achieving only a series of short-term truces. It was a far from stable situation that Dafydd inherited at Llywelyn's death in 1240.

After six troubled years as the ruler of Gwynedd Dafydd died in 1246. He had been obliged to hand over his brother to the English in 1241, and until Gruffudd's death in 1244 the possibility that he might be released into Gwynedd to claim what he saw as his proper inheritance was a constant threat to Dafydd. The fragility of Dafydd's position in Gwynedd obliged him to accept the loss of all control over other Welsh lordships in the treaty of Gwerneigron with Henry III in 1241, which also saw him abandon to the king the easternmost *cantref* of Gwynedd, Tegeingl. Though Dafydd's later adoption of the title *princeps Wallie* showed that he had considerable ambition, he was never able to assert a meaningful control over Wales beyond Gwynedd, and even maintaining his hold on that region proved difficult enough. At the time of his death Dafydd was embroiled in a war with Henry III, and had been pinned within Gwynedd.

Dafydd was succeeded by two of his nephews, Owain and Llywelyn, sons of Gruffudd, who were forced to cede the whole of eastern Gwynedd (the Perfeddwlad or the Four Cantrefs) to Henry III.[64] Having agreed to divide western Gwynedd between them, they were joined by 1252 by a third brother, Dafydd. With several parts of Gwynedd above the Conwy having been seized by other, more distant, members of the royal house, a conflict could hardly be long delayed, and in 1255 Llywelyn ap Gruffudd defeated and imprisoned his two brothers.[65] In stages he secured control over western Gwynedd, and then following a period of consolidation swept into Gwynedd below the Conwy.

LLYWELYN AP GRUFFUDD AND
THE PRINCIPALITY OF WALES

The later 1250s and the early 1260s saw Llywelyn extending his rule over most of *pura Wallia* and into the March.[66] By 1258 he could appear at the head of most of the lesser Welsh rulers in negotiating an agreement with the Scottish lords. Llywelyn on that occasion used the title *princeps Wallie*. Though he seems to have drawn back from using that title in the years that followed, from 1262 he employed a more fulsome version, 'prince of Wales and lord of Snowdon', which echoed and amplified the title adopted by his grandfather at the height of his power.[67] His princely title and his rule over a less than perfectly defined principality of Wales were recognized by the English government in the Treaty of Montgomery in September 1267. Confirmed in his possession of the lordships of Brecon, Gwerthrynion, Builth, Ceri and Cedewain, Llywelyn was now to possess the homages of all but one of the Welsh barons of Wales – a concession that had been denied even to Llywelyn ab Iorwerth.[68] The homage of Maredudd ap Rhys of Ystrad Tywi had not been conceded to Llywelyn in 1267, but he was able to purchase it in 1270.

The title acknowledged by Henry III in 1267 was the formal expression of a dignity accorded to Llywelyn by the panegyrists at his court, who lauded him as the 'true king of Wales' and as a 'Welsh emperor'.[69] But the Treaty of Montgomery, in which it was stated that the king wished to 'magnify the person of Llywelyn, and to honour those who should succeed him by hereditary right' came at a cost. The prince was to pay to the king 25,000 marks in instalments. The mark was worth 13s. 4d, so the total obligation at that point was approximately £16,666. The first instalment (of 1,000 marks) due within a month, the second (of 4,000 marks) by Christmas and then

3,000 marks each Christmas. The financial clause of the treaty stipulated the financial penalties which would be incurred should Llywelyn fail to pay any instalment on time. This represented a very heavy financial burden for Llywelyn's principality to bear, and it is still a matter for debate whether it was actually possible for Llywelyn to meet his new financial obligations, or whether he had over-reached himself in accepting conditions that he could not meet.

The principal facts are as follows: Llywelyn discharged the obligations due under the treaty, more or less on time, up to and including the payment due at Christmas 1269. By that time he had paid 11,000 marks. By 1272 he had paid some 15,000 marks, but was already incurring late-payment surcharges.[70] It was during this last period that Llywelyn began to claim that he was withholding payments as a result of the English government's failure to uphold the terms agreed at Montgomery. He had obtained the homage of Maredudd ap Rhys in 1270, and should have paid – immediately – a further 5,000 marks for this, though it is clear that that money was not in fact handed over. There are thus signs that Llywelyn was beginning to struggle to keep up payments by the early 1270s, though this did not deter him from adding to his debt in 1270. In early 1277, in an attempt to stave off a damaging war, he had assured Edward I that if satisfactory terms could be agreed he was able to pay 6,000 marks to compensate for troubling the king, for a confirmation of the peace and for the delivery to Llywelyn of his bride, Eleanor de Montfort, then held by Edward. All this was to be paid fifteen days after doing homage to the king. In addition Llywelyn promised the 5,000 marks owing for the homage of Maredudd ap Rhys and his heirs, and all the money still owing under the terms of the Treaty of Montgomery. In a further development, Llywelyn offered 11,000 marks plus the 14,000 marks which he calculated he still owed under the treaty.[71] Either Llywelyn had the money or he was bluffing on a monumental and surely a catastrophic scale, but this remains uncertain as his offers failed to prevent an exasperated king from launching a major war, after which the Treaty of Montgomery was effectively a dead letter. But it is at least evident from the darkening political atmosphere of the 1270s that the governmental structures at the disposal of the prince, and the loyalties and tolerance of his subjects, were now put under very great strain.

DEVELOPMENTS IN GOVERNANCE

Institutional developments certainly lay at the heart of the pursuit of a single Welsh polity. Sir John Lloyd depicted that pursuit primarily in terms of the great rulers who had led it, but it is increasingly clear that there were factors other than the resolution of rulers or the waging of wars, the making and breaking of military alliances and the interactions of governments which were central to the evolution of Wales in these centuries. In the first place it is clear that the princes of the twelfth and thirteenth centuries did not govern alone. They were subject to the exhortations of their court poets, aided by the advice of their counsellors and they were supported by a cadre of officials who were of great importance.

Within several Welsh polities of that period we can detect the growth of a major governmental office, that of the *distain* or steward (*senescallus*), whose role developed into something approaching an omnicompetent chief minister of the ruler. Such officials are visible in Gwynedd, in northern and southern Powys, and in Deheubarth and the south-east. In Gwynedd, and also by association in southern Powys, the steward came to be designated the *Justiciarius*, or justiciar, presumably in imitation of the great English official who bore that title. It is probable that the steward exercised considerable influence on policy-making, and we can see signs of this in the case of Ednyfed Fychan in Gwynedd, who acted as steward from *c.*1215 until his death in 1246, and who was clearly important in managing the succession of Dafydd ap Llywelyn. Three of Ednyfed's sons occupied the post of steward, and one of them, Goronwy, left a reputation for sagacity; his death in 1268 may well have been one element in a subsequent perceptible deterioration in the quality of the diplomacy and the decisions of Llywelyn ap Gruffudd. In southern Powys a similar hereditary succession to the office of steward is visible, and Gruffudd ap Gwenwynwyn clearly relied on his steward Gruffudd ap Gwên to a considerable extent.[72]

It is noticeable that as the great rulers of the twelfth and thirteenth centuries advanced further towards making a principality of Wales a reality rather than simply an ambition, their regimes developed a new complexity. By the principate of Llywelyn ap Gruffudd we can see a senior financial officer, a *vice-camerarius* or vice-chamberlain, a title which developed, it seems, into that of *thesaurarius*, or treasurer. We can also see a senior clerical official who is designated as the *cancellarius*, or chancellor. Amongst the men who served the princes we find senior clerical and religious figures, such as Master Instructus/ Osturcius, noted on one occasion as 'archpriest of Caer Gybi' who acted for Llywelyn ab Iorwerth in the period 1204–31. He seems to have been succeeded by Master David, the archdeacon of St Asaph, who appears as an envoy of Llywelyn ab Iorwerth in the 1230s, and who is probably to be identified as the Master David designated as *cancellarius* in the time of Dafydd ap Llywelyn. In the 1250s the clerical servants included David, the archdeacon of Bangor, active between 1257 and 1260. In that last year he appeared as the prince's envoy along with the bishop of Bangor and this acts as a reminder that the bishops of Bangor and St Asaph are frequently found in the service of the princes, as are abbots of Aberconwy.[73]

At a more local level, old offices, such as those of *maer* and *canghellor*, are replaced by those of *rhaglaw*, the 'lieutenant' – essentially the ruler's deputy in the locality – and a host of others, including the *rhingyll*, or summoner, an officer of the judicial structure, and the *ceisiaid*, or serjeants of the peace. To these should be added the forester or woodward (found as *forestarius* or *wtwrt/wodwardus*), the keepers of the vaccaries, the great upland cattle-farms which were in use in the time of the thirteenth-century rulers of Gwynedd.[74] The local administrative areas within which officials discharged their duties and exercised their powers also underwent changes. The pattern of division of Wales into *cantrefi* was already established by the start of our period but in the course of the twelfth and thirteenth centuries *cantrefi* were increasingly subdivided into two or more commotes or *cymydau*. There are faint signs that still further layers of administrative structure were introduced, as when we find an official of Llywelyn ap Gruffudd designated as the *senescallus de Ultra Berwyn*, 'the steward of [the lands] beyond the Berwyn', the mountain range which effectively acted as a barrier between Gwynedd and parts of Powys.[75]

As the major polities of the later twelfth and thirteenth centuries began to be characterized by the building of stone castles, whose significance was administrative and political as much as military, we find castle staff, castellans and castle clerks. Such castles were relatively numerous in Gwynedd, appearing throughout that land, as at

Dolbadarn, Dolwyddelan, Castell y Bere, Degannwy, Ewloe, Dinas Emrys, Carndochan and Cricieth, but were also built or developed by the rulers of Gwynedd or their allies in locations beyond the heartland of the Llywelyns, as at Dinas Brân above the Dee, Dolforwyn in Cedewain, Bryn Amlwg at the point where Ceri, Maelienydd and Clun lordships met, and Rhyd y Briw (Sennybridge).[76] In other territories, less amenable to Venedotian control, regional lords maintained important castles at Pool (Powis Castle), the caput of southern Powys, and Llandovery, Dinefwr and Dryslwyn in Ystrad Tywi.[77] The very look of the land in *pura Wallia* was changing: castles, courts and towns had a greater appearance of permanence; governance was making its mark.

We can thus see that the political and military achievements of the princes were facilitated, at the very least, by substantial developments in the machinery and personnel of governance. At an even more fundamental level economic growth was also crucial to political innovation: the foundation of trading centres, boroughs and ports, was a phenomenon imported into *pura Wallia* from the March and beyond, and was both stimulated by, and helped to produce, a major thirteenth-century development of commutation of revenues and rents formerly rendered in kind into ones paid in cash. There were numerous flourishing market centres in and near the eastern and southern March in the twelfth and thirteenth centuries, and the importance of their trade with Wales can be judged by the quickness of English governments to ban trade with Wales at times of Anglo-Welsh war.[78]

The importance of such markets to the rulers of the developing Welsh polity is apparent also in the nervousness of Llywelyn ap Gruffudd about access to the market of Leominster. In what seem to be references to events in 1276 the prince had apparently ordered his bailiffs of the eastern March not to go beyond their bailiwicks to damage the English marchers; notwithstanding this, his bailiff of Buellt wrote to him to say that even after the making of the truce, Llywelyn's merchants from Buellt, Gwerthrynion, Elfael and Cardigan who had gone to the market of Leominster had been despoiled by Roger Mortimer's bailiffs, and some had been imprisoned.[79] An apparently related document addressed by the prince to the Archbishop of Canterbury, tells how over one hundred and twenty of Llywelyn's men had been seized at the markets and fairs of Montgomery and

Leominster, and that two deans and one deacon had been killed, even though a truce had been arranged between Llywelyn's bailiffs and Roger Mortimer, which had purportedly guaranteed that the prince's merchants could attend the fairs in peace.[80]

But urban centres, with markets and fairs, also began to appear in *pura Wallia*. Within Gwynedd, the growth of a cash economy was aided by what seems to have been the minting at Rhuddlan of short-cross pennies modelled on English currency by rulers of Gwynedd in the late twelfth and early thirteenth centuries.[81] In Gwynedd above the Conwy we see trading centres developed at Llanfaes in Anglesey, at Nefyn and, to a very limited degree, at Pwllheli in the Llŷn peninsula. In eastern Gwynedd Rhuddlan appears to have been a thriving market centre long before the Edwardian conquest, and was certainly the site of a mint.[82] In southern Powys a vibrant urban centre developed in the mid-thirteenth century at Pool (*Pola*, Welshpool); the economic importance of Pool is suggested by the virulence with which its market rights were disputed by the burgesses of the nearby royal foundation of Montgomery.[83] The development of Pool was followed in the last decades of the century by a number of urban foundations within the same lordship. In northern Powys it is possible that there was market development at Wrexham and at Llangollen as early as the first half of the thirteenth century; there was certainly an urban foundation at Llanarmon Dyffryn Ceiriog by 1279, part of a plan by the ruler of part of northern Powys, Llywelyn Fychan ap Gruffudd, to break the commercial dominance exercised by Oswestry.[84]

It is clear that during the thirteenth century more and more cash was coming into use in many parts of Wales, and this both stimulated and was encouraged by the growth of market centres. Commutation of renders and services into cash payments was a relatively easy matter for those who produced a surplus which could be sold in markets, but for those who farmed at a subsistence level it was a far more daunting prospect. Social change, most importantly an apparent growth in the proportion of freemen and a corresponding decline of the bond population, appears also to have gone hand in hand with politico-military changes. Particularly in Gwynedd, the old differentiation between the freemen, who did armed service in the rulers' armies, and the unfree, who performed only duties of carriage and digging, was being made obsolete. Thus the century which saw the rise of a Welsh polity under the Llywelyns also witnessed socio-economic changes that were for many, especially in the free community, far reaching and often disturbing.

THE COLLAPSE OF LLYWELYN'S PRINCIPALITY

It is clear moreover that the development of the principality of Wales was viewed with dismay by many of the Welsh magnates who found their ambitions restricted and their status diminished by the prince's dominance. Stories of plots against Llywelyn began to circulate, and his brother Dafydd, and his most prominent vassal, Gruffudd ap Gwenwynwyn of southern Powys were forced into exile in England in 1274, and their lordships were occupied by Llywelyn, while Gruffudd's eldest son, Owain, was held as a prisoner in the prince's court. The fact that Dafydd ap Gruffudd and Gruffudd ap Gwenwynwyn were sheltered by the English government, and even encouraged to harass the prince from their bases in the borderland served to embitter Llywelyn's relations with Edward I, who had succeeded his father Henry III as king in 1272. Llywelyn's refusal to perform homage to Edward, and his failure to maintain the payments due under the Treaty of Montgomery made a confrontation virtually inevitable.

Llywelyn's construction of an extensive Welsh polity was an impressive testimony to his drive and vision, but it was an edifice that Edward I's armies brought low in the war of 1277 which saw Llywelyn lose most of Wales beyond western Gwynedd. Humbled by the outcome of the war, Llywelyn was then frustrated by what he saw as Edward's refusal to grant him a fair hearing of his claim to the mid Wales land of Arwystli, which he claimed from the reinstated lord of southern Powys, Gruffudd ap Gwenwynwyn. Dafydd ap Gruffudd had fought against Llywelyn in the war of 1277, and had been rewarded by King Edward with extensive lands in eastern Gwynedd; but by March 1282, driven by grievances of his own, he launched a surprise attack on English territories, which rapidly escalated into full-scale war. Llywelyn appears at first to have held aloof from the conflict – though he did not move against his brother – and then in mid-1282 he seems to have joined the uprising and to have put himself at its head. The forces opposing Edward I enjoyed some successes, but the massive force assembled by the king ensured that those successes simply delayed the outcome: breaking out of Gwynedd, where Edward's armies pressed ever harder upon him, Llywelyn attempted to find support in the Middle March, but met his death in an encounter near Builth in December 1282.

Llywelyn died without an acknowledged heir. Married late in his life to Eleanor de Montfort in 1278, he had produced a daughter, taken into custody by the English government.[85] Of his brothers, Owain, whom he had kept imprisoned until forced to release him in 1277, appears to have died by 1281; Dafydd, who had been released by Llywelyn in late 1256, deserted him in 1263, was reconciled in 1269 and deserted again in 1274. It had been Dafydd, apparently dissatisfied at his treatment by Edward I's government, who had begun the war of 1282, and after the death of Llywelyn he assumed leadership of the resistance to Edward's advancing armies, and presented himself as the prince of Wales. But in 1283 he was captured, and executed at Shrewsbury.[86] A fourth brother, Rhodri, had never taken Llywelyn's side, and survived, living in England in comfortable obscurity. Such was the end of the realistic attempts to create and consolidate a polity of Wales, under a single Welsh ruler.

Edward's destruction of the polity developed by Llywelyn ap Gruffudd had been no easy matter. The king had had to mobilize forces on an unprecedented scale, employing not only English levies but also Welsh troops from regions whose lords were hostile to Llywelyn – from southern Powys, Ystrad Tywi and the Middle March, from which troops were raised both from the Mortimer land of Maelienydd and from the lordships which had been under the prince's increasingly fragile rule from the early 1260s.[87] Forces were also called in from far afield – knights and crossbowmen from Gascony, while castle-builders were brought in from Savoy. And the massive expense entailed by the wars and the arrangements for holding on to the captured lands were met in part by Edward's turning to Italian banking houses.[88] Such a massive governmental effort betokened a determination on Edward's part to bring the Age of the Princes to an end.

POST-CONQUEST WALES

With the deaths of Llywelyn ap Gruffudd and his brother Dafydd in 1282–3, a milestone in the history of Wales had indeed been reached.

The dynasty that had dominated attempts to construct a Welsh polity in the previous century and more was effectively extinguished, and an English king enjoyed an unprecedented supremacy over much of Wales. In large parts of the country Edward I was now the direct lord, particularly in the case of the north-west and west, and in the north-eastern cantref of Tegeingl (Englefield), fused administratively if not territorially with the detached lands of Hopedale and of Maelor Saesneg, into the county of Flintshire.[89] Elsewhere he was able to dispose of Welsh territory to his favoured nobles and commanders, creating thereby a large extension of the March, in many parts of which the new lords were able to organize large-scale migration from England, which must have entailed a corresponding contraction of the economic resources available to the native Welsh population.[90]

A few Welsh lords survived: Gruffudd ap Gwenwynwyn (d.1286) and his eldest son Owain (d.1293) were able to maintain, and even extend, the large lordship of Powys, and to savour their eventual triumph over their dynasty's old enemies of the ruling house of Gwynedd. In Edeirnion and Dinmael, and in some contiguous areas a cluster of descendants of Madog ap Maredudd were able to hang on as Welsh barons, holding their small lordships by a privileged tenure; they included Gruffudd Fychan, the ancestor of Owain Glyn Dŵr, who clung on – albeit precariously – to the land of Glyndyfrdwy, and whose son Madog was to secure in addition half of the commote of Cynllaith.[91] Of the descendants of the Lord Rhys, Llywelyn ab Owain ap Maredudd retained the half-commote of Is Coed Uwch Hirwen and half of Gwynionydd together with a scatter of smaller territories, while Rhys ap Maredudd, holding most of Cantref Mawr and part of Ceredigion, could be called, with pardonable exaggeration, 'lord of Ystrad Tywi', and continued to act the part of a Welsh prince in his castle of Dryslwyn.[92]

In the north-west and in west Wales lands that had fallen under Edward's control were organized into a new principality; in the north new counties were created, that of Flintshire becoming in effect an extension of the (royal) earldom of Chester, while in the north-west the counties of Anglesey, Caernarfonshire and Merionethshire were created. In west Wales the counties of Carmarthenshire and Cardiganshire, whose history as English royal outposts long pre-dated the Edwardian wars, were continued and entrenched. Montgomery and Builth were administered as separate lordships, not dependent on any of the counties or other contrivances of Edwardian administration. In the counties the office of sheriff was introduced, and regional centres of government were created, Caernarfon in the north and Carmarthen in the south. The office of justiciar was created – so powerful that it was regarded by some Welshmen as a continuation of the office of *distain* – and other significant, and well-rewarded, posts emerged, such as the northern and, by 1299, the southern chamberlains.[93]

The statute of Wales issued at Rhuddlan in 1284 brought criminal law on the English model into the royal lands of the north-west (the 'northern principality'), and an English-style system of courts and coroners was established.[94] The change was not perhaps as dramatic as may be thought, as the criminal law, particularly in Gwynedd, had been developing under the thirteenth-century princes. In civil law, many of the aspects of Welsh law were retained. Even where apparent changes were introduced, as in the specifications that land might pass to daughters if there were no sons, or that widows might expect a dower share of a third of their husbands' lands, they were not entirely new, as in many regions Welsh practice had already been moving towards such rules.[95] In the royal lands administration at the level of the commote (i.e. below the county level) remained under the control of officials who were Welsh, usually local to the areas for which they were responsible, and who held offices familiar from the days of princely governance. The same pattern was visible in the newly created marcher lordships, apart from the introduction of some novel senior administrative posts such as that of the Receiver. Throughout much of the March administrative and legal structures were effectively fossilized, and for the historian they reveal much about the institutions which applied before the age of Edwardian conquest.

What seems to have been new was the drive in the first generations after 1282–3 to enquire into and establish the range of established obligations, fiscal and personal, which were owed to the new rulers in Wales. We have no evidence for the holding by the Welsh princes or lords of enquiries which resulted in the extents and surveys which exist, or are known to have existed, in Crown lands and marcher lordships and episcopal lands alike. The counties of north-west Wales were surveyed in 1284, the lordship of Bromfield and Yale in 1315, that of Dyffryn Clwyd in 1324, that of Chirkland in 1332 and that of Denbigh in 1334, while the estates of the bishopric of Bangor were surveyed in 1306 and those of St David's in 1326.[96] And in an even more striking sense, the number and size of castles throughout much of Wales was dramatically increased as a result of the wars of 1277 and 1282–3. The ring of coastal castles created by Edward I, Rhuddlan, Flint, Conwy, Caernarfon, Harlech, Aberystwyth, is well known. Montgomery castle continued to guard the central March, and was supplemented by a new castle, built in stone, at Builth. To them we must add Beaumaris, built a few years later, while castles such as Cricieth and Castell y Bere in the north and Dinefwr in the south which were of earlier, princely, origin were absorbed into the new system.[97]

Royal castles, often supplemented and supported by adjacent walled boroughs, do not exhaust the fortifications constructed after the Edwardian conquest: marcher castles in stone, some again developed from Welsh princely structures, were numerous, and include, in central and north-eastern Wales, Dolforwyn, Holt, Denbigh and Ruthin, while in the south we find the greatest of them all at Caerphilly.[98] Pool castle (today's Powis), destroyed by Llywelyn ap Gruffudd, was rebuilt by Gruffudd ap Gwenwynwyn and his son Owain ap Gruffudd of Powys, who had transformed themselves into Welsh lords of the March; by 1309 it had passed by marriage into the hands of the first of the Charlton lords of Powys. Wales had been heavily castellated – by earthwork and timber structures – since the later eleventh century; now the Edwardian settlement was buttressed by some of the greatest and most intimidating stone castles in Europe.

The post-1283 dispensation did not however pass without challenge. In Ystrad Tywi a combination of frustrated ambition, particularly his failure to obtain the ancestral castle of Dinefwr, and resentment at his treatment by royal officials such as Robert Tibetot, the Justiciar of west Wales, drove Rhys ap Maredudd to rebellion in 1287 and to his execution in 1292.[99] The effects of the lay subsidy levied throughout Wales in 1292–3 were an important factor in the wave of revolts which swept through most of Wales in 1294–5. The most threatening movement came in Gwynedd, and was led by a member of that branch of the old ruling dynasty which had been associated with Meirionnydd, Madog ap Llywelyn. But there were other uprisings: in west Wales they were led by Maelgwn ap Rhys, a descendant of the Lord Rhys, and in central Wales by Cynan ap Maredudd; in

Glamorgan a rising was prompted primarily by local issues, and was led by Morgan ap Maredudd, representative of an old princely lineage. An insurgency in Gwent was led by Meurig ap Dafydd, who, ironically, had been one of the two chief assessors of the lay subsidy of 1292 in the lordship of Abergavenny.[100] The preponderance amongst these leaders of men drawn from former ruling dynasties is notable. Some of the leading figures of the risings were executed, including Cynan ap Maredudd; some, like Maelgwn ap Rhys, were killed. Madog ap Llywelyn, after a defeat at Maes Moydog near Welshpool against the earl of Warwick, whose force included Powysian troops, was captured and imprisoned in the Tower of London. Care was taken to maintain him in some state, and he was still in the Tower in 1312. His son Maredudd was to become one of the king's esquires and to recover some of the family lands.[101] Morgan ap Maredudd, who insisted that his movement was not aimed at the king but at Gilbert de Clare, earl of Gloucester and lord of Glamorgan, not only survived but prospered greatly as a royal official.[102] The risings were widespread and serious, affecting both royal and marcher lands, and their suppression required a third massive military effort from Edward I.

The upheavals of 1294–5 were not the end of disturbances in Wales. Glamorgan again was shaken by the revolt of a man of princely ancestry, Llywelyn Bren, in 1316; the insurrection disturbed neighbouring territories.[103] When Llywelyn Bren gave himself up to forces led by Humphrey de Bohun and Roger Mortimer, his captors made a plea to King Edward II for clemency. Two years later Llywelyn was executed by Edward's favourite, Hugh Despenser, an action which appalled marcher and Welsh opinion alike.[104] Further north the great barony of Powys was torn for two decades after 1312 by a violent succession dispute between Owain ap Gruffudd's daughter Hawise and her husband John Charlton on one side, and Hawise's uncle, Gruffudd Fychan, on the other, ended only by Gruffudd's death in 1332.[105] Beyond these local issues, Wales was stripped of its young men as Edward I and then his son recruited amongst Welsh communities a huge proportion of the soldiery for their many wars beyond England. And the country was gripped by the factional struggles of Edward II's reign, particularly given that the king's greatest opponents were great lords in the March, and in some cases prominent in royal government in Wales. The woes of the land were compounded by the agrarian crises and famines of the second decade of the fourteenth century.

One of the main, and sometimes neglected, aspects of the events of 1277–83 was that Edward's conquest effectively made Wales more administratively fragmented than it had been for much of the thirteenth century. Over half of Wales consisted of marcher lordships, often at odds with one another, and on occasion at odds with the king, as in the case of Edward I's bruising collision with Humphrey de Bohun, earl of Hereford and lord of Brecon and Gilbert de Clare, earl of Gloucester and lord of Glamorgan in the early 1290s.[106] Gone was the dream of a single Welsh polity. The post-Conquest regime in Wales was truly one in which division was a principal motif. Wales became uniform only in one sense: the crushing of native rebellions, in 1287 and 1294–5, and the humiliation of marcher magnates both demonstrated that Wales was subject to a resolute and ruthless English king. Much of the land was, in the formulation of Rees Davies, 'Colonial Wales'. In one way or another it could be regarded as 'under the heel'.[107] It is thus possible to paint the state of Wales in the late thirteenth century and the first generation of the fourteenth in consistently dark colours.

Nor, in some respects, did the situation improve in the reign of Edward I's successor, Edward II. The latter, born at Caernarfon, and created prince of Wales by his father in 1301, might be said to have had a special relationship with Wales, and this was something that he sometimes emphasised. But his reign saw upheavals that featured prominent members of Welsh society, as in the case of the challenge offered by Gruffudd Fychan de la Pole from 1312 onwards to the establishment of John Charlton as lord of Powys, or the rebellion of Llywelyn Bren in Glamorgan in 1316 – but these were primarily, even though not entirely, localized affairs.

Crises such as these were exacerbated, no doubt, by the economic hardship which affected much of northern Europe in the years 1315–17. There are clear signs that the rebellion of Llywelyn Bren combined with economic severity to produce crisis conditions in some parts of Wales. Neath and Llantarnam abbeys were hard hit, and even in the north, the monks of Aberconwy abbey, since 1284 relocated to Maenan, some miles upstream on the Conwy, lamented the lean years and the debt into which they had fallen.[108] Official nervousness was increased by the abject failure of Edward II's attempt to deal with Robert the Bruce at Bannockburn in 1314, and the threat of Scottish intervention in Wales in the following year.[109]

The fact that one of Edward's favourites Hugh Despenser, was lord of Glamorgan, and that many of the king's opponents and enemies, such as Roger Mortimer, Humphrey de Bohun and Thomas of Lancaster, were major marcher lords, meant that Wales was closely involved in the turbulent politics of Edward II's reign, a fact that offered both danger and opportunity to leading members of the Welsh lordly class. But the political troubles of Edward II's reign meant that he was forced to seek support wherever he could, to exploit his relative popularity in north and west Wales, and the connections that he had developed as a result of his time as prince of Wales. The result was that the decades after his accession in 1307 were a time when Welsh magnates, sometimes of princely, sometimes of ministerial, descent had a pronounced, and sometimes crucial, influence on events in Wales.[110]

2

The Age of the Princes: shifting political cultures and structures

We can now begin to probe behind the events summarized in the previous chapter and to identify some important underlying developments in the polities of *pura Wallia* in the two centuries before Edward I's destruction of the native principality of Wales. It was certainly the case that new forms of polities emerged. This process can be described in terms of the replacement of kingdoms by principalities and lordships, a process in which the twelfth century appears to have been crucial. While major rulers of a conservative disposition, such as Madog ap Maredudd of Powys (1132–60) continued to describe themselves in formal documents as kings – in his case as king of the Powysians – and while the title of *rex* or king was employed by the rulers of micro-polities, such as Hywel ab Ieuaf, king of Arwystli (1132–85), we have seen that a new wave of major Welsh rulers came to describe themselves as princes.[1]

FROM KINGS TO PRINCES

The shift in nomenclature is seen in the case of transitional figures such as Owain Gwynedd (d.1170), who used both *rex* and (later) *princeps*. But the Lord Rhys (d.1197) may have used *princeps* more consistently, though the evidence is so thin that it is far from conclusive. When Gwenwynwyn ab Owain Cyfeiliog employed any title, which was not often, he generally used *princeps*.[2] Though Dafydd ab Owain Gwynedd, prominent in the politics of Gwynedd from the 1170s to the mid-1190s, seems initially to have reverted to *rex* as a title he also used *princeps* in some of his *acta*.[3] Dafydd's successors as the dominant rulers of Gwynedd, his nephews Gruffudd ap Cynan and Llywelyn ab Iorwerth, and the latter's son and grandson, Dafydd ap Llywelyn and Llywelyn ap Gruffudd, were more consistent in their use of *princeps*. Lesser figures tended to use the much less specific designation of *dominus* 'lord', or to employ no title.

The increasing use of *princeps* from the mid-twelfth century onwards does seem to have been one expression of a drive to create a single Welsh polity. That idea was not new, and had been realized, albeit for only a few years, under Gruffudd ap Llywelyn, but some of the developments described in the present chapter made it appear more of an attainable political objective. On occasions the notion of a single Welsh polity had come close to realization in a union of rulers and their forces in opposition to a threat from England. Such was the case in 1165, when a great number of Welsh rulers joined forces to frustrate Henry II's invasion. Not all Welsh rulers joined the coalition which gathered in the region of Corwen, but enough did to give some support to the chronicler's assertion that Henry was opposed by 'the host of Gwynedd … the host of Deheubarth … and the host of all Powys', together with the forces of the sons of Madog ab Idnerth, the rulers of the land between Wye and Severn.[4]

In the years that followed King John's invasion of Gwynedd in 1211, there emerged a coalition of Welsh rulers which is described in some of the chronicles in terms of confederacy.[5] The same tendency is visible in the late 1250s, when Llywelyn ap Gruffudd was emerging as a leading, but not yet overbearing, force in *pura Wallia*. The Red Book of Hergest version of the *Brut* notes that in 1258 'an assembly of the magnates of Wales gave an oath of allegiance to Llywelyn ap Gruffudd' (*rodes kynnulleitua o dylyedogyon Kymry lw ffydlonder y Lywelyn ap Gruffud*). But in contrast the Peniarth 20 version of that chronicle records the agreements made in that year in rather different terms: 'all the Welsh made a pact together, and they made an oath to maintain loyalty and agreement together'.[6]

It is noticeable that it is particularly in the period of Llywelyn ap Gruffudd's rise to power that the relations between rulers are sometimes couched in formulae which mention *amicitia*, *unitas*, *unio* and the like.[7] The tendency towards submission to a single prince was therefore on occasion paralleled, and perhaps facilitated, by the use of concepts of confederative union. And that tendency may well have been encouraged by the poets' depiction of a circuit, or a gathering, of the regions of Wales, which while emphasizing the existence of different regions, brought them all together in a single whole.[8]

The leading Welsh rulers from the mid-twelfth century onwards also acquired high-level diplomatic partners: the kings of France in the 1160s and in 1212, a faction of the Scottish nobility in 1258, English aristocrats of the quasi-regal status of the earls of Chester in the 1140s and 1150s, and again in the early decades of the thirteenth century.[9] They secured wives of such dynastic eminence as to set their husbands apart from other Welsh rulers (Dafydd ab Owain's wife Emma of Anjou, half-sister of Henry II, Llywelyn ab Iorwerth's wife Joan, daughter of King John, and Llywelyn ap Gruffudd's wife Eleanor de Montfort), while their sons and daughters married into the foremost families of the marcher lords.[10] Welsh princes became accustomed to sending diplomatic missions to the papal curia, of which correspondence and embassies in 1222, 1244 and 1276 are good examples.[11]

These foreign alliances and missions were not an entirely new phenomenon, for Welsh rulers had attended the courts of the English kings of the middle decades of the tenth century, and in the eleventh century Gruffudd ap Llywelyn had been the ally of Aelfgar of Mercia.[12] But the later alliances involved contacts from further afield and often at a higher level: they involved formal agreement, expressed in writing, rather than de facto cooperation. They are evidence of a growing sophistication and integration into the ranks of European rulers and aristocracy. The marriage alliances and the diplomatic engagement with European ruling houses were such that only the most prominent of Welsh rulers might hope to be involved in them. Their integration into the European elite was symbolized and reinforced by the increasing possession and use by Welsh rulers of equestrian seals, a sign of high status. Nevertheless, the fact that equestrian seals were possessed not only by the princes but also by lesser rulers also suggested a community of status and interest. But only the Llywelyns (and, it seems, Llywelyn ap Gruffudd's wife Eleanor and his brother Dafydd, who took the title *princeps Wallie et dominus Snowdoniae*) are known to have possessed an additional 'secret' seal, and this perhaps underscored their eminence, while Dafydd ap Llywelyn used a double-sided seal modelled on the great seal of England, suggesting the scope of his ambitions.[13]

The significance of the shift from *rex* (king) to *princeps* (prince) in the styles employed by the greater rulers of Welsh polities in the twelfth and thirteenth centuries calls for some discussion. In modern usage 'prince' tends to signify someone of lesser status than a king, but this was clearly not necessarily the case in the twelfth and thirteenth centuries, though 'anyone who exercised government at a fairly high level was a sort of prince'.[14] In the Welsh context the word clearly had a greater, and more precise, significance. It signified headship, pre-eminence and as such may have reflected the Welsh *pen*, head or chief: the title of the chief of the household guard, the *penteulu*, could thus be glossed in a Welsh lawbook as *princeps milicie* (head of the war-band).[15]

The force of the designation of *princeps* is perhaps encapsulated in the description by Llywelyn ab Iorwerth of Philip Augustus of France as *regum princeps* (prince/leader of kings, or 'foremost of kings') in 1212.[16] Once it had become established as a designation of the greatest Welsh rulers, no ruler who aspired to widespread control over *pura Wallia* reverted to the use of *rex* in formal documents.[17] But there is more to this issue than a merely nominal change: the appearance of the title of prince coincided with more fundamental changes in the nature of Welsh polities. Perhaps the most obvious of these is the transformation of the very nature of the political geography, as new forms of polities emerged.

CHANGING STRUCTURES OF WELSH POLITIES

Eleventh- and early twelfth-century Welsh kingdoms often appear to have been somewhat amorphous. The most striking feature of kingship which was exercised at anything above a very localized level would seem to be the fact that it was not generally contained within clearly fixed boundaries. It is indeed a moot point whether there were at this date precisely fixed boundaries of polities, which were frequently ignored in practice, or whether boundaries themselves were subject to constant change. Frequently, kings, and with them kingdoms, appear to have been constantly on the move across the face of the land. As such they resembled in significant measure the marauding bands of Norse raiders that are such a feature of the

Welsh chronicle accounts of the ninth and tenth centuries. Thus we can picture Gruffudd ap Cynan and his rival Trahaearn ap Caradog as attempting to secure a hold on a realm of Gwynedd, of indeterminate extent: but the decisive encounter between them, the battle of Mynydd Carn, took place in the far south-west of Wales, and also involved, as well as Rhys ap Tewdwr ruler of Deheubarth, a Powysian magnate, Meilyr ap Rhiwallon, and a ruler from the southeast, Caradog ap Gruffudd.[18] The degree of royal mobility involved is impressive.

In the following decades, Cadwgan ap Bleddyn emerged as a powerful ruler, opportunistically raiding into Dyfed in 1088 and 1093, and sending his war-band on a similar foray in 1096. His power base appears to have been in Ceredigion, but he also appeared in Gwynedd, leading resistance to a Norman invasion in 1094; he was in Gwynedd again in 1098, taking refuge in Anglesey, along with Gruffudd ap Cynan, from Norman attacks before leaving, also with Gruffudd, for a brief exile in Ireland. He was associated with part of Powys, as well as Ceredigion, in 1099, and was ultimately killed in the eastern parts of Powys in 1111. At some point he had sufficient power in Meirionnydd and Cyfeiliog to give those territories to Uchdryd ab Edwin.[19] Given that he had taken as one of his many wives a daughter of Picot de Say, lord of Clun, Cadwgan presumably also had a presence in the borderland.[20]

It seems that in the early decades of the period under review in this book a ruler's kingdom was defined by the constantly shifting areas in which he was able to enforce his will or his claim to be a king. Cadwgan ap Bleddyn may have had dreams of emulating the achievements of his father, Bleddyn ap Cynfyn, in controlling north Wales, or those of his uncle, Gruffudd ap Llywelyn, in dominating most of Wales, and so we may have to see the wide scope of his rule as a reflection of his ambitions to achieve a wide hegemony. But some of the fluid nature of the political geography of Wales in this period was perhaps the result not so much of the ambition of Welsh rulers but of their manipulation by English kings. This was never more so than in the case of Henry I. In 1102 he offered to Cadwgan's brother, Iorwerth ap Bleddyn, 'the portion it was his due to have of the land of the Britons ... That was Powys and Ceredigion and half of Dyfed ... and Ystrad Tywi and Gower and Cydweli.'[21] Many of these territories

– Dyfed, Gower, Cydweli – were ones with which Iorwerth's father had no known association; and it was in Ystrad Tywi that Bleddyn ap Cynfyn had been killed by the local magnates in 1075.

In the event, Henry not only failed to honour his offer to Iorwerth, but imprisoned him for several years. In his place he installed one Hywel ap Goronwy, a descendant of the shadowy mid Wales ruler Elystan Glodrydd, in half of Dyfed as well as Ystrad Tywi and Gower. In return Hywel appears to have given up his recently acquired territory of Brycheiniog, and his claims to Glamorgan. He too did not rule in the south-west for long, being killed in 1105.[22] But he serves to exemplify the sort of rootless monarchs, constantly on the move, who are characteristic of this age. They include men such as Uchdryd ab Edwin, whose family associations were with north-east Wales, but who was installed in Meirionnydd by Cadwgan ap Bleddyn, who 'had given Meirionnydd and Cyfeiliog to Uchdryd on this condition: that he should be a true, inseparable friend to him and a helper against all opposition that might come against them'.[23]

There does seem to have been a trend towards greater territorial definition of major realms in the course of the mid- and later twelfth century. Gruffudd ap Cynan (d.1137) in his later years, and Madog ap Maredudd, appear to have been primarily consolidators of a territory that they regarded as their hereditary right: Gruffudd in Gwynedd, particularly in Gwynedd above the Conwy, and Madog in Powys, as defined in the tale *Breuddwyd Rhonabwy* and in contemporary poetry.[24] Gruffudd's sons might strike out into neighbouring territories – especially into Ceredigion, and Madog might extend his dominion southwards into the land of the Iorweirthion (Rhwng Gwy a Hafren), but in general they avoided the constant roaming across regions that had characterized the kingships of the tenth and much of the eleventh centuries.[25] There were of course areas of uncertainty: Rhys ap Gruffudd of Deheubarth claimed Cyfeiliog, and Meirionnydd – claims that proved unsuccessful in both cases – though the Welsh chronicle noted that in 1167 Tafolwern – the site of the court of Cyfeiliog – 'was said to be within his bounds'.[26]

There was still conflict over territory in the later twelfth century, in all of the major polities which had begun to crystallize, but it was conflict within royal houses, and within recognized realms: the principal struggles were for Gwynedd, for Powys, and for Deheubarth. By the closing decade of the century Gerald of Wales could talk confidently of those regions as constituting the three major native polities, and the law books whose development we can trace to the later twelfth and the thirteenth century referred to the same territories as the main political divisions of Wales under native rule.[27] The union of the ruler and a defined territory is exemplified by the response of Llywelyn ap Gruffudd to the suggestion made to him late in 1282 that he might agree to abandon his principality – now reduced to Gwynedd above Conwy and a few outliers – in exchange for an English earldom. Llywelyn replied that he would not consider abandoning his inheritance and that of his ancestors, and that in any case his council would not allow him to renounce territory which was a part of the principality of Wales which he and his ancestors had held since the time of Brutus.[28]

Within the major polities of Wales that were beginning to assume a more lasting form the process of definition of boundaries was further strengthened by several interrelated institutional developments. Of great and still underestimated importance was the transformation, under Norman influence, of the structure of the church. The twelfth century saw a great advance in the ecclesiastical territorial framework within Wales. By mid-century, four territorially defined bishoprics had emerged, at Bangor, St Asaph, Llandaf as well as the long-established centre of St David's.[29] Each of these locations had claims to venerable traditions of spiritual eminence, but now these crystallized into precisely defined areas of responsibility and authority. There were of course disputes as to the extent of the lands within which each of the bishops had authority, but these only served to underscore the fact of growing territorial fixity: Llandaf and St David's collided in the early twelfth century over significant claims by the former to extend its territorial authority into lands that fell within the see of St David's, and in a celebrated incident Gerald of Wales succeeded in 1176 in foiling a bid by the bishop of St Asaph to annex Ceri – and apparently a wider swathe of territory in the land between Wye and Severn – from St David's.[30]

Above the level of the territorialized bishoprics there existed the tantalizing prospect of an archbishopric for all of Wales. An archbishopric of St David's was a project that Bishop Bernard of St David's (1115–48) – albeit that he was a Norman, and quite possibly because he was a Norman – fought strenuously to promote, and which half a century after Bernard's death Gerald of Wales made another determined but ultimately fruitless effort to realize.[31] Though there was to be no medieval archbishopric, the notion of an ecclesiastical authority extending throughout Wales was one of the conceptual underpinnings of the objective of a realm, or principality, of Wales; it ought not, perhaps, to occasion surprise if the records of support for a Welsh archbishopric by Owain Gwynedd and Llywelyn ab Iorwerth should turn out to be genuine.[32] The idea quite probably gained the support of key members of the dynasty of Deheubarth, including the Lord Rhys himself, whose support may be inferred from the fact that he chose St David's as his burial place rather than the abbey which he had re-founded at Strata Florida.[33]

Below the level of the bishoprics there emerged, in the same period, a range of new strata of ecclesiastical administration. Archdeaconries, offices commanding considerable power and prestige, whose holders were men of influence over both the church and the lay power, were developed under Bishop Bernard, and rapidly spread throughout Wales, covering both *pura Wallia* and the March. Below the archdeaconries, rural deaneries came into existence, while the whole structure of ecclesiastical governance was underpinned by the growing network of parishes with precise boundaries and specific powers and responsibilities.[34] These newly developing ecclesiastical structures had very close links with the frameworks of lay governance. Thus the layout of the dioceses often reflected patterns of lay power.

The diocese of St Asaph, created in 1141, extended through much of eastern Gwynedd and almost all of Powys and reflects the political closeness of Earl Ranulf de Gernon of Chester, whose forces controlled much of eastern Gwynedd, and Madog ap Maredudd of Powys.[35] The extent of the new diocese also reflected the fact that some territories were contested, such as Arwystli, which even in the Domesday Book had been revealed as a *cantref* contested between Normans controlling parts of Gwynedd and Normans moving into mid Wales from Hen Domen, Montgomery.[36] It therefore causes little surprise that Arwystli was not included in St Asaph, even though its king was closely aligned to the Powysian ruler Madog ap Maredudd in the mid-twelfth century, but was included, as a wholly detached deanery, in the diocese of Bangor.[37] It is quite possible that this, together with the creation of another detached Bangor deanery of Dyffryn Clwyd in the midst of St Asaph territory, was done to reconcile the rulers of Gwynedd, Owain Gwynedd and his brother Cadwaladr, to the new Chester/ Powys dominated diocese of St Asaph. It is perhaps significant that in 1141 Cadwaladr was closely associated with both Madog ap Maredudd and Ranulf of Chester.[38]

One of the potential political problems brought by the creation of the diocese of St Asaph was that it left the kingdom of Powys lacking an episcopal centre within its territory, in contrast to Gwynedd, which had Bangor within its heartland, or Deheubarth, which boasted St David's, and Glamorgan, in which lay Llandaf. But the problem was largely solved by the creation of an archdeaconry of Powys, centred at the ancient *clas* church of Meifod, in an area where Madog ap Maredudd was clearly attempting to develop a complex of structures, including a re-built church and a nearby newly built castle and court complex at Mathrafal, which would serve as a dynastic centre.[39] And the close relationship between political and ecclesiastical units was underscored in pronounced fashion in the early thirteenth century when Iorwerth ap Hywel, a son of the former king of Arwystli, described himself as 'dean and heir of Arwystli'.[40] Indeed, several members of ruling dynasties were noteworthy as ecclesiastical figures in the twelfth and thirteenth centuries: thus Maredudd, son of the Lord Rhys, became archdeacon of Ceredigion, while sons of Madog ap Gruffudd and Gruffudd ap Madog of northern Powys and of Gruffudd ap Gwenwynwyn of southern Powys entered the ranks of the clergy.[41]

In the south, the complexity of secular politics was recognized in the division of the see of St David's into four archdeaconries: St David's itself (corresponding to the diverse lordships of Dyfed), Brecon (corresponding to the Anglo-Norman lordship of that name and to the lordships and kingdoms and marcher lordships of Rhwng Gwy a Hafren), Cardigan (covering Ceredigion) and Carmarthen (covering the cradle of the dynasty of Deheubarth in Ystrad Tywi). A similar pattern, with archdeaconries reflecting constituent political units, sometimes corresponding to the ground plan of dynastic segmentation, applied in Gwynedd, with archdeaconries of Meirionnydd, Llŷn, Anglesey and Bangor.[42] It seems quite probable that these structures of ecclesiastical administration provided models for secular governance, and in part reflected and entrenched some of the territorial segmentary realities of the developing political geography of Wales in the twelfth century, just as a proliferation of deaneries may reflect, and may have encouraged, the development of units of local administration in the thirteenth century.

But the increasingly fixed and vertebrate nature of the Welsh polities was also emphasized by two other categories of ecclesiastical developments. The twelfth and early thirteenth centuries saw the foundation and patronage by Welsh rulers of many houses of reformed religious orders, particularly of the Cistercians. By the early thirteenth century it had become almost de rigueur for a Welsh ruling dynasty with pretentions to power and prestige to exercise patronage over a monastic establishment founded within its realm or lordship. Gwynedd had Aberconwy on the west bank of the Conwy, and Basingwerk in the eastern reaches of Gwynedd below Conwy. Southern Gwynedd, the territory in which the descendants of Cynan ab Owain Gwynedd continued to compete with Llywelyn ab Iorwerth and his successors for much of the thirteenth century, had Cymer. Northern Powys had Valle Crucis, a daughter house of Strata Marcella in the polity of southern Powys. Maelienydd in the Middle March had Cwm-hir; Deheubarth had Strata Florida in Ceredigion, and the Premonstratensian house of Talley in Ystrad Tywi.[43] In Gwent lay the house of Llantarnam or Caerleon, while there was an abortive attempt to set up a house within the lordship of Brecon at Trawscoed. The marcher lords of Glamorgan patronized the Cistercian houses of Neath and Margam, while in the uplands of Morgannwg, for long a bastion of native rule, there was an attempt to set up some form of monastic institution at Pendâr.[44] In the south-west, the abbey of Whitland lay on the very borders of lands contested by marchers and by native lords of Deheubarth.[45] The monastery thus founded and patronized would then act as a dynastic mausoleum, as an advertisement of the rulers' piety and generosity, and would provide important secretarial assistance, storage for valuables and, in its granges, residential facilities for the rulers, their entourages and officials. The obligation of the rulers to protect the monks and their often extensive properties, in particular the abbeys themselves, provided a further powerful incentive for each dynasty to become entrenched in a particular region.

That tendency to dynastic entrenchment was reinforced by another phenomenon which was particularly marked in the twelfth century: the foundation or re-building of local, subsequently parish, churches. The process can be pictured in the early decades of the twelfth century, in the reign in Gwynedd of Gruffudd ap Cynan. Gruffudd's *Life*, a product of the mid-century period, describes how under Gruffudd's governance,

> the people began to found churches, sow acorns, plant trees, and build orchards and gardens and surround them with pools, ditches and fences, to construct buildings, and to gather for use the produce and fruits in the manner of the Romans. Gruffudd also built large churches next to his palaces which he built and established beautifully, sparing no expense[46]

Many, perhaps most, of the churches that were built or significantly re-built in the twelfth century were ruined or replaced in subsequent ages, not least in the course of Victorian 'improvement', but even so much escaped destruction. Many ancient church sites are characterized by circular or sub-circular churchyards which suggest that they are of great antiquity, long pre-dating the developments of the twelfth century. But, all over Wales, fragments of church structures, walls, windows, doorways, arcading and fittings such as fonts bear witness to a great burst of church construction in the Romanesque style which betrays borrowing from Anglo-Norman and continental models.[47] The increased solidity of these structures – and the massy columns of Romanesque architecture speak of permanence – helped to anchor rulers more securely in regions in which their patronage was greatest. It was with such buildings, often constructed at great expense as 'prestige projects' as much as exercises in piety, that they identified, just as they identified their interests with the monastic houses which they and their families had founded and enriched and which were their dynastic mausoleums.

But the building of churches and the patronage of monasteries were not the only construction projects of the twelfth and thirteenth centuries which served to bring a new and important definition, sense of solidarity and identity to the polities of Wales. Much the same effect was produced by the widespread wave of castle- and court-building that characterized the Age of the Princes. Castles, especially earthwork and timber motte and bailey structures and ringworks, were introduced into Wales by the Normans, but it took only a generation for Welsh rulers to begin to make such strongholds.[48] By the later years of the twelfth century timber castles had proliferated throughout *pura Wallia*. The building of such castles seems to have entailed significant consequences. Some castles might serve to protect, and to keep guard over, the boundaries between polities. In this way they acted to reinforce the importance of demarcations of territory – and to emphasize the fixed nature of lordship.[49] Military effort might be directed against them, but it was now designed to extend the territory of one ruler at the expense of others, or to deny to opponents centres from which they might threaten other territories. The castle in other words was not only a defensive centre which served to protect the court of a particular dynasty, but a device for consolidating a ruler's hold on territory, and an administrative centre.[50] In this last capacity the castles came to be of increasing importance as centres of exploitation.

With the building of stone castles, beginning in most regions in the late twelfth century and flourishing in the thirteenth, the role of the castle was once again enhanced. The stone castle became the focus of a dynasty – was able to act as a centre for collection of dues, and in this respect it coincided with the development of a cash economy. This in turn made the ruler less necessarily mobile as itineration to consume the produce of the land became less of an imperative. In some regions, particularly Anglesey, it was complex courts – in part stone-built and apparently featuring decorative work of a high standard – rather than castles which became the focal points of political life, but they fulfilled many of the functions of castles.[51]

Dynasties began to be defined, and to define themselves, by reference to the castles and courts that they built and where they spent much of their time. The principality of Gwynedd was defined by, and focused on, Aberffraw, rather than its stone castles.[52] Powys was thought – though primarily by the jurists of Gwynedd – to be dominated by the castle at Mathrafal, though in practice it was the fortresses of Dinas Brân and Pool that were the central places of the Powysian dynasties.[53] Deheubarth was dominated by Dinefwr, described by Llywelyn ab Iorwerth in 1220 as the place to which, as if to the head of south Wales, all the privileges of south Wales had once belonged;

while in 1277 Rhys Wyndod, ruler of part of Ystrad Tywi, announced himself as the lord of Dinefwr, and thereby laid claim to a wide eminence.[54] The castle, dominating as it often did a wide landscape, as was certainly the case with strongholds such as Dinefwr, Dryslwyn, Dinas Brân, Pool, Dolwyddelan, Castell y Bere and Dolforwyn, and representing a resolve to guard territory from ravaging bands of troops and to secure the produce of its lands for its lord and his subjects, represents a visual reminder of another crucial shift in the political life of Wales which took place in the twelfth century and was continued into the thirteenth.

FROM DEVASTATION TO MEASURED EXPLOITATION

Wales in the eleventh and early twelfth centuries, as in previous centuries, was indeed marked by repeated raiding, involving pillaging and devastation of the land. That devastation was unleashed from many different directions, both inside and outside Wales, much of it the work of intruders coming across the Irish Sea, Hiberno-Norse or 'men of the Isles' and increasingly of Norman forces entering Wales from the east and roaming across wide expanses of territory.[55] But much of the destruction was caused by Welsh rulers, whose object was simply to seize spoil, or to reduce to ruin the lands associated with their opponents. In 1044, the chronicle tells how Hywel ab Edwin 'gathered a fleet of the Gentiles (Vikings) of Ireland, with the intention of ravaging the whole kingdom'. In 1047, to avenge a slaughter of his war-band, Gruffudd ap Llywelyn ravaged Dyfed and Ystrad Tywi.[56]

In 1081 there took place the murderous battle of Mynydd Carn in which, amongst great slaughter, three rulers were killed. One of the victors, Gruffudd ap Cynan, who sought to rule in Gwynedd, proceeded, according to the *Life* written in the following century, to devastate the immediate region (Dyfed) and then to lead his mainly Norse and Irish forces to Arwystli (a land from which his dead rival Trahaearn ap Caradog had emerged) 'where, raging with slaughter and fire, he dragged their wives and daughters off into captivity ... Finally he himself went off into Powys where he employed the greatest cruelty against his enemies to the extent that he did not even spare the churches.'[57] In 1105 Hywel ap Goronwy, having been dispossessed by Henry I, devastated his own former territories, 'and he burned the houses and the crops and ravaged the greater part of the whole land'.[58]

The destructive savagery of these years is perhaps symbolized by instances of the taking of the wives of prominent leaders by their victorious opponents. Thus in 1041 Gruffudd ap Llywelyn defeated Hywel ab Edwin 'and he seized his wife and made her his own'.[59] In much the same way, Owain ap Cadwgan, who had been installed in part of Powys by his father Cadwgan ap Bleddyn, made a night attack in 1109 on the castle of Gerald, the king's steward of Pembroke, at Cenarth Bychan, and after slaughtering the garrison and forcing Gerald to make a particularly undignified escape down a latrine-chute, Owain 'violated Nest (Gerald's wife) and lay with her and then returned home'. She was hardly to be distinguished from the cattle and the goods that had been taken by Owain from Gerald, as is implied in the chronicler's comment that Owain's father, frightened by the inevitable reaction by Henry I to the insult to his officer 'sought in every way to restore the woman and the spoil'.[60]

Not even the churches were immune from violence: we have seen that the churches of Arwystli and Powys were the targets of Gruffudd ap Cynan's rage in 1081. A generation later, when Cadwgan ap Bleddyn and his son Owain were attacked by a coalition consisting of their kinsmen Madog and Ithel, sons of Rhirid, Llywarch ap Trahaearn and Uchdryd ab Edwin, the forces of these latter rulers violated even the sanctuaries of the great churches of Llanbadarn Fawr and Llanddewi Brefi.[61] The same disregard for the rights of great churches to offer sanctuary was made manifest by Gruffudd ap Cynan in 1115, when, hearing that the southern leader Gruffudd ap Rhys was a fugitive in his land and had taken sanctuary in the church of Aberdaron (itself a revealing example of the way in which rulers might roam widely to escape their enemies as well as to secure plunder) 'he sent servants to drag him from the church'.[62]

Thus ravaging an opponent's lands, slaughtering his people, carrying off whole populations into captivity (effectively into slavery),[63] violating the churches which might have expected protection from him, even taking possession of his wife, were all signs of the depths of devastation and misery into which violent leaders of raiding bands had cast Wales in the eleventh and early twelfth centuries. That devastation came not only from raiders from overseas or from across the border with England, but from Welsh rulers engaged in conflict with Normans and with their fellow countrymen. In such a climate measured exploitation by rulers of their lands was a near impossibility. Instead revenue came largely from raiding and expropriation, while prestige was in large measure derived from a reputation for violence and rapacity. It is no surprise that the law texts contain elaborate rules for the sharing out of plunder.[64]

Already, however, by the final third of the eleventh century it is possible to trace change. The notice of the death of Gruffudd ap Llywelyn in 1064 in the *Brut* emphasizes his achievement in 'the taking of spoils and treasures of gold and silver and purple raiment', whereas Bleddyn ap Cynfyn (d.1075) is noted as 'a defence for the weak and the strength of the learned and the honour of the churches and the foundation and comfort of the lands'.[65] However haltingly, a concept of good governance was developing. And if we shift the focus to the late twelfth and early thirteenth centuries, it rapidly becomes clear that a significant transition had continued. There was still much fighting throughout Wales, as the sons and grandsons of the Lord Rhys (d.1197) struggled for survival and supremacy within Deheubarth, the kin of Madog ap Maredudd fought similarly in Powys, and Llywelyn ab Iorwerth (d.1240) battled to assert his supremacy, first in Gwynedd against his near kinsmen, and secondly in much of Wales. But the attacks on Welsh territory from outside Wales had become much less frequent. A major assault by Henry II in 1165 came to nothing, and threatening manoeuvres by the same monarch against the Lord Rhys resulted in a politic agreement, encouraged no doubt by Henry's preoccupations with Ireland and with the church in the wake of Archbishop Becket's murder, which saw the southern prince recognized as the king's justice in all Deheubarth.[66] In the north Owain Gwynedd had driven English garrisons out of all the territory from the Conwy to the Dee by the close of 1167, and just three years earlier the Lord Rhys had ended Norman control of Ceredigion. Even in Glamorgan, Ifor Bach, lord of Senghennydd, had launched a daring raid on Cardiff Castle in 1158, when he had captured William, earl of Gloucester, his countess, Hawise, and their son Robert. The family were held by Ifor until his demands for a restoration of lands were met.[67] The episode is symptomatic of the changes taking place: a Welsh lord had learned how to deal with a strongly built and guarded castle, and instead of inflicting

savagery on its lord and his family, held them as key assets in a nego-
tiation. The daring of Ifor Bach in seizing the earl and his family is
impressive, but equally so is the purpose to which their capture was put.

In the context of the coastal regions of Wales, the later twelfth
century still saw the appearance of threats from intruders coming
across the Irish Sea: we have seen that forces from Man arrived in
1193 to help Rhodri ab Owain Gwynedd, who had married the king
of Man's daughter, to take possession of Anglesey. But the fact that
this episode was recalled as 'the Gaelic summer' serves to underscore
the rarity of such events. In the eleventh century the presence of Irish
forces in Wales had been commonplace; by the close of the twelfth
century such presence had become exceptional.

There is certainly by the early thirteenth century a new tone to
warfare, both amongst Welsh forces and between Welsh and English.
We hear much more of agreements to avoid conflict, as in 1202, when
Llywelyn ab Iorwerth of Gwynedd and Gwenwynwyn of southern
Powys looked certain to join battle, but we then read of 'the inter-
cession of men of the Church and laymen arranging peace between
Llywelyn and Gwenwynwyn'.[68] When Llywelyn ab Iorwerth moved
against his son Gruffudd in 1221 because of the latter's oppressions
in Meirionnydd it seemed that war between them was inevitable, but

> when wise men on either side saw that there was excessive dan-
> ger … they urged Gruffudd to surrender himself to his father's
> will. And they also urged Llywelyn to receive him peacefully and
> mercifully and to remit to him all anger from a good heart.[69]

Similarly, the prospect of conflict between two brothers, Owain and
Llywelyn sons of Gruffudd, who were both potential successors to
Dafydd ap Llywelyn in 1246, was averted when they 'by counsel of
the wise men of the land, divided the territory into two halves between
them'.[70]

It is significant in this context that when Llywelyn and Owain,
sons of Gruffudd ap Llywelyn, lords of western Gwynedd, made
an agreement with Maredudd ap Rhys Gryg and his nephew Rhys
Fychan, lords of Ystrad Tywi, in 1251, they were careful to insert a
clause designed to avert future conflict. That clause stated that if any
conflict should arise between any of the lords in question, it was to be

settled by the immediate election of suitable men, by the consent of each of the parties involved.[71]

We also begin to hear of arrangements to mitigate the violence of warfare, as in 1196, when Gwenwynwyn was attacked by a combination of English and Gwynedd forces. The evidence of court poetry suggests that the Gwynedd forces carried out a campaign of devastation, in particular in the region of Mathrafal. But the English siege of Gwenwynwyn's castle of Pool came to a conclusion when, after undermining the motte, the English force allowed the garrison to march away in safety, bearing their weapons. And when in due course Gwenwynwyn besieged an English garrison which had been installed in Pool Castle, he returned the courtesy, allowing them a dignified withdrawal.[72] And in a conflict between descendants of the Lord Rhys who were struggling for territory and power in Deheubarth, Rhys Gryg captured the castle of Llandovery in 1210, when it was surrendered to him by the garrison 'upon their being given their lives and their safety and what was theirs and all their chattels free and sixteen steeds'.[73] Three years later the Welsh chronicle records that Rhys Gryg fortified the castle of Dinefwr – that is, prepared it for an attack – and that it was besieged by his nephew, Rhys Ieuanc.

> From without archers and crossbowmen were shooting missiles, and sappers digging, and armed knights making unbearable assaults, till they were forced before the afternoon to surrender the tower. And they gave three picked hostages that they would surrender the castle unless help came to them by the following day, upon their being allowed in safety their lives and their limbs and their arms. And so it happened.[74]

In 1262 Llywelyn ap Gruffudd, to the astonishment and suspicion of some, allowed his cousin Roger Mortimer and his men to march out of Cefnllys Castle when he apparently had them cornered there.[75] In such episodes as these, we have evidence of the introduction into Wales of chivalric culture, and also of the calming influence of ecclesiastics and other elements in what was essentially a new political class.

It is also clear that there had been considerable change over the course of the twelfth century in the objectives and forms of warfare in Wales. War had become in large measure a competition for control of castles – a point which in turn emphasizes once more the importance of the castle, and increasingly of the stone castle. The prominence of the castle is revealed in the pages of the Welsh chronicle: in its far from comprehensive account of the events of the first decade of the thirteenth century, it mentions no less than twenty-four instances of the construction, capture or destruction of castles in Wales.[76] In other words, warfare was becoming less a matter of raiding and devastation, and more a struggle for possession of castles. The castle may be seen as simply a stronghold offering defensive qualities and providing a base for offensive action. It was both of these things but as we have seen it became much more. Castles offered secure storage, for goods and records; they constituted statements of political power – the power to mobilize human and material resources for their construction, and the power to confine enemies in varying degrees of discomfort. Crucially, they were centres from which surrounding territory could be dominated and its population controlled.

And indeed, control of territory for the purposes of future exploitation was becoming more important than devastation as a means of asserting power. By the thirteenth century the chronicles are no longer full of accounts of pillage; instead we read of victorious leaders taking possession of the land of their opponents. Thus in 1202 Llywelyn ab Iorwerth planned to attack Gwenwynwyn of Powys and 'to gain possession of his territory'.[77] Foiled on that occasion, Llywelyn was finally able to achieve his objective in 1208 when Gwenwynwyn was held prisoner by King John, with the result that the northern ruler 'made for his territory and gained possession of it and his castles and his townships'.[78] Gwenwynwyn recovered his lands in 1210, but in 1216 he was once more driven out by Llywelyn, 'who subdued for himself all his land and gained possession of it'.[79] In the next year the sons of Gruffudd ap Rhys in Deheubarth reacted against Reginald de Braose, their uncle, who had abandoned his alliance with the Welsh rulers and made an agreement with the English government: as a result 'they rose up against him and took from him the cantref of Builth, and gained possession of it all, except the castle'.[80]

By the third quarter of the thirteenth century the actions which followed the assertion of ascendancy by a Welsh ruler had become transformed. Two episodes underscore the change. In the first, the agreement that Llywelyn ap Gruffudd made with Gruffudd ap

Gwenwynwyn in 1263, by which the Powysian ruler was restored to his territory of southern Powys, included the provision that Gruffudd was to decide whether to uphold or reject any grants of lands made by Llywelyn in that territory.[81] Here was a clear demonstration that territory seized from a defeated lord (in this case in 1257/8) was now occupied and used to reward those who were in the prince's favour. In other words warfare was concerned with long-term exploitation rather than with pillage. And in the second case, when Llywelyn ap Gruffudd drove Gruffudd ap Gwenwynwyn from Powys in 1274, in contrast to the murderous retribution on Arwystli and Powys practised by Gruffudd ap Cynan in 1081, the Welsh chronicle records simply that he 'placed officers of his own in every place in the territory'.[82] It was probably not an entirely gentle transition, but essentially all that happened was a change in the personnel of administration. There could hardly be a better illustration of the fact that the economic base of Welsh polities had moved from the seizure of plunder to more regular and measured exaction.

The degree of instability in eleventh-century Wales (and indeed in previous centuries) and the shift to polities more subject to systematic governance rather than pillage and destruction is a potent explanation for the fact that the eponyms of many of the *gwelyau* (i.e. units of settlement of members of a particular lineage) recorded in fourteenth-century and later extents can be reckoned to have lived in the twelfth or thirteenth centuries. It is surely not the case that this phenomenon reflects a shift from a semi-nomadic society to settled agriculture in that period, but rather that the greater stability generated by twelfth-century political developments encouraged population growth and allowed settlement to become much more enduring than had been the case in the pre-twelfth-century period.[83] And a more enduring settlement pattern provided a sounder basis for agricultural production, which in turn facilitated the exaction of dues by the ruler. It is surely no coincidence that it is from the second half of the twelfth century that we can trace complaints against the increasing pressure of governance on the free population which was being imposed by rulers.[84]

There were of course still moments in the early thirteenth century when devastation was unleashed in and on Wales. As well as the destruction caused by English invasions, there are still references to pillaging carried out by Welsh rulers. But increasingly Welsh devastation was often targeted at towns and areas of English settlement in the March, as will be made clear in the next chapter. And even when he was launched on a campaign of devastation in the March, Llywelyn ab Iorwerth was prepared to come to agreement, for a cash payment, as in Brecon, 1217, when he took 100 marks to spare the town.[85] Rulers continued to be spurred on to violent action by their enthusiastic and often blood-thirsty poets, but the exhortations to destruction were increasingly balanced by more politic considerations, the product, perhaps, of advice from administrators, ecclesiastics and lawyers.

THE CHANGING ETHICS OF DYNASTIC ELIMINATION

A further indication of fundamental shifts in the political climate in Wales is provided by the way in which those who sought Welsh hegemonies became less concerned with removing rulers from other dynasties and more prepared to accommodate them by ensuring that they held lands under the hegemonists' suzerainty. This even applied to those with whom they had come into conflict, as in the case of Elise ap Madog of Penllyn and Edeirnion, who had refused to join Llywelyn ab Iorwerth in an attack on Gwenwynwyn of Powys in 1202; Elise was deprived of much of his territory by Llywelyn, but he was not killed or maimed or driven out entirely: instead 'Llywelyn of his mercy allowed Elise the castle of Crogen and seven small townships along with it'.[86]

It was however in 1216 that Llywelyn demonstrated his ascendancy most effectively by supervising a partition of Deheubarth amongst the descendants of the Lord Rhys, whose sons Maelgwn and Rhys Gryg, and grandsons Rhys Ieuanc and Owain sons of Gruffudd, all received substantial territories.[87] In the same year, when Gwenwynwyn of Powys refused to accept Llywelyn's suzerainty and was driven into England, some of the rulers who had helped Llywelyn to expel him were rewarded with parts of southern Powys: Maredudd ap Rhobert of Cedewain took the lands between Rhiw and Helygi, and Gwenwynwyn's brother Caswallon appears to have been confirmed as the lord of some of the lands abandoned by the departed ruler.[88]

When Rhys Ieuanc of Deheubarth died in 1222 his brother Owain succeeded to some of his territory, but the chronicle notes that 'he received only a portion of his brother's patrimony; and the other portion Llywelyn gave to Maelgwn ap Rhys'.[89] Llywelyn, acknowledged as the dominant force in Wales, was adjusting the political balances of *pura Wallia* by making important adjustments of territory. The same pattern in which a prince re-allocated lands amongst subordinate lords was repeated in the period of Llywelyn ap Gruffudd. To take just one example, the chronicle entry under 1256 records that, having made himself master of Gwynedd, Llywelyn turned his attention to territories further south, seizing Edward's land in Ceredigion which he gave to Maredudd ab Owain, together with the lordship of Builth; he also turned on Rhys Fychan of Ystrad Tywi, 'expelling him from his territory and giving it to Maredudd, and keeping naught for himself, only fame and honour'.[90]

A similar and related shift is also visible in the methods and ethics of elimination of rivals within and between dynasties. In the late eleventh and early twelfth centuries it appears that the standard means of dealing with a rival was to kill or maim him, the latter by blinding, an atrocity sometimes complemented by castration. A veritable orgy of killing and maiming of near kinsmen amongst the ruling dynasty of Arwystli in the few years after 1127 is only the most extreme example of a practice that was widespread.[91] Savage elimination continued for some time: in 1152 Owain Gwynedd 'caused Cunedda ap Cadwallon, his nephew ... to be castrated and his eyes to be gouged out of his head'; in 1175 Hywel ab Iorwerth of Caerleon seized Owain Pencarn, his uncle 'and he gouged his eyes out of his head and castrated him, lest he should beget issue who might hold authority over Caerleon', while in 1193 Anarawd ab Einion, a kinsman of the Lord Rhys, 'in his greed for worldly power' seized his two brothers, Madog and Hywel, 'and had their eyes gouged out of their heads'.[92]

But such atrocities were becoming rare. The later twelfth and thirteenth centuries saw the replacement of 'casual' blinding, emasculation and killing by trial and imprisonment and sometimes by the loss of territory. Thus Gruffudd son of Llywelyn ab Iorwerth was imprisoned by his father in 1228. Released and granted extensive territories in 1234, by the end of the decade he was deprived of many of his lands by his brother Dafydd, who finally imprisoned him in Cricieth Castle in 1240.[93] So, too, Owain and Dafydd sons of Gruffudd were imprisoned by their brother Llywelyn after the battle of Bryn Derwin in 1255; Dafydd was soon released, but Owain was held, probably at Dolbadarn Castle, for over twenty years.[94] And in 1259 the southern lord Maredudd ap Rhys was judged to have betrayed Llywelyn by an assembly called to Arwystli, and was imprisoned in Cricieth Castle until he provided suitable guarantees of his future loyalty.[95] A similar fate befell Owain, eldest son of Gruffudd ap Gwenwynwyn of southern Powys, taken as a hostage by Llywelyn ap Gruffudd after he and his father were accused of infidelity to the prince at a gathering at Dolforwyn Castle in 1274.[96]

The reasons for the changes in aspects of political culture noted above are complex, and much work remains to be done before they can all be unravelled, but they include the example offered by English royal practice. The actions of the English kings were not above reproach, of course, but they were played out against a background of expectations that proper process would be observed. The apparently murderous elimination by King John of Arthur of Brittany was not without repercussions.[97] Again, increasingly organized and powerful clerical and monastic establishments might provide rulers with guidance and might also confront them with the prospect of spiritual sanctions should they stray too far from what the Church regarded as proper behaviour. On the one hand a bishop of Bangor (Anian) might lament in 1277 that he had not been able to stir a foot except under the power of Llywelyn ap Gruffudd, but on the other a bishop of St Asaph (Anian II) was able to launch a widely publicized and longrunning campaign against the same prince in the 1270s in defence of the bishop's conception of the liberties of the Church.[98]

THE INCREASING COMPLEXITY OF PRINCELY GOVERNMENT

A further factor involves developments in what we may call the organisational infrastructure of Welsh polities. The twelfth and thirteenth centuries saw the development of visual expressions of princely and lordly power and prestige. At least in some cases, the stone castles, as well as the more prominent *llysoedd*, were adorned with impressive stone decoration which enhanced the prestige of their lords.[99] They were also complex structures, affording an element of privacy, even secrecy, to the rulers. Thus Gruffudd ap Gwenwynwyn's wife Hawise Lestrange was said to have kept documents relating to a conspiracy against Llywelyn ap Gruffudd in a chest in Pool Castle – and this perhaps suggests that she had a private apartment in which to store such material.[100] And at some point before the war of 1277, when Archbishop Kilwardby sent messengers to Llywelyn ap Gruffudd who was holding his court at Llanfaes, the prince was able to administer a diplomatic snub by refusing them admission to his presence. The envoys had to be content with discussions with the prince's ministers and members of his household.[101]

The environment in which the rulers moved was becoming more complex, and not only in terms of the buildings within which they operated. The court of a Welsh ruler, particularly of a ruler with aspirations to hegemony, was becoming more numerous and more diverse in the course of the Age of the Princes. In terms of the range of people to be found at the ruler's court, and the variety of business – and pleasure – transacted there, Welsh court politics were becoming 'denser' and far more complex. It is now well established that by the thirteenth century there existed a core of experienced ministers who were engaged in financial, diplomatic and military affairs, and general administration of the ruler's lands and castles.[102] Many of the most senior of the ministerial elite had experience of travel in England and even in continental Europe. They were known and welcome at the English royal court and in the castles of marcher lords. Some of them were married to women of Welsh ruling dynasties and of families of marcher lords.[103] They brought, as did several ecclesiastics to be found in the princes' entourages, a crucial breadth of experience and acquaintance to the princes' councils. It is hardly a coincidence that the surviving poetry of the Gogynfeirdd in the thirteenth century reveals an increasing representation of poems to members of just that ministerial elite.[104] The twelfth and thirteenth centuries indeed witnessed the rise of experts in a wide range of professions: poets, lawyers, physicians, military engineers and specialist soldiers.[105] The Age of the Princes was thus also increasingly an age of professional expertise, and governance was thereby rendered still more complex.

Some of the shifts in the political culture and structures of Wales discernible in the twelfth and thirteenth centuries meant that as well as nurturing an increasingly important 'ministerial aristocracy' princes had to encourage, intimidate and conciliate dependent rulers. Such glimpses as we have of the princely courts reveal a regular presence of lesser rulers, particularly but not exclusively on important occasions. The presence of lesser rulers may be assumed at the 1176 'eisteddfod' organized by the Lord Rhys at Cardigan, the 1238 Strata Florida assembly at which dependent lords swore fealty to Dafydd ap Llywelyn, and the 1259 Arwystli gathering at which Maredudd ap Rhys of Ystrad Tywi was convicted of infidelity to Llywelyn ap Gruffudd.[106] Such a presence can be clearly demonstrated at the assembly which witnessed the 1258 agreement between Llywelyn ap Gruffudd and other Welsh rulers and Walter Comyn, earl of Menteith, and his allies. Llywelyn appears at the head of seventeen lesser lords as well as his key ministerial entourage.[107] Again, the 1274 *causa accusationum* at which Gruffudd ap Gwenwynwyn and his son Owain were judged to have offended against their fealty to Llywelyn ap Gruffudd was attended by six subordinate lords and many of the ministers of both Llywelyn and Gruffudd.[108]

Amongst those who do not generally appear in the witness lists of the princes' *acta*, or are not listed as present at major events, the rulers' wives were undoubtedly important. It was certainly true that wives of Welsh birth sometimes wielded great influence over their husbands: the determination of Cristin, wife of Owain ap Gruffudd, to promote the interests of her sons, Dafydd and Rhodri, at the expense of sons born of other partners may provide an instance.[109] A little later, in 1188, Gruffudd ap Madog of northern Powys was persuaded by Archbishop Baldwin to put away his wife, Angharad, on the grounds of consanguinity; but it is clear that Angharad continued to be an important presence in the court, even in the period of their son, Madog.[110] On occasion the wives may be seen working assiduously in their husbands' interests, as in the case of Senana, wife of Gruffudd ap Llywelyn. When Gruffudd was held in captivity by Dafydd ap Llywelyn Senana was able to gather a most significant array of Welsh and marcher lords and notables to stand surety for her offer of money to Henry III to secure Gruffudd's release and re-instatement in Gwynedd. Her campaign was eventually unsuccessful, but was none the less impressive.[111]

Such prominence was particularly the case when wives were drawn from marcher nobility or, even more significantly, from English royalty. Into the former category came such eminent women as Margaret Corbet, wife of Gwenwynwyn of southern Powys, Hawise Lestrange, wife of his son Gruffudd, Joan Corbet, wife of Gruffudd's son Owain, Emma Audley, wife of Gruffudd ap Madog of Bromfield (northern Powys), Matilda de Braose, wife of Gruffudd ap Rhys of Deheubarth, and a later Matilda de Braose, wife of Rhys Mechyll ap Rhys Gryg, as well as Isabella de Braose, who married Dafydd ap Llywelyn of Gwynedd. Welsh rulers' wives who were drawn from English royalty were Emma of Anjou, sister of Henry II, Joan, daughter of King John, and Eleanor de Montfort, whose mother was also a daughter of John.[112]

Such wives could not be pushed into the background at their husbands' courts: it is clear that several of them were formidable personalities. Matilda de Braose, for instance was credited in the *Brut* with handing over Carreg Cennen Castle to 'the French' out of hostility to her own son, Rhys Fychan.[113] The implication is that Matilda was capable of independent, and dramatic, action, and that she was able to control possession of a major castle. But apart from such personal qualities as they possessed they represented significant conduits for information and support from the March or the English royal court, and might make valuable, and in some cases vital, interventions in the relationship with the English kings. Into the last category come the actions of Joan, wife of Llywelyn ab Iorwerth, who interceded with her father to spare Gwynedd further destruction when John launched his great attack on Llywelyn in 1211; the following year she intervened once again, when John was gathering his forces for a second and even more crushing assault, by informing him that there was a plan amongst his nobles to kill him while he was on campaign in Wales. Her warning served to deter John from his planned attack, and quite possibly saved Llywelyn from destruction.[114] Joan's involvement in Anglo-Welsh politics extended into the reign of her half-brother Henry III, when she worked to mend relations between her husband and the king in the troubled early 1230s.[115] Eleanor, wife of Llywelyn ap Gruffudd, also played a significant part, if we can assume that the letters sent in her name reflect her own wishes and actions, in attempting to improve relations between Llywelyn and her kinsman Edward I in the years after her marriage in 1278.[116] It is a matter for speculation how far it was a response to his marriage to Emma of Anjou that caused Dafydd ab Owain to be characterized by Gerald of Wales as one of the rulers who had observed strict neutrality between Welsh and English.[117]

We must begin, therefore, to envisage the princely courts as places where the ruler was subject to many different forms of counsel, including members of the ministerial elite, representatives of the elders, the *seniores* or *optimates*, of lands under their rule, monks of favoured houses who sometimes acted as diplomatic envoys on behalf of their princely patrons, ecclesiastical dignitaries and their envoys.[118] They would be likely to listen to the views of members of their families including their wives, and their own sons and on occasion their nephews who appear in records from some regions as giving consent to rulers' grants, and who might be entrusted with military responsibilities and lordship over regions within the wider realm.[119] They would hear advice and entreaty from dependent lords, such as Maredudd ap Rhobert of Cedewain, a close confidant of Llywelyn ab Iorwerth, and who was described at his death as 'the chief counsellor of Wales', or Maredudd ab Owain of Ceredigion, described in his obituary notice in the *Brut* as 'the protector of all Deheubarth and the counsellor of all Wales'.[120] And they would be the targets, as well as the beneficiaries, of the praises sung by the court poets. It is to this last group that we now turn.

The court poets were the professional propagandists of the ruler's court. They were not mere sycophants, for they might on occasion turn against their patron, though at some considerable risk and at some cost, as their production of *cerddi dadolwch*, poems seeking reconciliation, indicates.[121] But most of the working life of a court poet was devoted to composing poems, for public recitation in song, praising their patrons; some of these poems were *marwnadau*, elegies for a dead ruler. But where they were composed in praise of the living, they frequently urged the patron on to greater deeds – usually deeds of martial valour. We are becoming aware of some at least of the 'diplomatic' tasks of the court poet: recent important studies have shown poets acting in the interests of the Llywelyns attempting to secure reconciliations with other important rulers: Llywarch Brydydd y Moch composed a poem to Rhys Gryg of Dinefwr in 1220 as part of Llywelyn ab Iorwerth's attempt to reconcile Rhys to his overlordship, and Bleddyn Fardd sang to Rhys ap Maredudd of Ystrad Tywi in 1277 in a vain attempt to persuade him to support Llywelyn ap Gruffudd and not Edward I.[122] We must not assume that the poets undertook these ambassadorial ventures alone: it is probable that experienced diplomatic representatives of the northern princes accompanied them. The poems were for performance in the courts of Rhys Gryg and Rhys ap Maredudd and were almost certainly part of a multi-pronged approach to them. Behind the poetry, hard bargaining surely took place.

In many ways the court poets seem, like the jurists to whom they were sometimes related, to be the proponents of a traditional order of things. The court poets do not, for example, praise rulers for making agreements with the English kings; they do not praise them for accepting English subsidies: even when Iorwerth Goch of Powys was receiving a subsidy of over £90 per year from Henry II at the time of his death, his *marwnad* by Cynddelw records him as the enemy of the English.[123] The poets were an important feature of the rulers' courts; their exhortations were powerful and vividly expressed, and added to the mass of often conflicting counsels which the princes had to weigh. The task of ruling and reconciling different views and interests was becoming complex.

It may be significant that in the case of Einion ap Gwalchmai, the only poet who is known from record sources to have been a member of the circle of administrators, envoys and legal experts close to a prince – in this case Llywelyn ab Iorwerth – most of his few surviving poems are addressed to God, and only one is a praise poem to the ruler. This last poem is only eighteen lines long, and is in significant measure somewhat formulaic. It praises Llywelyn's martial qualities, and his exploits against the English, but pictures him primarily as a defender of his land.[124] There is a certain lack of the rejoicing in violence and aggression which characterizes much of the poetry of the Gogynfeirdd. When allowance has been made for the problems of survival, it raises a suspicion that Einion's other duties – judicial and diplomatic – meant that his poetry was of a rather different stamp from that of some of the other court poets.

The political environment in which Llywelyn ap Gruffudd moved was very different from that of Gruffudd ap Llywelyn ap Seisyll, and even of Owain Gwynedd. By the thirteenth century we hear much more about rulers acting not just in council, or within their own courts, but in great assemblies such as the Aberdyfi gathering at which the partition of Deheubarth took place before Llywelyn ab Iorwerth, the rulers of Wales and the wise men of Gwynedd, that which made an agreement with Scottish magnates in 1258, or the assembly in Arwystli in the following year, in which judgement was passed on Maredudd ap Rhys. It is appropriate to recall in this context the statement in the prologue to the 'Judges' Test Book', a part of the thirteenth-century Book of Iorwerth, that no alteration should be made by a ruler to the law unless carried out in an assembly as large as that which the law books claimed had been called together by Hywel Dda, the reputed original codifier of the Welsh laws.[125]

The princes' courts were almost certainly getting bigger: new classes of administrators, of military experts and advisors – men with experience of siege engines, of castle construction, of cavalry tactics – ecclesiastics offering advice on estate management and on diplomatic contacts as well as spiritual guidance, the entourages of rulers' wives, and the poets and storytellers, huntsmen and falconers and an expanding corps of cooks and servers, as well as local officials bringing revenues to the court, all tended towards curial expansion. The report in 1285 that Llywelyn ab Iorwerth had brought 300 men with him when he visited the Penllyn lands of Basingwerk Abbey, but that Llywelyn ap Gruffudd had brought 500 hundred, is often interpreted as a sign of the latter's rapacity. It may also indicate the scale of the expansion of the court personnel.[126]

Many of the above developments involve a growing degree of cultural and practical 'convergence' between Welsh, marcher and English royal practice, with inevitable political consequences. While much rhetoric, such as English chroniclers' horror at Welsh 'savagery' or 'backwardness', English royal pronouncements to the same end, and English ecclesiastical condemnation of the backwardness and immorality of the Church in *pura Wallia*,[127] and Welsh chroniclers' and poets' rejoicings at defeats suffered by the English enemy, emphasized ethnic difference and collision, important underlying aspects of social and institutional development tended towards assimilation. That process made the task of a would-be conqueror of the polity forged by the Llywelyns much easier.

3

The other Wales: the March

T he history of the Welsh march in the eleventh to thirteenth centuries has hitherto generally been written and considered, even by Welsh historians, from an Anglo-Norman or English perspective. Emphasis has frequently been placed on the methods by which eastern and southern Welsh territories were subjected to conquest by Anglo-Norman lords, on the types of economic, legal and political structures which were imposed or tolerated by the marcher lords, and the relations of those marchers with the English Crown.[1] But there is another side, quite literally, to this story – the Welsh view of the mysterious and extensive border zone which developed in the course of the twelfth and thirteenth centuries between English counties and Welsh kingdoms, principalities and lordships and which signified Welsh territory held by lords who were usually but not invariably Anglo-Normans/English, and who increasingly claimed and exercised special privileges, a veritable quasi-regal status.

Most of the early Anglo-Norman encroachments into Wales had almost certainly not been thought of as creating a borderland, but were regarded rather as the stepping stones that would lead to the conquest of all Wales and which had by the later eleventh century seen not only broad swathes of eastern Wales but also much of western Gwynedd as far as Anglesey and Llŷn fall under Norman control, while even Ceredigion had suffered raids and Dyfed had been occupied. But, as we have seen, in the course of the twelfth century much of the western and northern parts of Wales had come once more under native political and military control, while some eastern regions had been reoccupied by Welsh rulers, as in the case of Oswestry in the 1140s and

1150s, or threatened, as in the case of much of Glamorgan in 1183–4. In the process it appears that *Marchia Wallie* had begun to develop as a region characterized by an ethnically mixed population, often serving as a zone of containment of Welsh territorial advance.[2]

A further aspect of the March in some of its northern expanses was the movement of Welsh population into lands to the east; there was considerable Welsh movement into the western parts of the lordship of Oswestry in the middle decades of the twelfth century. Welsh settlement units, *gwelyau*, are to be found in surveys of Oswestry lordship from the late fourteenth century, and in many cases their eponymous founders can be traced to the mid-twelfth century.[3] And by the later years of the same century, the landscape east of Montgomery had seen significant Welsh settlement and influence. Llywelyn ab Iorwerth had even had one of his daughters fostered in that area by a prominent Welsh magnate, whose wife was apparently a Corbet.[4] In this and other regions members of marcher families had already begun to marry into Welsh ruling dynasties. Here are reminders that the March might in some circumstances be made, or at least adapted, in circumstances of Welsh expansion and of coexistence as well as conflict.

But by the thirteenth century the March had largely stabilized as a broad band of territory running from north to south through much of eastern Wales, sometimes embracing neighbouring English territory, and along a similarly broad band, sometimes fluctuating in extent, along much of the southern coastal region, from the Severn estuary in the east to Dyfed in the west. These marcher lands were composed of numerous lordships of very varying size. The lords were English, generally of Anglo-Norman descent, and at the start of the thirteenth century, as in the twelfth century, their companions, their major tenants and their officials, were also overwhelmingly English. The Welsh element in marcher lordships was often concentrated, though not exclusively, in the west or north of the lordships, that is in the upland Welshries in which Welsh law and custom and population continued to prevail throughout the central medieval period.[5] In many lordships there was thus a form of segregation in operation, with much of the urban development and the better lands in English-dominated areas, though some regions, in particular Gwent, were in significant measure free from the rigid division between Englishry and Welshry which characterized many marcher lordships.[6]

THE MARCH AS A ZONE OF CONFLICT

The developing March was a zone of often contradictory character-istics. It can easily be portrayed as a land marked by oppression of the indigenous Welsh by brutal incoming lords and their minions, as in the case of the blinding of a Welsh hostage, Cynhaethwy, by William earl of Gloucester (1147–83) and lord of Glamorgan, or that of the killing by William de Braose or his associates in 1175 of the Gwentian lord Seisyll ap Dyfnwal, his son Geoffrey and a group of six other magnates when they were lured to Abergavenny Castle under safe conduct on the pretext of discussing peace.[7] De Braose had compounded the offence by ravaging Seisyll's lands and captur-ing his wife, and killing his 7-year-old son. Just over two decades after Seisyll's killing something similar overtook Trahaearn Fychan of Brycheiniog, described in the *Brut* as 'a brave eminent man of gentle lineage, with the niece of the Lord Rhys as his wife'. The chronicle recounts how

> He came incautiously to Llan-gors, to the court of his lord, William de Braose, and there he was seized and imprisoned. And as a pitiful example and with unusual cruelty he was bound by his feet to the tail of a strong horse, and was thus drawn along the streets of Brecon as far as the gallows; and there his head was struck off and he was hanged by his feet; and he was for three days on the gallows, after his brother and his son and his wife, niece of the Lord Rhys, had fled from such peril as that.[8]

It is tempting to see such behaviour as typical of the activities of the marcher lords, for many more examples of oppression on their part and that of their followers could easily be adduced. And yet other incidents reveal a different side to the story. A rather different aspect of Welsh–marcher relations is revealed in a story recounted by Gerald of Wales relating to an incident a few years later in the twelfth century. Gerald tells how the ruler of Deheubarth, the Lord Rhys, came to a meeting at Hereford in the 1180s where he encountered the bishop of Hereford, and Walter fitz Robert, both of them members of the great house of Clare. Also present was Gerald himself, who by his own account teased Rhys about the struggles that he had had with the Clares, who were not only lords of Glamorgan but had for a time possessed Ceredigion. But Rhys replied with wit and with polish:

> It is true that long since we lost [part of] our inheritance to the house of Clare, but since we had to lose it, we are glad that we lost it, not to sluggards of ignoble birth, but to men of such high fame and renown.[9]

Less surprising than the Lord Rhys's courteous fatalism were the repeated attacks by Welsh forces on the lands of the March. In the twelfth century Welsh onslaughts on marcher territories were often desperate attempts to regain lands lost to incoming Anglo-Norman lords and their forces. Territory under these circumstances might change hands rapidly – as in the case of the Mortimer seizures of land in the Middle March: the Welsh chronicle records that in 1144 Hugh son of Ralf de Mortimer, who had almost certainly been driven out of Maelienydd in 1136 by the forces of Madog ab Idnerth, repaired the castle of Cymaron 'and for the second time subjugated Maelienydd'. In the following year Hugh seized and imprisoned another member of Madog ab Idnerth's family, Rhys ap Hywel, and in 1146 he killed Madog's son Maredudd.[10] Thereafter, for the best part of a century the Mortimer grip on Maelienydd was repeatedly shaken and on occasion the land was retaken by Welsh forces, now led by a ruler of Powys, now by descendants of Madog ab Idnerth and now by the prince of Gwynedd. The conflict and the hatred thereby generated became marked by obsessive resolve on both sides: Roger Mortimer (d.1282) secured a somewhat fragile, and still contested, hold on Maelienydd in the mid-1260s, but it was not until the power of Llywelyn ap Gruffudd in the marchland was broken in the war of 1277 that his family was able to build a more enduring lordship there.[11]

In the thirteenth century the power of the marcher lords was matched by the increasing strength of the armies and weaponry of the major Welsh princes. The process was exacerbated by the distraction occasioned by political crises in England – in which many of the marcher lords, as significant barons of the English polity, were inevitably involved. The March became an ever more tempting target for Welsh attacks. Those lands were clearly a place where profit and renown might be won, by re-conquest, by settlement and by plunder. The following are simply a few examples from many instances of Welsh onslaughts on the March.

In the south, after a long period of hostility, Rhys Ieuanc ap Gruffudd, grandson of the Lord Rhys of Deheubarth, and his uncle Maelgwn ap Rhys were reconciled in 1215, and the Welsh chronicle records that 'together they fell upon Dyfed, and they subdued all the Welsh of Dyfed except for Cemais. The castle of Arberth and the castle of Maenclochog they burned, and Cemais they plundered.'[12] At this point Rhys Ieuanc struck out on his own:

> he moved his host to Cydweli, and he subdued it and the commote of Carnwyllion, and he burned the castle. And thence he went to Gower, and set fire to the castle of Loughor and burned it. And he made for the castle of Hugh de Meules at Talybont, and the garrison sought to hold it against him. But he took it by force and burned some of the garrison and slew others. And on the following day he made his way towards Swansea, and for fear of him the garrison burned their town. But he, not desisting from his plan, made for the castle of Oystermouth, and on the first day he took the castle, and there he encamped that night. And on the following day he burned the castle and the town. And he took all the castles of Morgannwg before the end of three days. And he returned, joyful with victory.[13]

For the inhabitants of some of the lands thus devastated it was not the end of their tribulations. Over the winter of 1215–16 forces drawn from all over *pura Wallia* returned, and destroyed the castles of Swansea, Cydweli, Carmarthen, Llanstephan, St Clears Laugharne, Trefdraeth, Cardigan and Cilgerran. The comment of the Welsh chronicler that 'while that war lasted, so great was the mildness of the air and the fine weather that a winter as mild as that was never seen nor heard of before' can hardly have been much consolation to the inhabitants of a region which had been so thoroughly devastated.[14]

And less than two years later the Gower region was hit again: Rhys Gryg, lord of the Tywi Valley and the great castle of Dinefwr, attacked the southern March, and he

destroyed the castle of Swansea and all the castles of Gower. And
he drove all the English away from that land and took from them
of their chattels as much as he pleased: and he drove with them
their wives and children without a hope of their ever returning.
And he divided their lands for Welsh men to occupy.[15]

It almost seems as though the southern March was being used as a
place where Welsh rulers might demonstrate their power – in a period
when the English government, absorbed in internal problems and a
French invasion, was not in a position to intervene.

In 1231 Llywelyn ab Iorwerth of Gwynedd, in all but name the
prince of Wales,

destroyed Baldwin's Castle (the town of Montgomery) and Brecon
and Hay and Radnor and burned them all. And thence he went
towards Gwent; and he came to Caerleon and burned all the town
to ashes, losing, however, gentlefolk in the fighting. And thereupon he took the castle of Neath and the castle of Cydweli, and
threw them to the ground.[16]

Two years later that same Llywelyn was back in the March: he

and a mighty host along with him, went to Brycheiniog, and
he burned all the towns and castles that were in that land,
and he carried many spoils away with him. And he manfully laid
siege to the castle of Brecon every day for a whole month with
catapults, and he threw the walls to the ground. And yet he left
the castle for fear, and burned the whole town. And as he was
returning he burned the town of Clun, and gained possession of
the land that was attached to it, that is, the valley of the Teme.
And thereupon he marched to Castell Coch [Castell Bryn Amlwg,
on the borders of Clun, Maelienydd and Ceri] and razed it to the
ground; and he burned the town of Oswestry.[17]

At times an assault on the marchland seems to have taken on an
almost ritualistic aspect, marking a successfully negotiated alliance between Welsh rulers. We have already noted the attacks on
marcher territories launched by Maelgwn ap Rhys and Rhys Ieuanc

ap Gruffudd in 1215 to mark their rapprochement. It was not an isolated instance. It is quite possible that Llywelyn ab Iorwerth of Gwynedd and Rhys Gryg of Ystrad Tywi were celebrating an accord reached in 1220 when they attacked Penfro and Rhos in that year.[18] In 1257 Llywelyn ap Gruffudd of Gwynedd gained the support of the ruler of northern Powys, Gruffudd ap Madog, or Gruffudd of Bromfield. The Chester Annals record the sequel: 'About the feast of St. Michael [29 September] Gruffudd of Bromfield, having deserted our lord the king, returned to Llywelyn, and with him laid waste the marches of Hereford and Salop.'[19] In the same year Llywelyn ap Gruffudd is recorded in the *Brut* as having made peace between the leading rulers of Ystrad Tywi, Maredudd ap Rhys and Rhys Fychan, following which 'they subdued the castle of Trefdraeth, and thence they went together and burned all Rhos except Haverford'.[20] And to celebrate their political accord in 1263, Llywelyn ap Gruffudd and the lord of southern Powys, Gruffudd ap Gwenwynwyn, launched a similar campaign of devastation, for a scribe at Alberbury Priory dated a charter by reference to 'the year in which Llywelyn ap Gruffudd and Gruffudd ap Gwenwynwyn came together with a great army to destroy the marchers, and especially Roger Mortimer'.[21]

There were other motivations behind Welsh incursions into the March. On occasion such forays, particularly when launched by Llywelyn ap Gruffudd, may have been intended to drive both marcher lords and the royal government to negotiations which might result in a proper recognition of the power and status of a Welsh ruler who from 1262 was presenting himself openly as prince of Wales and lord of Snowdon.[22] Again, the marcher lordships contained some of the more productive land in Wales, as well as monastic houses of non-Welsh foundation which were relatively defenceless, and thus tempting targets, and urban foundations where stores of goods and cash invited pillage.[23] Gerald of Wales, with all the pride of a man whose roots were in Manorbier, remarked on the productive nature and the attractive quality of that area in particular, and of Dyfed in general. Gerald also noted, with the authority of an archdeacon of Brecon, that in Brycheiniog there was 'a great amount of corn ... ample pasture, and plenty of woodland, the first full of cattle, the second teeming with wild animals. There is no lack of freshwater fish, both in the Usk and the Wye.'[24] Just to the north-east, in the marcher lordship of Elfael, it was reported in 1265 that the lords 'could have in pasture one thousand oxen and cows, two thousand sheep, five hundred horses and swine as many as they willed without number'.[25]

The depredations lamented by the Margam chronicler are a telling commentary on the wealth, and thus the attraction to raiders, of the March, even when we take into account the success of the Cistercians in pastoral farming. Under the year 1223 he recorded the loss of more than a thousand sheep, and in the following year he noted the loss of 400 sheep in an attack by Morgan ab Owain. Further losses of oxen and sheep were recorded at the granges of Pennarth and Resolven in 1227, with many cattle being taken away by attackers at the latter, and still more being taken from Theodoric's grange, while in attacks on several abbey farms large numbers of sheep perished by fire.[26]

On occasions cash might be extorted by a raiding force as an alternative to pillage. We have already noted that the burgesses of Brecon bought off Llywelyn ab Iorwerth for 100 marks in 1217; the *Brut* records that in the same year Llywelyn offered the burgesses of Haverford the choice of finding a 1,000 marks of silver to escape pillage, or of surrendering themselves to him and holding all their land from him.[27] The Margam annals note a payment by the abbey to the same ruler of 60 marks in 1231, while the Tewkesbury annals record, under the same year, that the prior of Leominster was forced to pacify Llywelyn at the cost of 'a great sum of money'.[28]

The economic benefits of successful raids into the March are obvious. Herds might be re-stocked, and cash and other valuables acquired. Raiding led by a ruler enabled him to present himself as a gift-giver in the aftermath of successful – and lucrative – military action. A strong current of expectation of reward in return for fighting in the service of a ruler appears in the law books and runs through the poetry of the twelfth and thirteenth centuries. We have already noticed that the law books make frequent references to the detailed sharing out amongst officers of the court of the booty which is taken from raiding a 'strange country'.[29] The details may be increasingly archaic by the thirteenth century, but the spirit of raiding pervades the law books, and that that 'strange country' was often located in the March is made clear by the poets and the chroniclers.

The chroniclers usually describe depredations in the March without any imputation of motive, but in a few cases they make it clear that this was the course of action expected of a ruler with aspirations to a national ascendancy. Thus Gwenwynwyn's ill-fated assault on Painscastle in 1198 was ascribed by the *Cronica de Wallia* to his wish to restore to the Welsh their original dignity and the bounds that they had lost.[30] Gruffudd ap Rhys was mourned in the notice in the *Brut* of his death in 1201 as the man who would 'in a short while have restored the March of all Wales' a rendering of a Latin original which obviously seemed credible to the early fourteenth-century translator even if it probably rests on a misreading of *Marchiam* for *Monarchiam*.[31]

For the poets, carrying war into the Marches – although they hardly use the word or make precise reference to the concept – was still one of the characteristics of a true leader. Llywelyn ab Iorwerth's exploits in the southern March in 1215–17 were recalled by Llywarch Brydydd y Moch as he gleefully listed his patron's onslaughts on Swansea, Cydweli, St Clear's and Haverford, as well as his attacks in the Shropshire borderland, including actions against Shrewsbury and Montgomery.[32] The same poet, addressing Rhys Gryg of Ystrad Tywi in 1220, similarly lists the destruction that Rhys had wrought in Rhos and Penfro earlier in the year.[33] Llywelyn ap Gruffudd's exploits in that same south-western March in 1257 are praised by Llygad Gŵr, with an emphasis on destruction: killing, burning and destroying castles in Rhos and Penfro.[34] The same poet later – in the period after 1277 – urged Llywelyn ap Gruffudd ap Madog of northern Powys to solve his difficulties with the men of the northern Shropshire March by burning Whittington and assaulting Ellesmere.[35]

The raising of such expectations may account in part for some of the incursions into the March by, say, Llywelyn Fawr – establishing himself as a national leader, while enriching his troops and dependents. The March might thus act as a conduit for the carrying out of acts of violence and devastation which had the effect of satisfying, and were perhaps calculated to satisfy, a current of opinion, most clearly articulated by the poets, which regarded the provision of opportunities to amass spoil from raiding as one of the essential functions of a ruler, and which demanded of a ruler periodic demonstrations of his recognition that it was his duty to continue the tradition of engagement with the age-old foe, still pictured in terminology more appropriate to the Dark Ages, as the Bernicians and Deirans. But the March was not simply regarded as a territory in which to hold military exercises by

Welsh rulers, even though there were times when it was seen to fulfil just that function. By the 1260s Llywelyn ap Gruffudd was still making inroads into the March, but in a development which reflects rather earlier changes, already noticed, within *pura Wallia* that prince was now becoming more interested in annexation and potential exploitation than in devastation.[36] By the mid-1260s he had become in effect not only the prince of Wales, but also a marcher lord of the first rank.

ANGLO-WELSH MARRIAGES IN THE MARCH

Raiding was not however by any means the only aspect of the Welsh response to the March. Already by the later twelfth century Welsh lords had begun looking with some regularity towards the March not as a military but as a matrimonial target. For them, the March had become a marriage mart. Intermarriage between Welsh and Normans began early: we have seen that Cadwgan ap Bleddyn, perhaps the most prominent Welsh ruler of the late eleventh century, included amongst his several wives a daughter of the lord of Clun, Picot de Say.[37] And Gerald of Wales was able to trace his descent from a marriage between Nest, daughter of the southern lord Rhys ap Tewdwr, and Gerald of Windsor, steward of Pembroke and lord of Carew, a marriage which the later Gerald described as intended to give the Norman lord a firmer foothold in Wales.[38] Many subsequent marriages into marcher families seem in contrast to have been intended by Welsh rulers to give them and their families a firmer foothold in the March.

It is perhaps Llywelyn the Great, ruler of Gwynedd and much of Wales in the period 1200–40 who brought marriage into the ranks of the marcher lords to its high point. Himself the husband of a daughter of King John, he knew well the advantages that a cross-border marriage might bring. He secured a marriage for his sole legitimate son and designated heir, Dafydd, to Isabella de Braose, which brought the lordship of Builth as a dowry. And he married daughters into a number of the great families of the March: Gwladus Ddu first to Reginald de Braose and subsequently to Ralph Mortimer; Margaret to John de Braose and subsequently to Walter de Clifford; Gwenllian to William de Lacy, and Elen to John the Scot, the future earl of Chester.[39]

In Powys, more closely bound by geography and sentiment to the borderland, Gwenwynwyn married Margaret Corbet, a member of the family which held the lordship of Caus and much contiguous territory; his son Gruffudd married Hawise, daughter of John Lestrange, lord of Knockin; of Gruffudd's sons Owain married Joan, one of the Corbets of Moreton Corbet, Llywelyn married Sybil, daughter of Hugh Turberville of Crickhowell and widow of Grimbald Pauncefoot, while their sister Mabli married a FitzWaryn, and Owain's son Gruffudd married Ela, of the important family of Audley, which had a long history of involvement in the March. The Audley family also supplied a wife, Emma, to the lord of northern Powys, Gruffudd ap Madog.[40] It is interesting that these Powysian marriages all relate to the borderland adjacent to Powysian territory. This suggests that rulers of Powys were determinedly employing marriage as a way to re-establish themselves in the English territories to their east, which they looked on as rightfully theirs.

In Deheubarth one of the sons of the Lord Rhys, Rhys Gryg (d.1234), lord of Ystrad Tywi, which he ruled from the great castle of Dinefwr, married Matilda, a sister of Gilbert de Clare, earl of Gloucester and lord of Glamorgan, in 1219; his son Rhys Mechyll (d.1244) in turn married Matilda, daughter of Reginald de Braose.[41] Another son of Rhys Gryg, Maredudd, lord of Ystrad Tywi, married Isabel, daughter of William Marshal II, earl of Pembroke. Their son Rhys married Ada, daughter of Henry Hastings, whose family were lords of Abergavenny.[42] An earlier Matilda de Braose had married Gruffudd (d.1201), the designated heir of the Lord Rhys.[43] Of the daughters of the Lord Rhys, one, Angharad, married William fitz Martin lord of Cemais, while Gwladus married William Cantington, another of the lords of the south-west; a third daughter, Gwenllian, married a Talbot.[44]

These cases are by no means exhaustive – other, more minor, Welsh dynasties also pursued marriages into the Norman and subsequently English families of the March. In Glamorgan, for instance, Morgan Fychan, lord of Afan (d.1288), whose predecessors had mounted a stern resistance to Norman over-lordship, signalled the integration of his house into marcher society when he married a daughter to Walter de Sully, of one of the old knightly families of the Vale of Glamorgan.[45]

Marriage between members of the families of marcher lords and those of native Welsh ruling dynasties certainly on occasion had an impact on the nature of Welsh/marcher relations. Welsh lords might be drawn into the sometimes bitter feuds between marcher magnates. Such was the situation that followed Gruffudd ap Gwenwynwyn's marriage to Hawise Lestrange in the 1240s. The Powysian lord was soon embroiled in the conflict between his wife's family and the family of his mother, Margaret Corbet of Caus. That process was accentuated by Gruffudd's own dispute with the Corbets over possession of the Gorddwr, a territory adjacent to the south-eastern parts of his lordship of southern Powys.[46] In turn, involvement in marcher conflicts meant that Welsh lords might become familiar with the mechanisms for mitigating the effects of such disputes.

An example of these mechanisms was the love-day (*dies amoris*), a meeting of marcher lords to iron out their sometimes deadly differences. It was not unlike the *cydfodau* between Welsh regions that are clearly visible in the later Middle Ages, but which certainly had earlier roots.[47] On one occasion we have a record of a love-day called in 1255, to attempt a settlement of the tensions between Gruffudd ap Gwenwynwyn and Thomas Corbet of Caus.[48] That the event went seriously wrong when Corbet quarrelled with his vassal, Fulk fitz Waryn IV, a Lestrange ally, and Fulk, moved to great anger, renounced his homage to Thomas, merely illustrates the depth of the tensions which sometimes existed between marcher lords and lordships, which prompted marchers to seek whatever allies they could find, even, and in some cases especially, amongst their Welsh neighbours. In the case of Gruffudd ap Gwenwynwyn (admittedly somewhat exceptional in that his childhood, youth and early manhood had been spent in exile in England), his marcher links became so strong that in later years it was an easy matter for him to declare, when it suited him, that he was one of the lord king's barons of the March.[49]

Patterns of marriage between marchers and Welsh lordly families also went hand in hand with political and military alliances. An early example is provided by the well-known marriage between Nest, daughter of Rhys ap Tewdwr of Deheubarth, with Gerald the steward, one of the foremost Norman magnates of Dyfed in the early twelfth century. That marriage had the dual effects of creating conflict, as when Nest was abducted by Owain ap Cadwgan, but also cooperation, exemplified by Gerald's subsequent provision of protection for Nest's brother Gruffudd, and in the next generation the collaboration between William fitz Gerald, son of Nest and Gerald, and the sons of

Gruffudd ap Rhys in the 1147 attack on Wiston Castle. Twenty years later one of the sons of 'the king of Wales', presumably the Lord Rhys, apparently joined the force of Flemings from Dyfed who went to Ireland to fight for the reinstatement of the exiled ruler of Leinster, Diarmait Mac Murchada. Early in the third decade of the next century William Marshal the younger, earl of Pembroke, allied with Cynan ap Hywel, a grandson of the Lord Rhys. It was later recalled that William gave Cynan two baronies 'to hold down the Welsh through him'. Another grandson of the Lord Rhys, Maredudd ap Rhys Gryg, husband of Isabel Marshal, joined with his wife's uncle, Gilbert Marshal earl of Pembroke, in the early 1240s to carry out a highly successful series of annexations which significantly advanced the territorial possessions of both men – for some time, at least.[50]

It is clear that the bonds of kinship had, by the thirteenth century, extended across the division between *pura Wallia* and the March. Nor did such marriages take place solely at the level of ruling families: members of the burgeoning Welsh official class also contracted marriages with the children of marcher lords, as was the case with Rhys ap Gruffudd ab Ednyfed, whose father and grandfather had both held the office of *distain*, or steward, of the princes of Gwynedd. Rhys married a Lestrange.[51] It remains uncertain whether this link – which involved him with a family that provided spouses for the dynasty of Powys – was the cause or the effect of Rhys ap Gruffudd's decisive breach with Prince Llywelyn in the later years of the latter's principate.

It is clear that the two zones of Wales, which modern maps of medieval Wales depict as characterising the fundamental divergence between the north and west and the south and east of Wales, were not in fact sealed off one from the other – as we have seen in the case of elite marriages. It must of course be recognized that though marriages might build bridges, they might also create problems. There were surely times when the marriages that created links between *pura Wallia* and the March appear to have been less than happy. When marriage brought into Welsh polities wives drawn from the March, those women arrived with expectations – such as a right to dower lands which amounted to one-third of their husbands' real property – which ran counter to the rules of older 'classical' Welsh law. The case of Emma Audley in northern Powys gives us insights into the tensions which sometimes ensued.[52] Nevertheless, by the period of the

Edwardian conquest, a widow's right to dower – and particularly if not exclusively the right of a widow who had come from the March – had apparently become accepted as normal in *pura Wallia*.[53] Here we have an example of cultural change within Welsh native polities which seems to have been at least in part brought about by contact with the March. As will become clear, it is not a unique case.

THE MARCH AS A ZONE OF TRANSMISSION

A further category of contacts between *pura Wallia* and the March is that which focuses on the social and cultural impact of the marcher lords on Welsh society and the Welsh polities of *pura Wallia*. In many ways the March was much less a barrier to contact between English and Welsh, but rather a conduit. This idea is perhaps an extension of the analysis of Welsh/marcher marriages, and can be examined by reference to a series of specific incidents. That relations with marcher lords were not always marked by extremes of violence is demonstrated by the way in which members of the dynasty of the small mid Wales kingdom of Arwystli, which had been annexed by Powys in 1197, were able in the early years of the thirteenth century to take refuge from the Powysian ruler Gwenwynwyn in the lordship of Ystrad Yw, held by the Pichard family.[54] In many respects, Welsh rulers came to mix in constructive, even in some instances amicable, fashion with their marcher neighbours. Llywelyn ab Iorwerth has been shown to have borrowed the idea of the twin-towered gateway of Cricieth Castle from the model provided by the castle of Beeston, newly built by Ranulf of Chester, whom the Welsh prince visited during negotiations for that dynastic marriage of Llywelyn's daughter Elen with Ranulf's heir John the Scot.[55]

Again, borough foundation in *pura Wallia* was in part inspired by Welsh contact with marcher towns, sometimes as a reaction against the marcher markets which drew commerce, and thus profit, away from the lands of the lords of *pura Wallia*. A similar situation is also evident in the case of the foundation of Welshpool as a chartered borough in the mid-1240s – a move that countered the attraction of Montgomery, founded some two decades previously, as a market centre. Certainly the development of the market and fairs of Welshpool was bitterly resented by the burgesses of Montgomery, who tried for decades to secure its removal.[56] Monastic foundation also owed at least something to the marcher example – especially the spread of the Cistercians. Cistercian houses, and those of the Savigniacs who merged with the Cistercians in 1147, first appeared in the March in the 1130s and 1140s, culminating in the re-foundation of Whitland in 1148 by William fitz Hay, lord of St Clears;[57] they then spread into *pura Wallia* when Strata Florida, the foundation of the constable of Cardigan Castle, Robert fitz Stephen, was taken over and re-founded by the Lord Rhys in 1165.[58] From that point, Cistercian abbeys sprang up over the next generation in all major Welsh polities.

Of course, even if we attempt to put it in a context of generally high levels of violence throughout much of Wales, for much of the twelfth, and indeed in the first years of the thirteenth century, life for the Welsh communities in the March appears to have been marked by the constant threat, and the periodic occurrence, of extreme violence, whether from the lords of the March and their followers, or from attackers from *pura Wallia*. That aspect of life, and death, in the March can hardly be denied. But again, it is not the whole story.

INTER-ETHNIC COOPERATION IN THE MARCH

Close analysis of the charters and related documents of the marcher lordships reveals that an important change was taking place in the course of the thirteenth century. In the twelfth century, in most regions of the March, charters issued by lords were witnessed by their leading Anglo-Norman tenants and officials. There were few Welsh witnesses.

But in the thirteenth century this situation changed. An early sign comes in the great charter issued by Roger Mortimer to the abbey of Cwm-hir in Maelienydd in 1199.[59] The witness list is headed by the abbot, the prior and one canon of the Mortimer foundation of Wigmore Abbey; they are followed by a member of the grantor's family, William Mortimer, and a number of men who were clearly drawn from Roger Mortimer's household and leading tenants, but the list closes with four Welshmen, notables of the Middle March; one of them, Gruffudd ap Heilyn, reappears as a witness to a charter of Madog ap Maelgwn of Maelienydd of about 1212, as does the son of another of the witnesses of 1199, Gruffudd *Velu*.[60] It is quite probable – and an early example of political accommodation between marchers and native Welsh dynasts – that Madog ap Maelgwn had succeeded in recovering some territory in Maelienydd as a result of an agreement with the then lord of that land, Roger Mortimer.[61]

Thus the marcher lords were absorbing more of their Welsh tenants into their administration, and were beginning to make agreements with representatives of Welsh ruling houses. Absorption of another sort is indicated by the habit of some native dynasties, who began to regard themselves as fully integrated into the ranks of the marchers, and as if to prove this point adopted 'Frenchified' family names which signalled their new status: the lords of southern Powys, taking a name from their castle of Pool, became known as the de la Pole family; already the ruling family of northern Powys were appearing as lords 'de Bromfield'; and the Welsh lords of Afan went even further when they transformed themselves into the lords d'Avene.[62] The success of Welsh lords in breaking down barriers between themselves is evidenced in striking fashion in the Anglo-Norman romance *Fouke le fitz Waryn*. This survives in a fourteenth-century prose version, which is however derived from a lost thirteenth-century verse original, parts of which can be reconstructed from the prose version. The most probable date for the construction of the verse text is some point in the mid-1260s; it clearly emerged from a marcher baronial milieu.[63] The key point in the present context is the respectful way in which the Welsh rulers who appear in the romance are treated by the author. Thus Owain Cyfeiliog is noticed as a brave and proud knight (*un chevaler hardy e fer*), while his son Gwenwynwyn is pictured leading his troops, who were strong and brave (*qe fortz e hardys furent*).[64]

And other, more dramatic, forms of acculturation were taking place. This is evidenced by events in the south-east in October 1252, when Robert de Chandos, lord of Wilmaston, in the Golden Valley, and a following that included some of his esquires, men with 'French' names and at least one Welsh accomplice, gathered in Monmouth, travelled through Archenfield to the manor of Sir John de Turvill, which they burned and from which they took considerable spoil. They moved on through the land of Sir Robert Tregoz (Ewias Harold), along the edge of the land of the king, into the territory of Sir William de Cantilupe (Abergavenny). They stayed a night in the land of Sir Robert Turberville (Crickhowell), and went finally to the land of Rhys ap Gruffudd. He can be identified as the lord of Senghennydd.

There the spoil was divided, with Rhys taking fifteen oxen and one warhorse, as his share in return for harbouring the raiders.[65] They were still living under his protection in December of that year.[66] By the middle of the thirteenth century Rhys ap Gruffudd and other Welsh lords were beginning to learn how to profit from the disorder that ensued when offenders were able to move rapidly from one lordship to another.

In many marcher lordships evidence of mixing between Anglo-Normans and Welsh is provided by the witness lists to charters, which increasingly include names of people of both ethnic backgrounds. In some instances this intermingling may be deceptive: in Glamorgan, Welshmen were sometimes joined by members of Anglo-Norman families in witness lists, but generally only in the case of grants by Welshmen; those made by Anglo-Normans were usually witnessed only by Anglo-Normans. The suspicion must arise that the Welsh were not considered good enough to validate grants by settler gentry, and that Anglo-Norman attestation was thought desirable to confirm the presumably less trustworthy grants made by the Welsh.

Much more significantly, and in the main peacefully, Welshmen were also appearing as officials of some at least of the marcher lords. In the lordship of the Three Castles in Gwent, the constable of White Castle in the 1270s was Philip ap Goronwy;[67] in 1251 the castellan of the castle of Bronllys in the Clifford lordship of Cantref Selyf in Brycheiniog was one Rhys ap Meurig;[68] eleven years earlier the bailiff of Cantref Selyf was Gruffudd Fychan.[69] In the south-western marchland, the constable of Cemais in the 1240s was Gwilym ap Gwrwared, a figure discussed more fully below.[70] Indeed, some Welsh officials of the marchland were to rise to very considerable heights in the second half of the thirteenth century. Prominent amongst them was Hywel ap Meurig, who may well have been the brother of Rhys ap Meurig, the Bronllys castellan of 1251.

Hywel ap Meurig had emerged as a royal negotiator by 1260.[71] He may already have entered the service of Roger Mortimer but the first unambiguous reference to him as a Mortimer official relates to 1262, when he appears as the constable of the Mortimer castle of Cefnllys in southern Maelienydd. Hywel, his wife and his sons were captured when the castle fell to local troops in that year, but it seems that he and his family were freed when Roger Mortimer appeared on the scene.[72]

In 1271 Hywel can be found in Cantref Selyf in northern Brycheiniog, amongst a group of Welsh supporters of John Giffard, the successor to the Clifford lords, who was driving prince Llywelyn out of the region.[73] In 1274 he acted as a Mortimer agent, gathering intelligence about the movements of Prince Llywelyn in Cedewain and Clun.[74] In the next year he appears in royal service as a surveyor of castles and lands in Carmarthen and Cardigan.[75] Unsurprisingly in the context of the worsening relations between Edward I and Llywelyn, Hywel's royal and marcher connections provoked the hostility of Llywelyn and by 1276 he had been obliged to surrender his son John to the prince as a guarantee of his future loyalty. It is possible that John was released when his father found sureties totalling £100 for his loyalty to the prince. The money was put up by many of the leading Welshmen of the Middle March, and included a pledge of £40 from the abbot of Cwmhir.[76] But whatever the pressures on him to remain obedient to the prince he emerged as a royal commander in the war that Edward unleashed against Llywelyn in 1276. He can be found leading a force of some 2,700 troops from the marchland against Llywelyn in 1277. It is striking that of the twenty-seven centenars, leaders of detachments of 100 troops, who were in Hywel ap Meurig's force, twenty were Welsh, and many can be identified with confidence as men of the Middle March.[77]

Following the war of 1277 many honours and responsibilities came Hywel's way: he was appointed to take charge of the building of Builth Castle for Edward I and had a grant of the mine nearby; he undertook a number of judicial commissions for the royal government in the March and in west Wales and in particular was appointed to the Hopton Commission to hear cases arising in the aftermath of the war of 1277.[78] At some point before his death in 1281 he was knighted. His continuing association with the Mortimers is revealed by the fact that his name and coat of arms appear in St George's Roll, a Roll of Arms associated with the Mortimer family.[79] As we shall see, Hywel's descendants continued to be of great importance and influence as administrators for many decades.[80]

It is becoming increasingly clear that the Middle March was characterized by a significant number of Welsh notables who were at the very least reluctant to accept the rule of Prince Llywelyn in the marchland: we shall see that such men fought, and conspired, against the prince's power.[81] These men had grown used to the established political dispensation in the eastern March, they and their families had learned how to prosper under the governance of the marcher lords and had, like Hywel ap Meurig, developed loyalties to them. It is probable that their outlook was in significant measure dictated by self-interest. They had established a place in the society of the March not unlike that of their counterparts amongst the ministerial elites which were developing in *pura Wallia* in the thirteenth century. In that period some had come to be lords of manors, to live in fortified residences, to hold important offices and to move apparently freely between marcher and royal service. Into this last category of course comes Hywel ap Meurig; but he was not alone, and the many examples are not limited to the Middle March. A particularly good instance of progression from marcher to royal service relates to an important Welsh family in the Dyfed lordship of Cemais.

Gwilym ap Gwrwared, along with other members of his family, was prominent as an adherent both of the Fitz Martin lords of Cemais and the English king. Gwilym appears as a witness to charters issued by, or relating to, Nicholas fitz Martin, lord of Cemais, who came of age in about 1231 and died in 1282. One of the charters is dated 1241, and Gwilym appears, as he does elsewhere, as constable of Cemais.[82] In 1244, a year in which he appears as holding land from the Earl Marshal, lord of Pembroke, he joined in an attack by the marcher lords of the south-west on Maredudd ab Owain of Ceredigion.[83] By 1250 Gwilym himself was holding land from the king 'in [the] Welshry' in Ceredigion and in 1252 he is reported in the Welsh chronicle to have been the king's steward of the lands of Maelgwn Ieuanc in northern Ceredigion.[84] In 1258 Gwilym was acting as a royal negotiator dealing with problems relating to the truce arranged with Llywelyn ap Gruffudd, and in 1262 he appears as the royal constable of Cardigan, which had been committed to his care by the king's son, the future Edward I. It is a sign of Gwilym's social and administrative upward mobility that he promised to return the castle to Edward in as good a state as it was in when he took it over. He undertook to do this in a letter which was in essence identical to that issued in the name of Nicholas Fitz Martin, lord of Cemais regarding the castle of Carmarthen.[85] Gwilym was being treated in a similar way to the lord of Cemais. Another indication of Gwilym's growing importance is his appointment in September 1267, alongside one English official, Guy de Bryan, by Henry III to do and complete all things relating to south Wales contained in the peace which was then being finalized between the king and Llywelyn ap Gruffudd.[86]

Thus, in an age when some Welsh rulers were being encouraged by their poets to burn and ravage the lordships and towns of the March, there were Welsh notables who were active in attempting to safeguard from such harm the lands of lords of the March to whom they owed allegiance, and to remove the hard rule to which Prince Llywelyn had subjected marcher territories. The appeals to ethnic unity made by the propagandists of imperialistic rulers such as the princes of Gwynedd were balanced, and often overborne, by the attraction of both loyalty to settled local lordship and local or regional sentiment, as well as by the desire of increasing numbers of Welsh officials to maintain a system from which they were beginning to benefit. That such forces as these were often crucial in determining the loyalties of the Welsh political class of the central Middle Ages is only now becoming appreciated with respect to major native polities such as Powys or Ystrad Tywi. But they applied no less to the communities, English and Welsh, of the March. Within the March, Welsh populations had become, by the second half of the thirteenth century, accustomed to rule by English marcher lords. And some had learned to thrive in that situation, and to develop not just an acceptance of, but a loyalty to, those lords. When those loyalties, and the careers that were built around them, were disrupted by Llywelyn ap Gruffudd's seizure of much of the March in the 1260s, that prince found that the extension of his principality threatened him with more problems than rewards.

The March clearly exercised a fascination for the princes who strove for an ascendancy throughout Wales: it became, particularly in the thirteenth century, a political arena in which highly significant alliances might be formed – as in the case of Llywelyn ab Iorwerth's complex manoeuvres with the de Braose family in the second decade of the century, his growing closeness to Ranulf of Chester in the following decade and his alliance with Richard Marshal in 1233. Llywelyn ap Gruffudd's relations with the Mortimer family were the cause of periodic speculation and suspicion: he certainly made an apparently far-reaching alliance with his cousin Roger Mortimer in 1281, and it seems entirely likely that it was the prospect of an agreement of an even more dramatic sort with Roger's sons in late 1282 which drew Llywelyn to his fateful foray into the marchland.[87]

For Llywelyn ap Gruffudd, the lure of extending his princely power over the Welsh lords and communities of the March was irresistible and fateful. His establishment of dominance in the Middle March in the early 1260s was apparently welcomed by many of the Welsh population of that region, but as the tensions and impositions of princely rule began to bite, significant disenchantment set in, particularly by the 1270s. And even before that troubled decade, even as the Treaty of Montgomery acknowledged Llywelyn's grip on much, though crucially not all, of the March, it was evident that it was there that his rule would face some of its most destructive challenges. Armed confrontation with Gilbert de Clare in the uplands of Morgannwg and, apparently, in Elfael had already begun by January 1268, and would spread in the early 1270s to similar clashes with Humphrey de Bohun and others in Brecon.[88] The provisions of the 1267 treaty relating to Maelienydd, where Roger Mortimer was left in control, but Llywelyn was given some hope of establishing his lordship, made it almost inevitable that that cantref, too, would become a source of resentment.[89] It was perhaps in the March more than anywhere else that the principality of Wales would begin to unravel.

4

The limits to princely power

It is clear that the twelfth and thirteenth centuries saw important developments in the scope and the apparatus of governance exercised by the Welsh princes. But it is also becoming apparent that the effectiveness of such developments was often diminished by the emergence of countervailing forces. The limitations on princely power took several forms, which were often interrelated. They involved issues of geography and geo-politics, economic and financial weaknesses, the contradictions that emerged from attempts to develop the structures of governance, tensions involved in the relations of the princes with the Church, the bitterness that often characterized inter-dynastic confrontations, and the similar and very damaging weakness engendered by intra-dynastic rivalries. A further factor in the limitation of hegemonic aspirations was the defence or promotion of regional ascendancies both by lords and, increasingly in the course of the thirteenth century, by local notables (*uchelwyr*). The collision between aspirations to 'national' and 'regional' power can only, for the present, be explored by means of a few case studies which are set out in the later stages of the present chapter.

PROBLEMS OF GEOGRAPHY AND GEO-POLITICS

Descriptions of the rigours of the Welsh landscape, combined with the vagaries of the Welsh weather are not uncommon in contemporary accounts. Celebrated examples include reports of the abortive invasion mounted by Henry II in 1165, when his army was effectively washed away from the slopes of the Berwyn Mountains by atrocious August storms.[1] The difficulties encountered by Archbishop Baldwin and his party as they moved along the periphery of Wales in the course of their journey to preach the Crusade in 1188 were graphically recorded by Gerald of Wales. Thus he notes Baldwin's wry remark to his exhausted party after a particularly arduous passage of mountainous terrain in Arfon, when they recalled that nightingales were never seen in those parts: 'If it never comes to Wales the nightingale is a very sensible bird. We are not quite so wise, for not only have we come here, but we have traversed the whole country.'

Unsurprisingly, Gerald remarks on the height and the forbidding aspect of several of the mountain ranges through or past which the party travelled, such as the mountainous terrain which included the Brecon Beacons and the Black Mountains: 'the lofty mountains of Morugge, called Elenydd in Welsh', in which he includes Pumlumon; Meirionnydd, 'the rudest and roughest of all the Welsh districts; Snowdonia, where the mountains 'seem to rear their lofty summits right up to the clouds'.[2] Gerald also notes the great rivers which he perceived as dividing Wales, amongst them the Severn, the Wye, the Usk, the Rhymney, the Taf, the Tawe, the Teifi, the Dyfi, the Mawddach, the Clwyd and the Dee. Elsewhere, he draws attention to the great expanses of forest land in many parts of Wales: thus he records his travels into Powys from the south, and his passage through the 'thick and shaggy forests of Powys'.[3] The difficulties posed by the dense woodland in many parts of Wales are evidenced by the frequent references in English records to the need to cut passes through them.[4] The picture of a land fragmented by its natural features is amply reinforced by the names given to the commotes into which the *cantrefi*, or major regions were divided. The commotes are often differentiated one from the other by being described as above or below a feature such as a river, a mountain or a tract of woodland.[5]

All of these features of the landscape might have advantages to those living in or near to them: the rivers brought fish as well as water, the mountains – as in the case of Snowdonia – might be praised for the pastures which sustained herds of cattle, and the forests provided a wide range of resources, in building materials and in food. The broken nature of mountain terrain also allowed rulers, when attacked, to withdraw their people into the wild uplands, which offered places of relative safety.[6] But these same features also served to divide the parts of Wales from each other, making travel, particularly between north and south, arduous and slow. The land hardly encouraged the formation and endurance of extensive Welsh polities. Indeed, the landscape, of river valleys interspersed with dense woodland or mountains and ridges, was conducive to the cohesion and isolation of relatively small communities, resistant to outside interference and the rule of those with no connection with their areas.

In geo-political terms, it is often instructive to think of Wales as a part of the 'Irish Sea zone' and to consider the importance of links with Ireland and with the Isle of Man. Particularly in the eleventh and twelfth centuries Ireland provided a refuge for political exiles from Wales, and also a source of military support for dynastic adventurers. And even in the last decade of the twelfth century 1193 became known as the 'Gaelic summer' as one of the contenders for supremacy in Gwynedd, Rhodri ab Owain, sought to strengthen his position in the contest with his kinsmen by a marriage to a daughter of the king of Man, a tactic that brought him enough Manx troops to enable him to secure a temporary hold on Anglesey.[7] The relationship of Wales with Ireland had however already begun to shift decisively, with the arrival in Ireland of the first waves of English troops in the later 1160s.

Initially the English involvement in Ireland had had a marked effect on Wales by facilitating the rise of the Lord Rhys. Many of the English lords of south and west Wales, who might have proved dangerous threats to Rhys's ascendancy, were diverted into Irish adventures. At the same time royal policy towards Rhys underwent a significant change. In order to enable him to focus on developments in Ireland Henry moved from hostility towards Rhys to a policy of establishing him as the royal representative in south Wales, a policy shift which helped considerably to facilitate Rhys's rise to pre-eminence.[8] But increasingly, as the English dominance of much of Ireland was more firmly established, Welsh rulers were sandwiched between England and its Irish colony. The latter became a source of support for English policy towards Wales. In the wars of Edward I against Llywelyn ap Gruffudd, for example, although Ireland contributed very little to the war of 1277 – largely because the justiciar was engaged in a conflict with the king of Leinster – in the war of 1282–3, Ireland contributed some £9,000 to Edward's war effort, and in the following years paid some £30,000 of the £80,000 expended on Edward's castle-building in Wales.[9]

Much remains to be written about the Irish Sea dimension of Welsh politics in the central Middle Ages, but it is fairly clear that developing English dominance in Ireland in the decades after 1167 made it increasingly difficult for Welsh rulers to look for support from, or refuge in, Ireland. With the declining prospect of an intervention from Ireland on behalf of Welsh princes, it was the proximity of the much larger, more powerful and well-organized polity of England which was to be crucial for Welsh political development.

The impact on Wales of its eastern neighbour was immense. England might serve as a model for political and military development, and as a source of support for contestants in the political struggles within and between Welsh polities.[10] Madog ap Maredudd had maintained close relations with Henry II, which had helped him in his confrontation with Owain Gwynedd, and his example had been followed by several later Powysian rulers.[11] The Lord Rhys had been able to use his appointment by Henry II as 'Justice in all Deheubarth' to consolidate his authority over the lords of central and southern Wales.[12] Llywelyn ab Iorwerth had seen the benefits of a marriage to a daughter of King John, and we have seen that the thirteenth century had been marked by a distinct tendency for Welsh lords to marry into the families of the English marcher lords.[13] Llywelyn ap Gruffudd had appreciated that the stability of the Welsh principality which he had constructed would only be secured by English royal recognition.[14] He thought that he had secured such stability in the Treaty of Montgomery in 1267, only to see that confidence shattered in the years that followed.

The more frequent impact of England upon Wales was indeed negative. It was from England that repeated intervention came, usually directed against polities that appeared as a threat to English interests, as in the case of Henry I's attacks on Powys in 1114 and 1121, Henry II's invasions of 1157, 1158, 1163 and 1165, John's destructive assault on Llywelyn ab Iorwerth of 1211, Henry III's incursions in 1228, 1241 and 1246–7, and of course Edward I's wars of 1276–7 and 1282–3. To these major campaigns could be added numerous lesser intrusions by English monarchs, and the frequent conflicts involving the lords of the March. The need to guard against English invasion and piecemeal annexation both spurred on Welsh rulers to develop the mechanisms of government, and also distracted them from the tasks of political consolidation. The proximity of a more powerful kingdom was therefore both formative and ultimately destructive.

ECONOMIC AND FINANCIAL WEAKNESSES

A second crucial factor that undermined the efforts of the twelfth- and thirteenth-century princes to create a polity of Wales was the fragility of the economic basis of such an enterprise. Much of *pura Wallia* consisted of relatively poor land, the productive extent of which was further reduced by the fact that so much of Wales was upland terrain, where the high altitude led to a reduced growing season, and by the prevalence of forest. The predominance of uplands is easily visible in Map 1. The importance of uplands and of dense forest is also attested by the frequency with which the descriptive terms *Is Mynydd* and *Uwch Mynydd* (below and above the mountain), and *Is Coed* and *Uwch Coed* (below and above the wood) occur in Welsh commote and other geographic names. The more fertile soils were all too often those of the Anglo-Welsh borderland, and these frequently lay under the rule of marcher lords, or were vulnerable to attack from England. In many regions the Welsh economy was in consequence lacking in diversity of produce, and this in turn entailed reliance on English markets.[15]

In addition to the limitations imposed by the limited productivity of the Welsh economy, there was a significant element of financial vulnerability. The Welsh princes might well have access to cash and the growth of commutation of renders in kind, or of labour services, into renders in cash is one of the important features of the thirteenth century.[16] But the fact remained that at times of crisis the Welsh princes could not look to sources of borrowing, such as existed for the marcher lords, or to arbitrary exaction on a scale available to English kings. Important to both of these limitations was the lack of a Jewish presence in Wales. It appears that in the whole of the twelfth and thirteenth centuries there was only one Jewry in Wales, and that was confined to Caerleon, existing only for a short period in the thirteenth century. It seems quite likely that this was a creation of William Marshal after his acquisition of the lordship in 1217, and that it came to an end by the 1240s. Not only was there no Jewry in *pura Wallia*, but there was no Jewry in the adjacent English territories of Cheshire or of Shropshire. There is a little evidence for some Jewish presence in the latter county, but it was on a very small scale and only short lived.[17] It appears as though Jewish communities were not encouraged to develop where they might have had ready access to the Welsh principalities. Though some ecclesiastics in Wales, even in Bangor, did arrange loans from English Jews, and several marcher lords were heavily dependent on such credit, there is no record of borrowing from Jews by Welsh rulers, and the absence of Jewries within their principalities meant that they were denied the option of the sort of exactions to which the English kings, particularly Henry III, subjected the Jews. And of course, in the period of decline of the English Jewish community in the 1270s and 1280s Llywelyn ap Gruffudd had no counterpart to Edward I's ability to borrow from the Italian banking consortia. A dimension of financial support was thus denied to those attempting to build a Welsh polity.

CONTRADICTIONS INHERENT IN DEVELOPING GOVERNANCE

A third category of problems – and it is an extensive one – was created by in-built contradictions in the structure of governance which the princes of the twelfth and more persistently of the thirteenth centuries were attempting to develop. This process may be illustrated in a number of ways. We have seen that one of the important developments of the Age of the Princes was the emergence, particularly striking in the thirteenth century, of an administrative elite, prominent as advisers, stewards, financial officials, diplomats and castellans and military leaders. Such a corps of officials needed to be rewarded by grants of lands, cash and privileges. In most parts of Wales the extent and nature of such rewards can be glimpsed only occasionally and dimly, but in the key region of Gwynedd, the core territory of the thirteenth-century hegemonists, the system of rewards for service is much clearer.[18] Members of a small number of families were particularly prominent in princely service, and it is clear that they received grants of land, and in many cases it is equally evident that their lands were to be held by hereditary tenures which involved immunities from most obligations, with the exception of military service. Such grants made service to the prince attractive, but they also reduced the ability of the princes to exploit their lands. Once begun – and it seems probable that Llywelyn ab Iorwerth was mainly responsible for the introduction of hereditary privileged tenures amongst his officials – the system must have generated serious structural problems for the princes of Gwynedd. In the first place we must assume that the system of hereditary tenurial immunities would have created expectations that service would be rewarded with similar grants. That in turn may have forced the princes to restrict entry to the ranks of the administrative elite, for to have widened the circle from which officials were appointed would have threatened to reduce the rulers' fiscal base. One probable consequence of this situation was that the princes became unable to appoint officials simply on the basis of proven ability, but were forced to restrict the official cadre to members of already privileged families. And amongst those families it appears that in some cases individuals sought to protect their privileges by looking to the English kings for protection against a prince such as Llywelyn ap Gruffudd, who was seen increasingly as a ruler who was encroaching upon the rights of those who were subject to him.[19]

TENSIONS IN THE PRINCES' RELATIONS WITH ECCLESIASTICAL INSTITUTIONS

In the pursuit of political dominance the princes relied to a significant extent on ecclesiastical support – we have seen that clerics and monks were important as diplomats, as administrators and as custodians of important documents, while the abbey granges and sometimes the abbeys themselves provided residences for rulers. But while the Church might prove a useful adjunct to princely power, it also imposed limits to the exercise of such power. The bishops and senior figures in the diocesan structures were of course valuable as diplomatic envoys and even as educated men who might undertake roles in the princes' administrations. But they were ultimately dependent on Canterbury, and thus had potentially divided allegiances, a problem that might become acute at times of conflict with England.[20]

The re-built or newly constructed churches of the Age of the Princes were of course expressions of spirituality, but they brought other, and worldlier, implications. Saints' cults might, in their distribution, reflect important political affiliations and also limitations. Thus there is a striking similarity between the distribution throughout southern Wales (south of the Severn/Hafren region) of churches dedicated to Dewi and the regions over which the Lord Rhys exercised authority in the period after his designation by Henry II as 'justice' in all south Wales. That authority seems not to have been confined to Deheubarth, but to have extended periodically into Rhwng Gwy a Hafren and even into south-eastern Wales.[21] But the northern half of Wales was devoid of Dewi dedications, and this may signal a profound barrier between Gwynedd and Powys on the one hand, and the southern polities on the other. The Lord Rhys certainly had ambitions in the lands to the north, particularly in Meirionnydd, but in them he was a stranger, without obvious dynastic roots, and perhaps he could not be seen as fully representative of a spiritual/cultural continuum.

Where saints' cults crossed boundaries between polities they might provide pretexts for aggressive political action. One may speculate whether Llywelyn ap Gruffudd's insistence on annexing Cedewain in 1261/2 may have been facilitated or even stimulated in part by the fact that it was in that region that church dedications, and hagiography, located the early ministry of Beuno, whose later career was focused on Llywelyn's heartland of Gwynedd and the great church of Clynnog Fawr.[22] Again, it seems possible that it was the existence in north Wales of churches associated with the cult of Tysilio that helped to give Owain Gwynedd, under the urging of Cynddelw, a justification for intervening in the politics of Powys, the heartland of the Tysilio cult.[23] Saints' cults may thus be classified amongst the elements which on occasion promoted 'imperial' tendencies amongst the princes. But this was not the case with all saints' cults, for they might become associated with local resistance to external control, and they might even act as signs of highly local identities: thus Powys might be identified as 'Tysilio's land', and specific local concentrations of cults, at a highly circumscribed level as in the case of the Tydecho dedications in Cyfeiliog/Caereinion, or of a more extensive type as exemplified by the Cadog dedications in the south-east, may have served to strengthen local and regional identities which perhaps transcended the spiritual and had implications for the socio-political life of the affected communities.[24]

Even more significantly, the princes had confirmed the bishops in possession of large estates and had endowed the monasteries with extensive lands and privileges. The large estates of the monasteries, and particularly of the Cistercians, had very usually been granted on remarkably privileged terms. A recurrent phrase in the rulers' charters of endowment was that lands had been granted 'free of all secular exaction and custom'.[25] Episcopal estates were very extensive, and they too were privileged.[26] The geographic extent and worth of episcopal lands is in some cases hard to establish with any certainty, but the extent of the lands of the bishop of Bangor drawn up in 1306 reveals that the episcopal estates in north-west Wales, together with some outlying lands in Arwystli and Dyffryn Clwyd were worth at least £100 per year – perhaps one-tenth of the value of the rents and services due to the prince from Gwynedd above Conwy.[27]

Welsh rulers had gained prestige by endowing religious orders with wide territories and privileges, and they had gained valuable support by acting as the protectors of the Church. But as the thirteenth century advanced, the tempo of endowment slowed and all but ended. A continued enthusiasm in Cistercian houses outside Gwynedd for the Llywelyns is evident, as in the case of Whitland in the second and third decades of the century, and in Cwm-hir a generation later, while most of the Cistercian abbots whose houses possessed lands in Llywelyn ap Gruffudd's principality wrote in his support in 1274 against the accusations levelled against him by the bishop of St Asaph.[28] But the temptation experienced by an over-stretched prince to encroach upon the rights and privileges of the Church and of the monastic orders can be seen in the clashes that Llywelyn ap Gruffudd had with the bishops of Bangor and St Asaph, and the complaints made by the abbot and convent of Basingwerk.[29]

Llywelyn appears to have remained on good terms with many of the Cistercian houses, though even with some of those the relationship with the prince was beginning to become fraught by the later years of Llywelyn's life. Aberconwy Abbey, formerly one of the mainstays of the regime of the princes of Gwynedd, was obliged to proffer £40 to Llywelyn ap Gruffudd in 1281 in order to secure the prince's benevolence.[30] Basingwerk Abbey in Tegeingl was absent from the list of Cistercian houses whose abbots wrote in support of Llywelyn in 1274, and it is clear that the same house was aligned to the English kings against the rulers of Gwynedd in 1241 and 1276–8. It seems likely that the Powysian house of Strata Marcella was similarly aligned against Llywelyn ap Gruffudd in the conflict of 1277, and this perhaps raises the possibility that the inclusion of that house in the letter of support for Llywelyn sent in 1274, when the prince had annexed southern Powys, may have been the result of a measure of coercion.[31]

TENSIONS ARISING FROM RELATIONS WITH OTHER WELSH DYNASTIES

By the thirteenth century ambitious princes relied to an increasing degree on the support of lesser rulers. The evidence points to a rather different situation in the twelfth century. Thus the chronicle accounts of the campaigns waged by the Lord Rhys seldom suggest that his forces were augmented by those of allied subordinate rulers, even though there were occasions, such as the conference with Henry II of 1175, when he could bring together many of the rulers in the southern half of Wales, perhaps by virtue of his role after 1172 as Henry II's lieutenant in that region. It is evident that he sometimes acted in alliance with others, as in the case of the great confederation of 1165 against the incoming Henry II. Rhys was again allied with Owain Gwynedd and Cadwaladr ap Gruffudd in an invasion of Powys in 1167, and later in the same year in the taking of Rhuddlan Castle from the English. The intervention in Powys was undertaken with the support of one of the Powysian rulers, Owain Fychan.[32] Most other references to military activity on Rhys's part imply that he acted alone, or with the support of some of his many sons. Rhys's ability to act without the military backing of other rulers was quite possibly related to the fact that most of his campaigns took place in the south, in areas adjacent to his power base in Ceredigion and Ystrad Tywi.

Gwenwynwyn, who may be regarded as having established a limited ascendancy following the decline and death of the Lord Rhys, engaged in military activity that was widespread and which was marked, perhaps necessarily, by cooperation with other rulers. His 1198 Painscastle campaign was undertaken 'with the help and support of all the princes of Wales' – many of whom are recorded as having been killed or captured.[33] Maelgwn ap Rhys in the south, and Maredudd ap Cynan in Gwynedd and Elise ap Madog in Penllyn and Edeirnion seem to have been amongst the rulers who accepted Gwenwynwyn's leadership.[34] And the ascendancy of Llywelyn ab Iorwerth, occupying most of the first forty years of the thirteenth century was clearly marked by that prince's ability to enlist the military support of several lesser lords. An illustration is provided by Llywelyn's 1215 campaign in south-west Wales, which involved a long list of allied leaders: Hywel ap Gruffudd ap Cynan and Llywelyn ap Maredudd from Gwynedd, Gwenwynwyn of southern Powys, the war-band of Madog ap Gruffudd of northern Powys, Maredudd ap Rhobert of Cedewain, the sons of Maelgwn ap Cadwallon of Maelienydd, Rhys Gryg and Maelgwn, sons of the Lord Rhys, and Owain and Rhys, sons of Gruffudd, grandsons of the Lord Rhys.[35] But as we shall see, the acquisition of allies by a would-be hegemonic ruler might well prove difficult to sustain when he proceeded to convert them into dependents and ultimately vassals.

In other and more complex ways success in extending princely dominion might bring with it damaging consequences. The extension of lordship over subordinate rulers who were often at odds with each other entailed problems of control in a principality riven by internal hostilities, and with inadequate resources to satisfy all of the contending parties. Thus, when a previously hostile lord accepted the lordship of a would-be hegemonic prince, that submission was almost always made on terms. But in the process of confirming to the new adherent a reasonable and perhaps an extensive territorial provision, the prince ran the risk of disappointing existing vassals amongst the Welsh rulers.

The situation in Ystrad Tywi provides a good example of this problem. It was a territory that had been ruled by one of the sons of the Lord Rhys, Rhys Gryg, who had died in 1234. His descendants subsequently engaged in a relentless struggle to assert mastery in the territories over which he had ruled. In 1240 Maredudd ap Rhys had seized the commotes of Catheiniog, Mabudrud, Mabelfyw and Gwidigada from his brother Rhys Mechyll. In 1256 Maredudd ap Rhys, once more disinherited, now by Rhys Fychan, the son of Rhys Mechyll, had joined with Llywelyn ap Gruffudd in a campaign in Gwynedd is Conwy, and had then been restored to his hereditary lands. But in 1257 Llywelyn is recorded as having made peace between Maredudd and Rhys Fychan. The latter recovered significant territories and Maredudd was thwarted in his evident ambition to control all of Ystrad Tywi.[36]

The terms of the agreement between Maredudd and Llywelyn ap Gruffudd in 1261 cannot conceal the fact that the territorial settlement contained in it satisfied neither Maredudd nor Rhys Fychan.

Something of the tension that existed between them is revealed by the clause which states that at Llywelyn's order, Maredudd is to lead all his forces with the (other) lords of Wales, or with some of them, except with Rhys Fychan, with whom he is not bound to campaign in person, unless sent help by Llywelyn from Gwynedd. Although not obliged to campaign with Rhys Fychan, Maredudd was expected to send his forces to go with Rhys.[37] The implication is clear: Maredudd and Rhys Fychan might both be vassals of Llywelyn, but they were not reconciled with each other, and this surely created a massive weakness in the political edifice that Llywelyn was building. By 1265 Maredudd was back in the allegiance of Henry III. His homage was reserved to the king in the Treaty of Montgomery of 1267 when that of all the other Welsh lords was confirmed to Llywelyn. Llywelyn bought Maredudd's homage for 5,000 marks in 1270 – though it is most unlikely that the money was actually paid.[38] But effectively Llywelyn had brought within the bounds of his principality the family that was amongst the most reluctant to accept his suzerainty. The homage of Maredudd and, subsequently, his son was an acquisition of very dubious value.

A similar situation obtained in Powys in 1263, when Gruffudd ap Gwenwynwyn came to terms with Llywelyn after it seemed that he could no longer rely on English governmental support to regain his patrimony of southern Powys. Given that the dynasties of Gwynedd and southern Powys had a long history of mutual distrust and conflict, it was hardly surprising that the relationship of Llywelyn ap Gruffudd and Gruffudd ap Gwenwynwyn would come under the sort of strains that underlay the complex events which came to a head in the alleged conspiracy of Gruffudd, his son Owain and Dafydd ap Gruffudd in 1273–4 and which accelerated the collapse of Llywelyn's principality. But it is also the case that Llywelyn had acquired in 1263 not only a potentially rebellious vassal, but also a delicate problem of balancing the interests of the lords of the two main branches of the Powysian dynasty, headed by Gruffudd ap Gwenwynwyn in the south and Gruffudd ap Madog in the north.[39]

It is possible to trace tensions between the rulers of southern and northern Powys back into the second decade of the thirteenth century. Rivalry for Powysian possession and leadership can at times be traced, while disputes over specific territories, such as Deuddwr, are also visible.[40] Once again, the inclusion of a prominent lord within Llywelyn's principality involved internal strains which were potentially destructive. In the years after 1263 Gruffudd ap Gwenwynwyn appears to have supplanted Gruffudd ap Madog as the most prominent of Llywelyn's great lords particularly given that the prince's brother Dafydd had left the principality and gone over to the English king.[41] But 1269 had seen both the finalization of an agreement between Llywelyn and his brother, which involved Dafydd's re-instatement in Gwynedd, and the death of Gruffudd ap Madog of northern Powys. After the latter's death Prince Llywelyn allegedly intervened in the succession to the lands of northern Powys in order to ensure that the lion's share of the lordship went to one of Gruffudd's four sons, Madog, who was married to the prince's sister Mared. That situation may have raised the prospect that Llywelyn might lend a sympathetic ear to any claims which Madog ap Gruffudd might make on lands held by Gruffudd ap Gwenwynwyn. Such developments may have contributed to the eventual breakdown of relations between the prince and Gruffudd ap Gwenwynwyn in 1274, and the conspiracy against Llywelyn which certainly involved Dafydd and Gruffudd ap Gwenwynwyn's son Owain.[42] It is surely significant that the name of Madog Fychan (ap Gruffudd), lord of Bromfield, appears second in the attenuated witness-list appended to the record of the proceedings of April 1274 which decided that Gruffudd ap Gwenwynwyn and Owain, having offended against their fealty to the prince, should be placed, with all their lands and possessions, at the mercy of Llywelyn.[43]

Neither in southern Powys nor in Ystrad Tywi were Llywelyn ab Iorwerth and Llywelyn ap Gruffudd able to bring the descendants of Owain Cyfeiliog or of the Lord Rhys to accept that the dominions which these regional lords strove to consolidate and to rule were likely to be secure or to prosper within the principalities of Wales which both of the northern lords were intent on creating. The case of southern Powys, the dynasty founded by Owain Cyfeiliog, has been investigated in detail, while that of the branch of the house of Deheubarth, which included Maredudd ap Rhys and his son Rhys ap Maredudd, is similarly prominent in the historiography.[44] Both families were persistent, if not entirely consistent, opponents of the Llywelyns, who were clearly seen as threatening their regional dynastic ambitions and, in some instances, survival. Members of both families, determined to secure their hold on the territories which lay at the heart of their dynastic heritage, moved from opposition to alliance with the Llywelyns, as the needs of developing situations dictated. And in both cases, there was always the prospect of turning to England for aid in resisting the expansionist plans of the rulers of Gwynedd.

Even when driven into exile, both Gwenwynwyn and his son Gruffudd threatened, with English help, the hold of the Llywelyns on southern Powys: such was the case with Gwenwynwyn in 1208–10, and Gruffudd in 1228–40, 1258–63 and 1275–7. Once restored to their patrimonial lands, they opposed the princes of Gwynedd, in 1210–12, 1241, 1244–7, 1256–8 and 1277–82. Only rarely, and often on terms more redolent of alliance than subordination, did they ally with the northern rulers, in 1212–16 and 1263–74. When the element of subordination became all too evident, a rift between prince and regional lord was almost inevitable

A somewhat similar situation obtained in the cases of two of the lords of Ystrad Tywi, Maredudd ap Rhys (d.1271) and his son Rhys ap Maredudd (d.1292). Maredudd displayed determined ambition to establish himself as the lord of Ystrad Tywi, the heartland of Deheubarth, containing as it did the significant castle and dynastic centre of Dinefwr. He was certainly prepared to cooperate with Llywelyn ap Gruffudd to further his ambitions, just as his father Rhys Gryg had cooperated with Llywelyn ab Iorwerth. An agreement made in 1251 between Llywelyn and his brother, Owain, on the one hand and Maredudd and his nephew Rhys Fychan on the other was phrased in terms which assumed, and proclaimed, equality between the parties.[45] But by 1259, with Llywelyn in the ascendant in much of Wales, and having presented himself in the previous year as prince of Wales, Maredudd was called before an assembly of nobles convened by Llywelyn, and convicted *de infidelitate*. Imprisoned for much of that year in Cricieth, Maredudd finally made an agreement with Llywelyn, which, though it provided for Maredudd's recovery of the lands which he held when he withdrew from unity (*unitate*) with Llywelyn, also made his feudal subjection to the northern ruler clear.[46] It is thus no surprise to find that as soon as he was able to transfer his loyalty to the English king, he did so, in 1265. Maredudd was obliged to become a vassal of Llywelyn in 1270, the year before his death, but his son Rhys abandoned the prince as soon as he could, in 1277.[47] The reluctance of

Maredudd ap Rhys and Rhys ap Maredudd to accept subordination to Llywelyn ap Gruffudd does not indicate any pronounced pro-English tendencies on their part, but rather a determination to recover control of Ystrad Tywi, a position that it was clear Llywelyn would not be able to accord them for fear of antagonizing their near kinsmen, the descendants of Rhys Mechyll.[48]

Gruffudd ap Gwenwynwyn's adherence to Llywelyn in 1263 would seem to have been an opportunistic move to re-establish himself in his lordship when it became clear that the English king was unlikely to be of help in that matter. It was not, however, unique. In southern Wales, the same patterns, and the same motives for adhering to a prince or an English king, can often be glimpsed. Thus in 1244, when a group of marchers staged a foray through the lands of Maredudd ab Owain in Ceredigion, Maredudd asked for a parley, at which he announced that 'it was unwillingly that he had withdrawn from the king, because of lack of maintenance and aid, and that he would willingly return to his fealty if he could obtain competent terms'. Maredudd pointed to lands that he thought should properly be his, and especially lands which were in the hands of the king's enemy, Maelgwn Fychan ap Maelgwn; if Henry would give him the lands that were held by Maelgwn, 'he would serve the king faithfully'.[49] And a generation later, when Rhys ap Maredudd became convinced that Edward I would not allow him to recover the lands, including the castle of Dinefwr, which would enable him to rule an undivided Ystrad Tywi, and that his autonomy would be restricted by the power of the justice of west Wales, he rebelled in 1287, with fatal consequences.[50]

Many treatments of the Age of the Princes have tended to focus on the heroic qualities and a supposed widespread acceptance within Wales of those great leaders such as Owain Gwynedd, the Lord Rhys or the Llywelyns, who are pictured as saviours of the Welsh people from the tyranny of the Normans and the English. Modern commentators have become more cautious, though such views continue to command significant attention at a popular level. The Welsh chronicles, and the court poets, are not slow to pick up and praise the commitment of leaders to the rights of the Welsh against foreign oppressors. Prydydd y Moch asked whether the Powysians wanted a ruler who was a true Welshman or one who was a 'Frenchman'

– seemingly a jibe at Gwenwynwyn.[51] It has already been seen that Gwenwynwyn himself was pictured in *Brut y Tywysogion* in the entry relating to the Painscastle campaign of 1198 as a leader who sought to restore ancient liberties to the Welsh, and much the same hope was expressed in the *Brut* under 1201, lamenting the death of a son of the Lord Rhys, Gruffudd, who would have restored 'the March of all Wales', where the Welsh text appears to misconstrue an entry in the Latin original which suggested that Gruffudd would have restored the monarchy of all Wales.[52] Gruffudd's death is duly and sadly recorded by the chronicler, who adds that he was 'a prince of Wales by right and inheritance'.

Indeed, for members of well-established dynasties with a tradition, however intermittent, of leadership of other Welsh rulers, the prospect of such dominance was undeniably alluring. But for many in the upper echelons of society in Wales, the rise of any would-be Welsh hegemonists was unwelcome. At times it is the absence of lesser rulers from the prince's proceedings which creates a suspicion that all was not well in the extended polity of a prince of Wales. This is most visible in the case of Llywelyn ap Gruffudd, perhaps the most overbearing and ambitious of the claimants to rule over Wales since Gruffudd ap Llywelyn in the eleventh century. We know that by the 1270s stresses were becoming apparent in the polity that Llywelyn had constructed, and it is in this context that the surprisingly limited number of lesser lords involved in the proceedings of 1274 against Gruffudd ap Gwenwynwyn at Dolforwyn have to be viewed. The record of the 'trial' and arbitration in that case, dated 17 April 1274, was witnessed by just one of the lords of northern Powys, just one of the southern lords, Hywel ap Rhys Gryg, and just one of the lords of Edeirnion.[53] The record of supplementary arrangements made on 18 April was witnessed by the three lords already noticed, together with two more of the lords of northern Powys and one other of the Edeirnion rulers.[54] The far more significant southern lords, such as Owain ap Maredudd of Ceredigion, or Rhys Wyndod and Rhys ap Maredudd of Ystrad Tywi were apparently absent, as were the lords of Elfael, of Ceri and other magnates of the Middle March. The whole episode may perhaps indicate not so much Llywelyn's might, but growing disillusionment with his ascendancy and the ways in which he was maintaining it.

LIMITATIONS ON PRINCELY POWER IMPOSED
BY INTRA-DYNASTIC RIVALRIES

It was perhaps inevitable that the aspirants to princely status should encounter serious opposition from within their own family, though beyond describing a prince's rise to power, often at the expense of near kin, the poets and chroniclers seldom make much of the point. But fuller consideration of the extent to which power was shared by sons, brothers, nephews or cousins makes it clear that few princes were able to exploit all of the territories with which they are credited in modern maps and by contemporary chroniclers alike. Thus Madog ap Maredudd of Powys settled his nephews Owain and Meurig, sons of Gruffudd in control of Cyfeiliog in 1149, and one of them, Owain (Cyfeiliog) had clearly established himself in eastern Powys, in the region close to the Breiddin, by 1156.[55] Owain's grip on territory in the whole region from Cyfeiliog in the west to Y Tair Swydd in the south-east of Powys was sufficient to enable him to take control of that land after Madog's death in 1160.

In the north, Owain Gwynedd was for many years obliged to share the territory of Gwynedd with his brother Cadwaladr. Even though Cadwaladr was more than once driven from territories, both in Gwynedd and in Ceredigion, he maintained his claims to extensive lordships, and though it is difficult to identify all of the territories which he possessed, it seems that he held Meirionnydd in the years before 1147, that he held a portion of Ceredigion in the late 1140s and that he exercised lordship in Anglesey in the early 1150s.[56] Cadwaladr lived as an exile in Shropshire from 1152 to 1157, when Henry II forced Owain Gwynedd to restore him and, in the words of the *Brut*, 'Cadwaladr received back his land.'[57] He can also be reckoned to have held extensive lands in Llŷn, both because he granted Haughmond Abbey lands in Nefyn and because his descendants had particular connections with that land, one as an official of Llywelyn ab Iorwerth, and one as the holder for several years of lordship in part of the peninsula.[58]

In the conflicts of 1165 and 1167 Cadwaladr is closely associated with Owain Gwynedd in the chronicles, and it seems that the two effectively shared control of Gwynedd. Something of Cadwaladr's eminence can be seen in the reference in the *Brut* to Owain and Cadwaladr as 'princes of Gwynedd', and his appearance in a much later confirmation of his grant to Haughmond of the church and land in Nefyn as '*quondam princeps Wallie*' and his description as *rex Waliarum* when he witnessed charters of Ranulf of Chester in 1147–8. At his death, Gerald of Wales recorded that Cadwaladr was buried with his brother in a double tomb in Bangor Cathedral, a further sign of equality of status.[59] A historiographic fixation with Owain Gwynedd has obscured the spasmodic but very significant part played in Gwynedd by his brother.

The eminence of the Lord Rhys, and the extravagant eulogy that he received in the chroniclers' notice of his death, have sometimes also obscured the extent to which his sons eroded his authority in the last decade of his life. In that period, he felt it necessary to imprison his son Maelgwn in 1189. The fact that the *Brut* records that in 1192 Maelgwn escaped from the prison of the lord of Brycheiniog may suggest that Rhys had handed him over to that marcher magnate as a safety measure.[60] In 1194 Rhys was imprisoned by 'his sons' until one of them, Hywel Sais, 'deceived Maelgwn his brother and released his father from prison'.[61] In the following year two more of Rhys's sons, Rhys (Gryg) and Maredudd took their father's castle of Dinefwr by treachery, and the castle of Cantref Bychan 'with the consent of the men of the land' but were in turn seized and imprisoned by their father.[62] Irrespective of the amount of territory held by Rhys's turbulent and often rebellious sons, the need to act against them and to be on his guard against them surely eroded his wider power and influence.

Llywelyn ab Iorwerth, whose ascendancy covered much of the first forty years of the thirteenth century, also had problems containing the ambitions and, when thwarted, the resentment of his son Gruffudd. Though Llywelyn planned to pass on the rule of the principality that he had created to his younger but legitimate son Dafydd, he nevertheless attempted to buy off the evident frustration of Gruffudd by settling him in extensive territories. Before he was removed by his father in 1221 he had been lord of Meirionnydd and Ardudwy. Gruffudd clearly held much of southern Powys in the years before his imprisonment by Llywelyn in 1228 and after his release in 1234 he was installed in southern Powys and, apparently, Llŷn, until he challenged his brother's succession in 1240 and was imprisoned for what turned out to be the final time.[63]

For Llywelyn ap Gruffudd the intra-dynastic problem was not the machinations of a disgruntled son, but those of his brother Dafydd, as well as the ambitions of cousins drawn from the Meirionnydd branch of the dynasty founded by Gruffudd ap Cynan in the early twelfth century. Dafydd was imprisoned by Llywelyn in 1255 after the battle of Bryn Derwin, but was released and joined Llywelyn by 1256. Clearly some provision was made for Dafydd by Llywelyn: he certainly held Dyffryn Clwyd and part of Llŷn. But this was not enough to prevent him from going over to the English in 1263, a move which the Chester annalist claimed was brought about because Dafydd wished to liberate his eldest brother Owain, who was not released but was held captive by Llywelyn for some twenty-two years after Bryn Derwin. In the Treaty of Montgomery of 1267, it was provided that Dafydd should be reinstated in the lands which he had held before 1263, but that if he was not satisfied with that arrangement, his claims should be settled by arbitration. The fact that he was not reconciled with Llywelyn until 1269 suggests that some very hard bargaining had taken place, though it is unclear whether Dafydd increased his territorial beyond what he had held before his defection. It is clear that in the years 1256–63 and 1269–74 Dafydd possessed extensive lands within Gwynedd and that this lessened the resources available to Llywelyn.[64] It is also clear that for much of the period 1241–56 Meirionnydd was in the hands of descendants of Maredudd ap Cynan, a cousin of Llywelyn ab Iorwerth, while even in 1278 a member of that family, Madog ap Llywelyn – who would assert his claim to be prince of Wales in 1294 – made a formal claim against Llywelyn ap Gruffudd to hold the whole land of Meirionnydd.[65] Hegemonic rulers, however mighty they appeared in the works of their panegyrists, were thus frequently debilitated and distracted by the activities and the plots of their close kin.

One of the motive forces in this respect was almost certainly the uncertainty that hung over the matter of succession to princely rule. It is often assumed that the succession to a Welsh kingdom or principality was governed by the same principles of partibility which applied to the descent of free lands; in other words there would be an enduring partition of the lands amongst a potentially broad group of co-heirs in each generation. J. Beverley Smith, in some highly important papers, has argued that in law the kingdom or principality was regarded as indivisible, and should descend to a chosen successor to the incumbent ruler. It was nevertheless possible to compensate other members of the ruler's family who were thereby deprived of lands by use of grants which resembled appanages. The case has been well made. But there remain doubts. Disputes over successions often produced what Smith describes as compromises, which involved in practice a partition amongst candidates. And such practical solutions might easily become precedents for future practice. And in one reveal-ing instance the Gwynedd law book of the principate of Llywelyn ab Iorwerth appears to recognize the problem. Discussing the *edling*, the heir apparent to a Welsh ruler, the law book notes that 'some say that each of these [the king's sons and his nephews and his male first-cousins] is an *edling*; others say that no-one is an *edling* save him to whom the king gives hope and expectation'. The uncertainty apparent in that comment was crucial and fateful.[66]

COLLISIONS BETWEEN 'NATIONAL' AND 'REGIONAL' ASCENDANCIES: SOME CASE STUDIES

We have examined some of the tensions that almost inevitably arose between claimants to hegemonic rule in Wales and the representatives of 'lesser' dynasties. But it is well to consider that in some instances the confrontations thus engendered were not simply between over-lords and recalcitrant underlings. Members of other dynasties might be inspired or provoked to assert regional ascendancies which were barely compatible with the ambitions of a prince with 'national' ambi-tions. And in those regions in which the combination of pressure from marcher lords and from princes of *pura Wallia* had resulted in the effective elimination of local dynasties that had exercised 'kingly' rule, as in the case of much of the Middle March, it is sometimes possible to pick out the resistance to princely rule offered by com-munities of local notables. Focus on the ambitions of princes such as the Lord Rhys, Llywelyn ab Iorwerth and Llywelyn ap Gruffudd may conceal the point that in many of the constituent parts of Wales there was a continuing strength of regional polities whose well-being might be seen by their dominant elites, whether they were men of 'royal' status or *uchelwyr*, to lie in autonomous development. That the vision of regional autonomy as the most effective guarantee of order was almost certainly a matter of the self-interest of the elites concerned does not diminish its importance. A few case studies will help to establish the continuing importance of the regional dynamic in Welsh politics.

The sort of competition that a regional ascendancy might offer to the claims of a hegemonic ruler can be illustrated by the case of the relationship between the Lord Rhys and Cadwallon ap Madog, one member of the dynasty of the lands that lay between Wye and Severn. Cadwallon was a son of Madog ab Idnerth, the ruler of much of that land in the 1130s. After Madog's death in 1140, his sons Cadwallon and Einion Clud appear to have succeeded to Maelienydd and Elfael respectively.[67] It is likely that Cadwallon had to recognize Madog ap Maredudd as his overlord in the 1150s, a situation that may lie behind Cadwallon's marriage to Madog's daughter Efa. It is difficult to gauge the nature of the relationship between Cadwallon and Madog. Cadwallon may have been installed by the Powysian king as dependent ruler of Maelienydd after Madog had, in all probability, displaced Hugh Mortimer there in 1155.[68] But as soon as Madog died in 1160, and Powys began to suffer attacks from Gwynedd, it seems that Cadwallon attempted to ally with the ruler of the latter territory. The *Brut* reports that in 1160 Cadwallon seized his brother, Einion Clud, and sent him for imprisonment to Owain ap Gruffudd, which is the designation often used by the chronicle for Owain Gwynedd.[69] But, with Owain Gwynedd's death and subsequent chaos in Gwynedd, Cadwallon's lands and those of other rulers between Wye and Severn became subject to the ambitions of the Lord Rhys, for a generation the most potent force in *pura Wallia*.

Rhys saw himself as the lord of the south – and perhaps the overlord of all Wales.[70] Such aspirations inevitably provoked resentment and in some case resistance. It seems likely that this was at an early stage the reaction of Owain Cyfeiliog, after 1160 the ruler of southern Powys. Owain engaged in several wars with Rhys, in 1153, 1167, 1171.[71] The last war may well have been triggered by Owain's foundation in 1170 of the Cistercian abbey of Strata Marcella, a move that appeared to signal a declaration of parity with Rhys, the re-founder of Strata Florida in 1165.[72] Perhaps as a result of the intervention of Henry II, the conflicts between Rhys and Owain subsided after 1171. But in the region south of the river Severn, a more serious opposition confronted Rhys.

Rhys's ascendancy over the southern regions of Wales was revealed in 1175 when he attended a gathering held by Henry II at Gloucester. The *Brut* records that Rhys took with him

> all the princes of Wales who had incurred the king's displeasure, namely: Cadwallon ap Madog, his first cousin, of Maelienydd, Einion Clud, his son-in-law, of Elfael, Einion ap Rhys, his other son-in-law, of Gwerthrynion, Morgan ap Caradog ab Iestyn of Glamorgan, his nephew by Gwladus his sister, Gruffudd ab Ifor ap Meurig of Senghenydd, his nephew by Nest, his sister, Iorwerth ab Owain of Caerleon, and Seisyll ap Dyfnwal.[73]

It was not to be the last occasion on which Rhys would seek to demonstrate his suzerainty over the southern lands that lay beyond his own realm of Deheubarth. When Archbishop Baldwin began his tour through Wales to preach the Crusade in 1188 he entered the country by way of Radnor – where he was met by the Lord Rhys. It was perhaps less a courtesy than an assertion of supremacy in the southern regions of Wales. That belief surely lay behind the last campaign that the Lord Rhys made, in 1196, the year before his death. The object of that campaign was the castle of Radnor, which he took and burned. He was then confronted by forces led by Roger Mortimer and Hugh de Say, whose forces he defeated before going on to take the de Braose stronghold of Painscastle.[74]

The ascendancy in central and southern Wales which Rhys evidently sought was however challenged for some years by Cadwallon ap Madog. That challenge may have been at least in part triggered by the reaction of Cadwallon and his brother Einion Clud to the events of 1175. Now ruling, respectively, Maelienydd and the neighbouring lordship of Elfael, Cadwallon and Einion had been amongst the rulers whom Rhys had taken to face Henry II at Gloucester. But though the Welsh chronicle notes that they and the other Welsh magnates had returned to their lands 'having made peace' with the king, it is clear from the evidence of the English Pipe Rolls that peace had come at a price for Cadwallon and Einion, who were burdened by Henry with a fine of 500 marks, equivalent to 1,000 cattle.[75] The brothers made an initial payment of £122 12.s, but failed to provide any further payments.[76] It is probable that such a burden, the result of the action of

Rhys as the king's officer, soured relations between the brothers, and in particular Cadwallon, with the southern lord.

Cadwallon's response to the events of 1175 seems to have taken many forms. These included an attempt to move at least some of his territories out of the ecclesiastical control of St David's, within which diocese the Lord Rhys was the dominant lay power. When in 1176 an attempt by the bishop of St Asaph to extend his diocese into Ceri, effectively the northern part of Maelienydd, was only narrowly foiled by Gerald of Wales, the archdeacon of Brecon, it seems clear that the bishop's plan had the backing of Cadwallon, and may have been his suggestion.[77] Gerald believed that if he had been successful in Ceri the bishop of St Asaph would have pushed his authority further south, into all of the land between Wye and Severn.[78] This would have taken all of Cadwallon's territory out of the control of St David's, and thus the sphere of influence of Rhys, and into the diocese of St Asaph, in which the dominant lay rulers were Dafydd ab Owain Gwynedd and Owain Cyfeiliog. The first of these may have seen himself as supplanting Rhys in the affections of Henry II, as he (Dafydd) had only recently married Henry's half-sister, Emma of Anjou. And the second of them, Owain Cyfeiliog, was a confirmed enemy of Rhys.

A second move by Cadwallon to assert his independence from Rhys's suzerainty was almost certainly made in imitation of a step taken by Owain Cyfeiliog a few years earlier: this involved the foundation in 1176 of a Cistercian abbey as a daughter house of Whitland.[79] This would have established Cadwallon as a monastic patron to rival Rhys, whose re-foundation of the abbey of Strata Florida, itself also a daughter-house of Whitland, had taken place in 1165. The political implications of monastic foundation, particularly the creation of a Cistercian house, are indicated by the fact that the foundation of the Cistercian abbey of Strata Marcella by Owain Cyfeiliog in 1170 was closely followed by the outbreak of war between Owain and the Lord Rhys the next year.

In a particularly assertive gesture in 1177 the Lord Rhys built a castle at Rhaeadr, on the Wye, facing into the land of Gwerthrynion.[80] Now it is clear from Cynddelw's *marwnad* for Cadwallon, composed in 1179, that the latter had been active in Gwerthrynion, which in 1175 had been in the possession of Einion ap Rhys, the son-in-law of the Lord Rhys. It thus seems that this was becoming a region of confrontation between Rhys and Cadwallon.[81] The building of the castle itself was certainly seen as a provocative move, for it is clear that it was destroyed, and having been re-built by Rhys in 1194 was immediately burned by Cadwallon's sons. So it seems that Cadwallon was extending his power into Gwerthrynion, and this had pushed Rhys into taking steps to protect his own interests.

In the same year as the building of the castle of Rhaeadr, Cadwallon's brother Einion was killed, though the identity of his killer is not clear. There also took place, after Einion's death, another meeting of Welsh rulers before Henry II, this time at Oxford. The developing ambitions of Cadwallon are revealed by the chronicler Roger Howden's description of him on this occasion as *rex de Delwain* (king of Elfael).[82] This indicates that Cadwallon had succeeded Einion Clud as ruler of the rich territory of Elfael, and had thus constructed a polity that embraced much of central Wales. Howden's designation of Cadwallon also suggests that he had risen into the front rank of Welsh rulers, for in the 1177 meeting the only others who were accorded the title of *rex* were the Lord Rhys and Dafydd ab Owain of Gwynedd, husband of Henry II's half-sister Emma. It would appear that the ascendancy of the Lord Rhys established in the early and mid-1170s may have driven or inspired Cadwallon to assert a regional primacy of his own. His apparently meteoric rise in the middle and later years of that decade was ended by his death at the hands of men of Roger Mortimer while returning from another meeting with Henry II.[83] Mortimer was duly chastised by King Henry. The principal beneficiary of Cadwallon's death was the Lord Rhys, though his tranquillity would be broken by the intrigues of his sons.

A grandson of Cadwallon ap Madog provides a further example of the tensions that the ambitions of an aspirant to princely status might generate. This was Madog ap Maelgwn ap Cadwallon of Maelienydd, who announced in a charter of 1212 that 'the nobles have sworn before many that they will never tolerate the lordship of any prince over them'.[84] It is tolerably clear that the object of his declaration was Llywelyn ab Iorwerth of Gwynedd. Madog ap Maelgwn had, it seems, been fostered or protected by Llywelyn when Roger Mortimer had overrun Maelienydd in the 1190s. But it is likely that Madog had recovered at least part of Maelienydd as a result of an agreement between him and Mortimer.[85] It is undoubtedly significant that the document in which Madog made grants to Cwm-hir and set out the hostility of the magnates of the land to any rule by a prince was witnessed by two men with Mortimer connections and by Maredudd ap Rhobert of Cedewain, who was a supporter of King John in 1211, alongside Gwenwynwyn of southern Powys.[86] It is quite possible that Gwenwynwyn's exclusion from his lands in the years 1208–10 may have served as an example of what princely rule might entail. In the event, Madog ap Maelgwn's opposition to Llywelyn's ambitions was cut short by his sudden execution by John in August 1212.[87]

Another instance of a collision between a national hegemony and a regional primacy involves the relationship between Llywelyn ab Iorwerth, prince of Gwynedd, and the southern lord Rhys Gryg, a son of the Lord Rhys. Rhys Gryg's career in the final decade of the twelfth and the early years of the thirteenth centuries was a turbulent one: he had been at odds with his father, eventually being imprisoned by him in 1195. In the following two decades he had moved in and out of alliances with the English as he struggled with his near kin to secure a part of the lands that had been held by his father.[88] But by 1216 under the supervision of the increasingly powerful northern prince, Llywelyn ab Iorwerth, Rhys Gryg, his brother Maelgwn and his nephews Rhys and Owain, sons of Gruffudd, had been induced to share out the territories of Deheubarth. Rhys Gryg's share was what most would have considered the heartland of that realm – in the first place the castle and dynastic centre of Dinefwr, all of Cantref Mawr except the commote of Mallaen, which went to his brother Maelgwn, who was tempted away from an alliance with Gwenwynwyn of Powys by the acquisition of an expansive lordship. There also came to Rhys Gryg the land of Cydweli, Carnwyllion, Cantref Bychan and Myddfai.[89] To these lands, indeed, were added more in the next year, when Rhys overran Swansea and Gower.[90] At that stage, therefore, he was profiting from accepting the overlordship of Llywelyn.

But in 1220 Llywelyn found himself pressed by the English government to fulfil obligations into which he had entered in the Worcester agreements of 1218: these included ensuring that the rulers of Deheubarth should perform homage to Henry III. By 1220 Rhys ap Gruffudd alone had done this. Rhys Gryg was recalcitrant, and had almost certainly signalled the extent of his ambitions by marrying a daughter of Gilbert de Clare, earl of Gloucester and lord of

Glamorgan.[91] Together their territories formed a solid bloc, extending across much of southern Wales. But in performing homage to Henry III Rhys would stand to lose lands that he had acquired in recent years. Cydweli, Carnwyllion and Gower were likely to be restored to the marcher lords from whom they had been taken and Gwidigada was likely to return to royal control.

In 1220 Llywelyn moved south to coerce Rhys into accepting his obligations. He reported to Henry III that he had occupied Dinefwr, which Rhys had dismantled and which was 'ruinous'.[92] It appears that there was also a confrontation at Carmarthen, in which some of Rhys's men were killed.[93] But it seems that Llywelyn and Rhys were reconciled. The evidence of a poem by Llywarch Brydydd y Moch suggests that after reaching an agreement, they both embarked on a great raid into Rhos and Penfro, as if to celebrate their accord.[94]

The patchy evidence, however, is at times problematic. Crucially, the chronicle sources are silent as to the clash of Llywelyn and Rhys in 1220. This silence may imply that the events at Dinefwr and at Carmarthen were not of any great importance, or perhaps that they had been exaggerated by Llywelyn in his report to Henry III. In the poem that was composed by Llywarch Brydydd y Moch, Rhys is hailed as 'hero of Dinefwr', a salutation that would seem decidedly tactless if that place had indeed been only recently rendered 'ruinous'.[95] Again, we should recognize that the poem gives very much a Venedotian view, picturing a reconciliation between a valiant Rhys Gryg and a Llywelyn who is the overlord. We do not have Rhys Gryg's reaction to this. The outcome of the events of 1220, however we construe them, is uncertain: Gower was indeed relinquished by Rhys, but other territory seems to have been retained by him. In the early summer of 1221 the English government ordered Rhys to hand over Cydweli and Carnwyllion to William Crassus, acting as custodian for the marcher heiress, Hawise de Londres. But it is clear from an agreement that Rhys Gryg made with the bishop of St David's in 1222 that he still held Cydweli and Gwidigada.[96]

Whether Llywelyn had returned to Rhys the commotes of Cydweli, Carnwyllion and Gwidigada, or whether Rhys did not actually lose his hold on them must remain uncertain. It is maybe significant that when it became clear that the territory of Cydweli and Carnwyllion was not being handed over to the custodian appointed by the English government, Rhys Gryg received a direct royal order to relinquish those lands; it appears that Llywelyn ab Iorwerth was no longer involved in the situation, and it is clear that he was no longer making any attempt to control Rhys Gryg.[97] The latter had emerged from 1220 with the great bulk of his lands intact. Even more than that, it appears that he may well have increased the territory that he controlled. The poem of Prydydd y Moch refers to him as *Rhys Derllys*, strongly suggesting that he had taken control of a commote which lay beyond the territories of Ystrad Tywi in Cantref Gwarthaf.[98] It would appear that Rhys had either been compensated or had compensated himself, in part at least, for the loss of Gower by the acquisition of Derllys. Similarly, it is evident from a chronicle entry for 1227 that Rhys Gryg held Llandovery Castle by that date, for in that year he was seized by his son Rhys Mechyll, and forced to buy his freedom by handing over Llandovery Castle. Hirfryn, the commote in which Llandovery Castle lay, had been part of the territories allocated to Maelgwn ap Rhys in 1216.[99]

The question of when Rhys Gryg replaced Maelgwn as lord of Hirfryn is an interesting one. Beverley Smith has suggested that it may have been in 1222. In that year, Rhys Ieuanc ap Gruffudd died, and his lands were divided by Llywelyn, acting as the royal agent, between his brother Owain ap Gruffudd and Maelgwn ap Rhys.[100] The chronicler's account suggests a degree of surprise at this redistribution, and at the fact that Owain ap Gruffudd had not been confirmed in all of his brother's lands. It is quite possible that Llywelyn had been obliged to compensate Maelgwn for the loss of Hirfryn. But if so it remains uncertain whether Rhys Gryg took Hirfryn in 1222, on the occasion of the distribution of lands that had been held by Rhys ap Gruffudd, or in 1220, in the aftermath of the handover of Gower. Whatever the exact date of the passing of Hirfryn from Maelgwn to Rhys Gryg, it seems to indicate that the latter was able to drive a hard bargain and to assert considerable autonomy.

Rhys Gryg was certainly amongst Llywelyn's allies in the war of 1223, and it is evident that it was in the aftermath of the fighting that he lost control of the lands of Cydweli, Carnwyllion and Gwidigada.[101] Llywelyn had proved incapable of maintaining his ally in the lands that Rhys had resolved to keep. In the following seven years it appears to have been royal, rather than princely, authority that was dominant in south-west Wales. In his later years Rhys seems to have stood somewhat aloof from Llywelyn ab Iorwerth. Whether this reflects his disenchantment with Llywelyn or Rhys's advancing years is uncertain. The *Brut* records that in 1231 Cardigan was attacked and captured by Maelgwn Ieuanc ap Maelgwn ap Rhys, and Owain ap Gruffudd and their men, and with them the men of the Lord Llywelyn.[102] There is no mention of Rhys Gryg as a participant. He did seal the truce between the king and Llywelyn which was agreed in November of that year and was clearly regarded by the royal government as a partisan of the prince, but that says little about the strength of his commitment to Llywelyn.[103] By contrast the chronicle does suggest that Rhys Gryg was involved in a campaign under the leadership of Llywelyn in 1233/4, when it notes that

> In that year Maelgwn Ieuanc ap Maelgwn ap Rhys and Rhys Gryg and Owain ap Gruffudd and their followers and all the leaders of Deheubarth, and with them the lord Llywelyn's host and the host of Richard earl of Pembroke all combined together, and laid siege to the town and castle of Carmarthen for three months at a stretch, and they destroyed the bridge on the Tywi, but it profited them little[104]

But it seems clear that Llywelyn was not present at Carmarthen. The *Brut* says only that his forces were present there, while in January he and Marshal attacked Shrewsbury, and after that was in negotiations with Henry's government.[105] It seems therefore that there is little reliable evidence to suggest that Rhys Gryg and Llywelyn engaged in a joint military campaign at any point after 1223. This may be a measure of Rhys's advancing years – after all in 1230 over forty years had elapsed since his first appearance in the record of the military affairs of Deheubarth. But alternatively, or additionally, it may also reflect a lack of commitment to the promotion of Llywelyn's cause, and a focus only on actions that might benefit Rhys himself. Rhys seems to have stirred himself to act in loose alignment with Llywelyn only when and in so far as their objectives coincided.

The greater principality of Llywelyn the Great which was signalled by his adoption of the title 'Prince of Aberffraw and Lord of Snowdonia' depended for its realization on regional rulers such as Rhys Gryg. Llywelyn had shown, in 1216 and in 1220, that he pictured himself as the dominant force in the south-west. And yet the evidence suggests that after 1216 he had never managed to establish consistent control over Rhys Gryg, whose activities reveal a continuing capacity for independent action. And the motive force behind that striving for independence – albeit a striving punctuated by cooperation with Llywelyn – is perhaps indicated even in Rhys's death. He had once promised his body to Strata Florida, but by 1234 he had clearly made another plan, for when he died at Llandeilo Fawr, in the environs of Dinefwr, his body was carried on the long and potentially dangerous journey to St David's, where he was buried close to the tomb of his father.[106] Also significant is the fact that Rhys's status as a king is clear in the poem that Llywelyn's bard Prydydd y Moch addressed to him in 1220, where he is the undoubted chief of kings (*diheuben teÿrnedd*) and a *tëyrn*. Rhys's royal status is even clearer in the *marwnad* composed by Prydydd Bychan, where he is memorialized as a king (*brenin, tëyrn*).[107] Even, and perhaps especially, in death Rhys Gryg laid claim to be thought the true heir of the Lord Rhys, a ruler who had called himself prince of Wales, and in whose day Welsh law books had accorded primacy to the court of Dinefwr.[108] In the expression of that claim, the suzerainty of Llywelyn ab Iorwerth was implicitly challenged.

We have already seen that Llywelyn ap Gruffudd had to face opposition to his ascendancy from the rulers of southern Powys (Gruffudd ap Gwenwynwyn) and of western Ystrad Tywi (Maredudd ap Rhys and his son Rhys ap Maredudd). The resistance to Llywelyn's aspirations of the rulers of substantial lordships whose near ancestors had entertained serious claims to an ascendancy of their own was to be expected. Less predictable, perhaps, was opposition from men whose ancestors were non-royal or only very distantly royal, and whom Llywelyn might have expected to be grateful for liberation from foreign rule or military pressure. Yet such opposition developed in the Middle March, where a significant group of local notables had risen in the service of the Crown and the marcher lords who had become established in the region before Llywelyn's significant conquests of the early 1260s. The crucial point is that a key element in the involvement of many of the men of the Middle March in the development of opposition to Llywelyn ap Gruffudd was the increasing pressure being applied to this region by the prince in the 1270s, against a background of signs that his control over the region was becoming fragile. The signs of that pressure are unmistakable, and can be found in the many documents which record that men of the Middle March were being forced to surrender hostages for their future good conduct, or to find substantial financial surety for their loyalty to the prince.

The attitude of prominent figures in the Welsh communities of the March may well have been formed by personal or family memories of events in the later years of Llywelyn ab Iorwerth, when we have seen that that ruler's forces repeatedly caused devastation in the marchland.[109] Llywelyn ab Iorwerth's grandson, in contrast, inflicted less chaos on the communities of the March, but, in a late manifestation of a development which we have seen in *pura Wallia*, concentrated rather on annexation and exploitation of lordships. The appointment of officials and the raising of revenues replaced pillage and destruction. But the imposition of princely governance throughout much of the March was not necessarily welcome to the community of Welsh magnates who had begun to prosper in a very different political order.

We have already noticed Hywel ap Meurig who served the cause of the Mortimers, the de Bohuns and the Crown in many parts of Wales in the decades before his death in the early 1280s.[110] But Hywel, although particularly prominent, was not alone. A good example of such figures is provided by Einion ap Madog, who first appears in accounts relating to the marcher lordships of the Three Castles and Abergavenny in the mid-1250s.[111] There he is recorded as having been on active service in Builth lordship, clearly as part of an attempt to defend the region against troops of Llywelyn ap Gruffudd, just beginning to extend his military power from his heartland of Gwynedd into other regions of Wales, including the central marches. Einion is recorded as receiving payments of 60s., and of £9 2s. The latter payment covered the half-year period from 3 June 1257 to 30 November, and works out at 1s. per day – the wage of a troop-leader. Einion ap Madog was clearly a valued soldier, as he also received a gift of £12 6s. 8d with which to buy himself a light horse, a robe, a shield, iron greaves, iron armour and other items of equipment for his work.[112] His early association with Builth is highly significant.

The advance of Llywelyn ap Gruffudd through many of the territories of the Middle March proved for a time to be irresistible, and much of the region was conceded to him in the Treaty of Montgomery, 1267.[113] The situation clearly presented problems for men who had been in the service of marcher lords and were anxious to build a career, and this may explain why Einion ap Madog reappears in May of 1276 as Prince Llywelyn's bailiff of Gwerthrynion, a territory bordering Builth.[114] This apparent change of allegiance did not last long, however. In the war of 1277, Einion ap Madog, acting as one of the troop-leaders of the army under the command of Hywel ap Meurig, led 100 men of Builth against the prince. Significantly, Einion's appearance in 1276 was as one of the sureties for John, son of Hywel ap Meurig. In the years after the war, we find Einion engaged in a land transfer, in which he obtained possession of extensive lands in the lordship of Builth.[115]

The men with whom Einion ap Madog was associated at various stages in his career are of great significance. He was not the only former official of Llywelyn ap Gruffudd who turned against the prince by the war of 1277, for another of the troop-leaders who served with him in the force led by Hywel ap Meurig was Ifor ap Gruffudd, one of two mounted constables at the head of 260 men of Elfael Is Mynydd.[116] Now, Ifor ap Gruffudd had been amongst the sureties for the release by the prince of John, son of Hywel ap Meurig of Elfael in 1276.[117] Amongst the other sureties on that occasion was Owain ap Meurig of Builth. Owain ap Meurig had acted, in 1259–60, as one of the envoys appointed by Henry III to make and receive amends for breaches of the truce between the king and Llywelyn ap Gruffudd.[118] He was one of the notables who witnessed, and sealed, a grant by Walerand ab Adam to Dore abbey in March 1276.[119] The grant was of lands in the forest of Severenny near Grosmont in the lordship of Three Castles. Those lands had been granted to Walerand ab Adam by Edmund of Lancaster, lord of the Three Castles and brother of Edward I.[120] Walerand himself was undoubtedly named after a former senior royal servant and steward of the Three Castles, Walerand Teutonicus.[121] Walerand ab Adam can thus be identified with some certainty as a royal partisan, and his relationship with Owain ap Meurig gains in significance. His grant to Dore was also sealed by the dean of Builth, who was accompanied by 'the whole chapter of Builth'.[122]

The connection between men of Builth and a Gwent lordship controlled in 1276 by a brother of the king, who would act as a leader of royal forces in the war of 1277 is interesting, and all the more so when we learn that in 1280 Owain ap Meurig pledged some of his lands in the Rhosferig area of Builth lordship, just to the north-west of Llanfair-ym-Muallt, to Einion ap Madog, whose career we have already examined.[123] Owain ap Meurig's continuing support for the royal cause is suggested by the fact that the man to whom Edward I committed the custody of the castle of Dryslwyn and associated territories which had belonged to the rebel Rhys ap Maredudd in 1290 was Philip ab Owain ap Meurig; it seems virtually certain that the new royal custodian was the son of Owain ap Meurig of Builth.[124] The deed which confirmed the transfer of the lands of Rhosferig from Owain ap Meurig to Einion ap Madog was sealed by Hywel ap Meurig, the king's bailiff of Builth, and by Philip, the dean of Builth.[125]

But the web of associations does not end there. Hywel ap Meurig, known as no supporter of Llywelyn ap Gruffudd, was one of the witnesses to a charter, probably given at the castle of Bronllys, relating to the rights of Dore Abbey in Cantref Selyf in the northern part of the lordship of Brecon. The charter was given in November 1271 and the witnesses were headed by Walter de Traveley, constable and steward of Bronllys, who was surely representing John Giffard and his wife, Maud Clifford, heiress of Cantref Selyf.[126] It suggests that Giffard had re-established himself in a lordship that had been allocated to Llywelyn ap Gruffudd in the Treaty of Montgomery, and strengthens the evidence that Llywelyn's hold on Brecon was already crumbling. The grantor was a man with lands in both Brecon and Elfael, Meurig ap Gruffudd. Before the end of the year he had been forced by the prince to find sureties for his future loyalty.[127] But as late as 1292 Meurig ap Gruffudd appears as the constable of Painscastle.[128]

Other witnesses to Meurig ap Gruffudd's 1271 charter included Rhys ap Meurig, who may have been Hywel ap Meurig's brother, and had been constable of Bronllys in 1251 under the Clifford lords, and Llywelyn ap Caradog. This last witness was amongst a group assembled at Builth in November 1271 to stand surety in the sum of £40 for the future loyalty to Llywelyn ap Gruffudd of one Iorwerth ap Llywelyn, imprisoned by the prince.[129] Willingness to stand surety for Iorwerth strongly suggests a degree of sympathy with him. Llywelyn ap Caradog also witnessed the charter of Walerand ab Adam to Dore Abbey of March 1276. His record suggests that he was an opponent of Prince Llywelyn. Others associated with Llywelyn ap Caradog in both Walerand ab Adam's grant and the record of sureties for the loyalty of Iorwerth ap Llywelyn were Llywelyn ap Madog and Moelwyn of Builth. Llywelyn ap Madog appears in 1277 as a mounted constable leading a force of 100 men from Builth against the prince, and Moelwyn of Builth, who was described as the *maer* in 1276, was responsible for organizing the sureties for Iorwerth ap Llywelyn in 1271. His son Ieuan was to go on to a prominent and very success-ful career as a royal official in Builth and in west Wales.[130] We may assume that neither Llywelyn ap Madog nor Moelwyn of Builth was a supporter of Llywelyn ap Gruffudd's regime in the Middle March.

There were many other notables of that region who can be con-fidently identified as opponents of the prince, or whose loyalty was at best lukewarm. They include Einion Sais of Brecon, and Meurig ap Llywelyn. The former, a significant magnate who was apparently the lord of a castle at Penpont in the Usk valley, west of Brecon, was obliged to appear at Llywelyn's castle of Rhyd y Briw (Sennybridge) in November 1271 to provide sureties in the very large sum of 200 marks for his provision of a hostage for his future fidelity to the prince.[131] The near coincidence of these proceedings with those relating to Iorwerth ap Llywelyn of Builth, noticed above, suggests a possible connection between the two men. Meurig ap Llywelyn appears in 1277 as a mounted constable leading 100 troops from Brecon against the prince; nearly six years before that he had to provide sureties of 100 marks to secure the release by the prince of a hostage, to ensure that if required by Llywelyn ap Gruffudd he would hand over that hostage once again, as a guarantee of loyalty to the prince. Very sig-nificantly, Meurig had to provide those sureties at Rhyd y Briw on the same day as Einion Sais.[132] The two men employed the same sureties. Meurig ap Llywelyn's loyalty to the prince, non-existent in 1277, had clearly been in grave doubt for many years.

Here then we have signs of a complex network of men from the Middle March whose fidelity to the prince was entirely suspect. It was surely no coincidence that the lands which Einion ap Madog acquired, in a deed that was witnessed or sealed by many of those men, can be identified as, in all probability, the very territory in the lordship of Builth to which Llywelyn ap Gruffudd was lured to his death in December 1282.[133] It is difficult to avoid the suspicion that Einion ap Madog and some of his associates were deeply involved in the cir-cumstances of the prince's death. In this last case opposition to the imposition of princely rule seems likely to have had ultimately fatal consequences for the prince himself.

An investigation of the various categories of resistance from within their dominions to the power and authority of those native rulers who claimed ascendancy within Wales thus suggests that the rule of the princes was never more than partially effective, and that resentment and fear amongst the rulers and magnates whom they sought to control frequently acted as a serious obstacle to the construction of hegemonic rule. Rees Davies argued with his customary skill and subtlety that in the thirteenth century 'the Welsh were winning the terminological contest, appropriating the term *Wallia* to describe that part of Wales which was still under their control'. But elsewhere he made it clear that by 'the Welsh' he meant the princes of Gwynedd and their supporters and propagandists.[134] Davies's 'contest' was one between the Welsh hegemonists – chiefly the rulers of Gwynedd – and the English government. He did not consider at all fully what *Wallia* might mean to other Welsh dynasties and communities, nor did he examine the significance and weight of *Wallia* when compared to other and older entities such as Deheubarth, Ystrad Tywi, Powys or indeed entities in the March such as Brycheiniog. It is also necessary to consider that still other and more complex political structures were composed of the webs of association and interest which cut across individual regions or lordships, and are exemplified by the network of possessions and influence constructed by Hywel ap Meurig, which extended from western Herefordshire, through Cantref Selyf and Elfael to Builth, and northwards into Cedewain.[135]

SOME REPERCUSSIONS OF THE AGE OF THE PRINCES: PARADOXES OF PRINCELY RULE

It is arguable that many of the developments which facilitated the princes' ascendancies also acted to limit or obstruct them. Thus the Treaty of Montgomery of 1267 may be viewed as the culmination of the drive to create a single enduring Welsh polity in the twelfth and thirteenth centuries, and as the greatest triumph of Llywelyn ap Gruffudd, in that it confirmed him in possession of territories which lay far beyond his heartland of Gwynedd, and brought him English governmental recognition of his status as prince of Wales, with the

homage of all of the native Welsh lords except Maredudd ap Rhys –
and even that was conceded to him in 1270. But there were of course
prices to pay. The most obvious were the financial obligations that
Llywelyn incurred in the Treaty of Montgomery in 1267, which have
been noted above.[136] But as well as the payments to which he committed himself at Montgomery, he had to find the money to construct
courts and castles, to acquire military equipment, to maintain an elaborate entourage as well as to meet the costs of increasingly extensive
and frequent diplomacy.

There are fairly clear signs that the financial effort involved in
constructing and maintaining his ascendancy in Wales was driving
Llywelyn to exert greater pressures on both the lay and ecclesiastical communities within his principality, and that this was provoking
widespread and significant resentment. The prince was beginning
to meet increasingly bitter opposition from ecclesiastical magnates –
of whom Anian II of St Asaph provides a most vocal and persistent
example, but certainly not a unique one. In addition there are clear
indications that leading figures from the administrative elite – both
within and beyond Gwynedd, were turning against Llywelyn, and
even signs that he was facing not only criticism but outright antago-
nism from some of the poets.[137]

The supremacies enjoyed by the princes were almost never what
they seemed, and certainly not as clear-cut as modern maps of the
territories subject to rulers such as the Lord Rhys, Llywelyn ab
Iorwerth and Llywelyn ap Gruffudd, purport to show. Ascendancies
were almost always won at a cost: the financial cost of building the
structures needed to enforce obedience, of payments to the English
in and after 1267, or political cost, as those who were once allies or
confederates became aware of their transition into dependents, and
were driven to resentment. The ultimate paradox of the growth of
princely rule was that it strained loyalties and resources to the point
at which it entailed the destruction of the native principality of Wales.

Llywelyn ap Gruffudd's principate was indeed the point at which
the efforts to construct a meaningful native principality of Wales were
put to the test. More precisely, that testing time came in 1277. It was the
war of 1282 that killed Llywelyn, but it was in the war of 1277 that he
was crushed, reduced to a shadow of his former eminence. Much of the
explanation for the completeness of Edward I's victory in 1277 is to be

found in the king's own resolve and in the massive force of troops and engineers that he was able to mobilize, and the huge amount of money that he was able to pour into his campaigns. But much of the explanation involves the strength of the Welsh reaction against Llywelyn and the nature of his rule in the years before the war. Of course, there were opportunists, those who saw the strength of Edward's armies, or who saw the chance for royal reward in place of princely parsimony. But many had loyalties and resentments that set them against the prince.

All those in southern Powys who had looked to the return from exile of the lord whose ancestors had been the rightful rulers of that land for well over a century marched with the advancing Gruffudd ap Gwenwynwyn to reclaim the lordship from Llywelyn. In northern Powys, those lords of the ruling house and their followers, who resented the prince's intervention in the region after 1269, turned against Llywelyn. In the Middle March, the magnates who had become accustomed to the rule of marcher lords, and had begun to develop loyalty to them, joined the forces of the region against Llywelyn. And in the same March, those who had been made to find sureties for their own, and their families' obedience to the prince, or had had to hand over to him hostages for their future good behaviour or to avert his anger and suspicion, put themselves in the van of those forces which drove back Llywelyn.

In Ystrad Tywi, Rhys ap Maredudd in his castle of Dryslwyn, who looked to restore the lost glories of the house of the Lord Rhys, turned against Llywelyn. In southern Powys, men waited for the return of their own hereditary lord, Gruffudd ap Gwenwynwyn, and when he approached in the early months of 1277, they went over to him in droves and abandoned any pretence of support for Llywelyn. In Gwynedd itself those, including members of the influential coterie of poets, who believed that the prince had done a grievous wrong by imprisoning for over two decades his elder brother Owain, turned against Llywelyn. Those who believed that the prince had offended against Mother Church and her bishops resisted Llywelyn. Even Dafydd, the prince's younger brother, had his supporters. He had escaped from Gwynedd into England in 1274 not as a solitary outcast, but at the head of a large band of soldiery, doing great damage as he went. Now those followers had the chance of reward and revenge, and they too fought once more against Llywelyn.

5

New ascendancies

By the close of 1283 Edward I's armies and their allies in Wales and the March had secured the death of Llywelyn ap Gruffudd, the capture and execution of his brother Dafydd, and the capture, death or surrender of the lords who had supported them. The accoutrements of princely rule and dignity had been seized: the portion of the True Cross, alleged to have been handed down from prince to prince, was taken to the king by some of Dafydd's men, while the seals of Llywelyn, his wife Eleanor and his brother Dafydd, were melted down and made into a chalice, given by Edward to Vale Royal abbey; Llywelyn's coronet was presented to the shrine of St Edward at Westminster.[1]

THE ESTABLISHMENT OF
ROYAL DOMINANCE IN WALES

The king emphasized his triumph in 1284 by the holding of a Round Table at Nefyn in the Llŷn peninsula.[2] Llywelyn had been eulogized as an Arthur, and by holding that most Arthurian of festivities Edward made it clear that he, and not the dead prince, was the true heir of Arthur; that point was made explicit when 'the crown of the famous King Arthur, for long held in great honour amongst the Welsh' was discovered and brought to Edward.[3] The reality of conquest was made evident by the continuation of the programme of castle-building begun by Edward after the war of 1277, which extended the stone manifestations of royal power into western Gwynedd.[4] And in the Statute of Wales of 1284, the new administrative structures of north-west Wales were established.[5] There could be no doubt that a conquest had been effected. New laws were made, new boroughs were created and beyond the Edwardian Crown lands newly conquered territories were parcelled up and given out to the king's noble lieutenants, in the form of marcher lordships.

From the 1280s onwards, the March represented the greater part of Wales, extending in a great arc from east of the Conwy to the Dee, excluding only the three discrete territories of Tegeingl, Hopedale and Maelor Saesneg which constituted the new county of Flintshire, dependent on Chester.[6] From the middle waters of the Dee the March then ran southward through much of eastern Wales. It included not only the bulk of the territories of the former northern Powys, but also the great barony of (southern) Powys, whose lords were determined to assume the status of Welsh barons of the March, and whose territory, extending as far west as the tidal reaches of the Dyfi, effectively severed the northern from the southern and western Crown lands.[7] Much of the Middle March was Mortimer territory, while to the south lay the de Bohun land of Brycheiniog which bordered the various lordships of Gwent and the great Clare lordship of Glamorgan, where the March turned westwards, running along the whole of the southern coastal region and its hinterland, as far as the south-western extremity of Dyfed. These marcher territories were not fixed after 1284; some, such as the lordship of Builth, were now part of the March and now in the possession of the Crown. The status of some, such as the well-recorded case of the Corbet lordship of Caus, remained for long a matter of dispute as to whether they were properly marcher territory or whether they came under the authority of royal county officials.[8] The lordships of the March had varying customs and laws, and one hears much of the laws and customs of specific lordships – of Brecon, for example, or of Powys.[9]

The March, then, normally covered a larger area of Wales than that which comprised the Crown lands. Edward I had conquered Gwynedd and its satellites; the problem which followed that conquest was how to deal with the power of the great marcher lords. But the March was not a unified territory. Some lordships had by the late thirteenth century developed traditionally bitter relationships with their neighbours. The tensions between southern Powys and the Corbet lands, for instance, are well documented.[10] It was the frequent disunity, and at times the mutual hostility, of the marcher lords that gave Edward his opportunity to establish his mastery of the March. The principal occasion for this was the dispute between Humphrey de Bohun, the lord of Brecon and Gilbert de Clare, lord of Glamorgan. Edward had shown that he was intent upon establishing his control over the March, and over even the greatest of its lords, in the 1270s and 1280s.[11] But the real confrontation came in 1291, when the king had turned on two of the mightiest of the marchers, Gilbert de Clare, earl of Gloucester and lord of Glamorgan, and Humphrey de Bohun, earl of Hereford and lord of Brecon. There can be little doubt that the king had resolved to bring Gilbert de Clare to heel long before this: at Caerphilly Earl Gilbert had founded one of the greatest castles in Europe, a massive statement of his wealth and ambition. And when Edward made a royal progress through Wales in 1284 he had been escorted though Glamorgan by the earl in person, and the latter had treated him less as a sovereign and more as a fellow ruler.[12]

In the late 1280s Gilbert de Clare had begun building a castle at Morlais, which de Bohun claimed was on land belonging not to Glamorgan but to his own lordship of Brecon.[13] The dispute reflected a long history of conflict between the men of the two lordships, and by 1290 violence had once more broken out. Humphrey de Bohun put his case before the king, who ordered an end to the fighting. Now, this cut across a traditional marcher right to settle disputes by private war, and it was thus no surprise when the bailiffs of Earl Gilbert raided into Brecon lordship, with the earl's banner displayed, and the earl himself took his traditional third of the spoils 'as it befits the lords to have in time of war, in accordance with the use and custom of the March'.[14] But later in the year Earl Gilbert married Edward's daughter, Joan of Acre, and celebrated the union with massive ceremony. Edward was however not inclined to allow his new son-in-law to pursue traditional rights at the expense of the royal majesty. As it was explained to the marchers, the king 'for the common good, is by his prerogative in many cases above the laws and customs used in his realm'.[15] This was a matter of urgency, especially when Earl Gilbert persisted in raiding into Brecon after the king had ordered the fighting to cease. A first hearing took place in early 1291, before many of the marchers, though Earl Gilbert failed to appear. The royal judges pronounced his bailiffs guilty, assessed damages and renewed the order against private war. Edward then convened a new hearing, before him, at

Abergavenny in the early autumn of 1291. It was established that some of Earl Humphrey's men had raided into Glamorgan; they had been arrested by their lord, but Humphrey had detained the cattle that they had brought back into his lordship. Earl Humphrey was pronounced guilty of contempt, and declared liable to be imprisoned and to have his land of Brecon taken into the king's hands. Gilbert de Clare was then subjected to the same punishment: he too was to be imprisoned and to lose his lordship of Glamorgan. In the event, their imprisonment was short, and they were restored to their lands, but the royal mercy cost Earl Gilbert 10,000 marks; Earl Humphrey, whose offence was not reckoned so grievous, had to pay 1,000 marks.[16]

Two of the most significant of all the marcher lords had been publicly humbled, and it was clear that Edward had established the point that marcher 'regality' would not prevail against the royal majesty. Edward was, throughout the proceedings, anxious to establish whether anything had been done 'in prejudice or contempt or injury of his crown or royal dignity'.[17] The king was master of the March, just as of the principality. And indeed, he was master of the March precisely because he was master of the principality: with Edward in control of *pura Wallia*, and with all of the Welsh rulers compliant, imprisoned or dead, he had far less need of the marchers. Moreover, the trial of the earls of Hereford and Gloucester was not the only process in the 1290s at which the same point had been made: the king repeatedly intervened to keep the marcher lords in order.[18] It was in the final decade of the century that it became clear that the future activities of marcher lords would be much more circumscribed unless like Hugh Despenser or Roger Mortimer in the reign of Edward II they could associate themselves with the king, or with the king's wife. And it was in that same decade that the dream cherished by some Welsh lords of successful rebellion was dashed.

It was in 1292, the year of the humbling of the earls of Gloucester and of Hereford, that Rhys ap Maredudd, rebellious lord of Dryslwyn, was finally captured, tried and executed.[19] But in 1294–5 Edward had to face Welsh risings that involved most regions of Wales.[20] The risings served as a reminder that the pride and traditions of the marcher magnates were not the only challenge which he faced, but that conquest might, for very good reason, engender dangerous resentments amongst the conquered. At least five leaders, from Gwynedd,

Ceredigion, Brycheiniog, Glamorgan and Gwent, were involved in almost simultaneous, if not concerted, uprisings, which posed a serious threat to Edward's hard-won control of Wales, and even involved a French plan to stoke up the fires of discontent.[21] But, albeit with considerable expenditure and effort, the risings were suppressed. At last Edward appeared to be master of Wales.

AN AGE OF CONTRADICTIONS:
OPPRESSION AND ADVANCEMENT

It is depressingly easy to point to the widespread oppression and discrimination suffered by the Welsh population in the decades after 1283 in many regions of Wales, where in matters of administration, law and economic opportunity, there was a rigid distinction, in theory at least, between the privileged English and the 'mere Welsh'.[22] The Edwardian boroughs were to be populated by English settlers, and the Welsh were to be excluded from the status and privileges of burgesses. In some of the new lordships English settlers were brought in considerable numbers, and given choice lands from which Welsh landholders were evicted and compensated with less useful lands elsewhere. A prime case was in the Honour (i.e. lordship) of Denbigh, where it is reckoned that by the early 1330s 10,000 acres of land had been occupied by English incomers.[23] The 1334 Survey of the Honour of Denbigh noted, amongst many such records, that in the vill of Tre Prys 'various proprietors from Llewenni, Ystrad Cynan, Gwenynog Cynan, Berain and Talybryn and elsewhere hold by way of exchange 879 acres and 25 pieces of land and waste in lieu of their patrimonies seized from them in the time of the earl of Lincoln'.[24] The lands from which those families had been removed were fertile, while the territory which they had been allotted consisted of vastly inferior rain-lashed upland heath on Mynydd Hiraethog.

Similar changes can be glimpsed within the principality lands. Thus the principal trading centre of the princes, Llanfaes in south-east Anglesey, was effectively suppressed after the war of 1294–5 to make way for the castle and new town of Beaumaris, and its inhabitants were moved across the island to the much less advantageous urban centre of Newborough.[25] It was estimated by E. A. Lewis, the pioneering historian of the boroughs of Snowdonia, that in the eighty years which followed the conquest, more than five thousand acres of generally very good agricultural land was absorbed into the lands of the boroughs of the north-west of Wales.[26] It is similarly easy to establish the case for ethnic discrimination when we turn to the administrative structures of post-conquest Wales. From the outset there was a clear tendency to exclude Welshmen from the chief official posts – including those of sheriff and constables of castles – of the new administrations of north and west Wales, though at the level of the commotes officials remained almost entirely Welsh.[27]

And yet, on closer examination, the uniformity and, after some years, the severity of the Edwardian settlement, begin to appear less clear. Particularly after the tensions expressed and created by the revolts of 1294–5 had begun to subside, a shift in the nature of the government of north Wales begins to appear. The creation by Edward I of his son Edward as prince of Wales in 1301 can easily be dismissed as a purely cynical manoeuvre by the king, but it does nearly coincide with important developments in governance. The figures put forward by Rees Davies in his discussion of the holders of the office of sheriff in the northern principality cannot be denied: 'of the names of forty or so sheriffs for the northern counties [in the period 1284–1343] only seven are Welsh'.[28] But if we focus on the three decades after 1300, and if we count years in office rather than names, a rather different pattern appears. It is true that in Caernarfonshire the post was held by a Welsh official for only some four years. But in Merionethshire the office was in the hands of Welshmen for nearly half of the period, while in Anglesey Welsh officials held the shrievalty for some eighteen years.[29] In other words Welshmen held the offices of sheriff in the three counties of the north for 40 per cent of the period 1300–30. Just as important is the point that many of these sheriffs were representatives of old families prominent as members of the ministerial elite under the native princes.[30]

At an even higher level, that of the chief officers of the administrative centres of Caernarfon and Carmarthen, the justiciars, chamberlains and receivers, Welshmen were effectively excluded from office. But it is a matter for some consideration that officials at this level often had deputies, and many of those deputies were Welsh. Thus Rhys ap Hywel, a son of the Hywel ap Meurig who was such a determined opponent of Llywelyn ap Gruffudd, was deputy justiciar of south Wales to Roger Mortimer in 1312–13, and was to be justiciar in 1326–7. Sir Rhys ap Gruffudd was deputy justiciar, not for the last time, in 1321–2, and Philip de Clanvow, a nephew of Rhys ap Hywel, was deputy justiciar in 1332, and twice more in the following years.[31] It is also notable that both Sir Rhys ap Gruffudd and Philip de Clanvow served as constables of Carmarthen Castle, the former in 1326 and 1335–42, and the latter in 1335.[32]

A somewhat similar situation developed in the boroughs created or developed under Edward I. It is clear that boroughs went hand in hand with castles as instruments of consolidation of the Edwardian conquest, and as such their burgess populations were expected to be English. There are plentiful signs of tension between the English burgesses and the Welsh of the surrounding countryside. In Carmarthen the burgesses had received in 1309 a grant of murage, the right to raise a local tax to strengthen the walls of the borough. In 1312 they petitioned the king for an extension of that grant, so that they might be secure against the Welsh 'who threaten from day to day to take the town'.[33] A set of royal ordinances, most probably issued after the revolts of 1294–5, attempted to reinforce the exclusively English character of the boroughs founded after 1283 in the principality.[34] But here again the barriers to the advance of the Welsh were not indestructible. Thus we have seen that when Edward I established the borough of Beaumaris after the events of 1294–5 the new foundation involved the re-settlement of the Welsh population of Llanfaes at a new settlement in the south-west of Anglesey which became known as Newborough. That resettlement was resisted by a number of the inhabitants of Llanfaes, led by the local physician, Master Einion. But it seems that Einion was keeping a foot in both camps, for he was also recorded in 1300 as a burgess of Beaumaris.[35]

Beyond the principality, in the new lordships, there were examples of boroughs in which the Welsh established a significant presence. It has been demonstrated by some minute research that in one of the new post-conquest boroughs, that of Ruthin, there was a significant degree of assimilation of Welsh and English burgesses. The tenements of the Welsh burgesses tended to be small in comparison with those of the English, and the Welsh were generally less wealthy than the English, but there was a significant degree of shared experience which brought the communities together. There are fascinating signs of a degree of collusion between the English and Welsh elites in the borough, as in an apparent agreement by the brewers of both ethnic groups to fix ale prices during the great famine of the second decade of the fourteenth century. Again, a tendency for Welsh and English to specialize in different trades can be pictured as complementary rather than necessarily divisive, as when the Welsh weavers were complemented by English tailors, or Welsh tanners by English cobblers: here were the seeds of mutual dependency and cooperation.[36]

A single incident underscores the ambivalence of ethnic relations in early fourteenth-century Dyffryn Clwyd: in 1321 there was a raid by Welsh insurgents on the castle and borough of Ruthin. This suggests the resentment of the Welsh rural community against institutions that were the result and the symbol of conquest – a phenomenon that is seen elsewhere at various times. But within the borough, there was an apparent reluctance on the part of Welsh townsfolk to join in the attack and turn on the English community: the urban groups, irrespective of ethnic origin, had a solidarity born of shared interest.[37] And a similar mixture of ethnic origins can be seen, perhaps predictably, in the boroughs of the lordship of Powys: while the 1292 lay subsidy assessment reveals that at Welshpool, near to the English border, English burgesses were in a majority, with a significant minority of Welsh, the same record reveals that the borough of Llanidloes, at the head of the Severn valley, had English and Welsh burgesses in equal numbers, while in the north-western borough of Machynlleth the burgesses appear to have been overwhelmingly Welsh.[38]

Indeed, there was a degree of ambivalence about many aspects of the new Edwardian order in Wales. The conquest – particularly if we extend the concept to embrace the wars that were undertaken to suppress rebellions in 1287, 1294–5 and 1316, as well as more localized fighting like that in Powys in 1312–32 – resulted in widespread deaths, either directly in combat or as a result of grievous damage to economic resources. The impact of fighting within Wales was then complemented by the fact that the English kings, especially Edward I, were particularly active in wars far beyond it. And they did not hesitate to call into their service large contingents of Welsh soldiery, both from the lands of the principality and those of the March.

The numbers of Welsh troops called into the service of the English Crown are impressive. The vast majority – some 88 per cent – of the troops involved in the war of 1287 against the rebellious Rhys ap Maredudd were Welsh, drawn from the Crown lands and marcher lordships. Welsh levies were also involved against the risings of 1294–5, but their numbers cannot be determined. Nearly three-quarters of Edward I's army of some 7,300 men active in Flanders in 1297–8 were Welsh, and 10,900 Welsh troops out of a total of 29,000 served in the Falkirk campaign of 1298. In further Scottish and other campaigns in the years after 1300 numerous Welsh soldiers were raised: 4,500 in 1301, 300 in 1306, over 2,800 in 1307, perhaps 3,200 in 1314, 2,500 in 1319 and 6,500 in 1322.[39]

Military involvement on such a scale assuredly had a profound impact on Welsh society. The men recruited must have represented a significant element in the Welsh workforce, and thus their absence on campaign may have been economically damaging. However, we should perhaps set an assessment of the consequences of employing large numbers of Welsh troops in distant campaigns in the context of the economic conditions of the late thirteenth and early fourteenth centuries. It is possible to paint a picture of the agrarian economy of much of Wales coming under increasing strain in this period. This putative economic fragility appears to have been revealed in stark form in the crisis years of the middle of the second decade of the fourteenth century, when a 'great dearth of victuals' was reported in Gwynedd, while escheats appear to have been unusually high in the north-east, and many of the cattle of Aberconwy abbey died in a murrain.[40] Similarly, a murrain of beasts and great dearness of food was noted in Glamorgan, and royal demands for what the community described as a ransom exacted because of their support for Llywelyn Bren's insurrection had to be remitted or delayed.[41] The men of Cantref Mawr in the county of Carmarthen were pardoned contributions to the fifteenth voted in 1318; the contribution of Merioneth to that tax fell from £566 in 1292 to £227 in 1318, and the chamberlain of north Wales was ordered in October to supersede until further notice the assessment and levy of the tax.[42] Consideration of such economic fragility led Keith Williams-Jones to point out that it was a 'grimly ironical fact' that wars, rebellions, occasional famine and, we may add, repeated military recruitment may have 'skimmed off some of the "surplus" population', and enabled the social order to persist longer than it would otherwise have done.[43]

We do indeed enter in the post-conquest decades into a period characterized by multiple paradoxes. The nature of Welsh society and the problems that it faced are indeed far more complex than can be summed up in the neat formulae of oppression. Undoubtedly many Welsh communities in the March were, or felt that they were, oppressed by their intrusive lords, just as those in the principality lands felt the pressures of royal governance. And yet one of the most striking features of royal governance in the lands of north and west Wales is the sensitivity of the king to complaints from the Welsh communities of those lands, and the resolve to rectify matters. This is particularly evident in the aftermath of the rebellions of 1294–5.[44] At the same time there are signs that some of the marcher lords were prepared – sometimes under royal pressure – to make some concessions to communities that were voicing opposition to their governance.

In the March, this appears to be demonstrated by the charters that the Welsh managed to extract, at a price, from their lords in so many lordships in the late thirteenth and early fourteenth centuries. Several such grants were made in 1297. The Welsh community of Maelienydd secured two charters from Edmund Mortimer at a cost of £500.[45] Further south the men of Brecon lordship similarly received a grant from Humphrey de Bohun, earl of Hereford, but only after severe royal pressure had been applied to the earl. Edward's officers – Walter Hakelute and Morgan ap Maredudd – were empowered to hear complaints of the earl's people of Brecon against the earl and his ministers, to defend and maintain those complaining until justice had been done, and to admit to the king's peace those people whom the earl had ejected from their lands and to reinstate them. In addition, similar grants were made within the lordship of Glamorgan.[46] In 1299 the men of Talgarth, Ystrad Yw and Crickhowell paid 100 marks for confirmations of their rights.[47] The Welsh of Tempseter in Clun lordship (i.e. the Welshry of Clun) had paid £200 for a charter of liberties in 1292.[48] A grant of liberties was made to all free men, both Welsh and English, in Cemais in 1278, and to all tenants and their men both Welsh and English of Gower in 1306.[49] All of these were established marcher lordships by the thirteenth century; but charters were also granted to the men of the more recently created lordships such as Chirkland, Denbigh and Dyffryn Clwyd.[50]

The terms of these charters are instructive. The 1297 Maelienydd grants may serve as an example. These were issued by Edmund Mortimer

> to his men of Maelienydd, on complaint by them that in the time of his father [Roger Mortimer (d.1282)] as well as in his own time they have been aggrieved by his bailiffs. The charter granted, inter alia, that if anyone claimed to suffer injuries or trespasses at the hands of Edmund or his father, he should bring his plaint into the court of Cymaron, where it would be determined by a jury, according to the laws and customs heretofore used there.

Further provisions establish that

> goods and chattels of the of the free men of Maelienydd should not be taken to Edmund's use, except in case of necessity, and then if their goods were saleable they should be taken at a just price, to be paid within three weeks; that if anyone should be taken and incarcerated and could find pledges according to the laws of that land, he should be liberated, and for any crime the common law should be granted without money ransom.

A second charter, granted on the same date, gave to the community licence to hunt and take deer throughout Maelienydd, except in the demesnes of Knucklas and Swydd, and in most of the lands of the abbey of Cwm-hir. Fixed penalties, in cash, for hunting stags, hinds, roe-deer and young hinds, boars and sows in the reserved places were established, and the community was also given licence to fish a specific length in the Ithon. The men of Maelienydd and their heirs were to hold these liberties as long as they kept themselves faithfully in the king's peace.[51] The terms of such charters as that granted to the men of Maelienydd suggest both that marcher lords were beginning to listen, at a price, to the complaints of their tenantry, and also that there had been past oppressions. The price that the community of Maelienydd was prepared to pay is perhaps an index of the concern felt about the loss of traditional rights and the development of arbitrary action on the part of the Mortimer lords. And the reference to the maintenance of the king's peace served as a reminder that the rights of the marcher lords existed in the shadow of royal power and supervision.

Such pressures to act in accord with past agreements and pronouncements also existed in the territories retained by the Crown after 1284, and in periods of crisis the communities of those lands were ready to take advantage of royal anxieties to press for redress of grievances. Thus the willingness of the royal government to listen to, and act on, complaints from the communities of north Wales and west Wales is very marked in the period after the risings of 1294–5. In September of 1295, for instance, a complaint by the community of north Wales prompted the issue of a commission to the justice of north Wales and the constable of Conwy castle to enquire into trespasses, injuries, oppressions and grievous losses inflicted on the community since that land came into the king's hands, by the sheriffs, bailiffs and other ministers of the king.[52] And in the following year four representatives of the 'good men and commonalty' of north Wales, the abbot of Aberconwy, Thomas Daunvers, Tudur ap Goronwy and Hywel ap Cynwrig, were sent to the king to relate a rumour 'which disturbed and grieved them, that the king held them in suspicion'. Edward responded by

> begging them not to believe such rumours for the future, as no sinister rumour of their state or behaviour has reached the king in these days, and he has no suspicion towards them, but rather, by reason of their late good service, holds them for his faithful and devoted subjects.[53]

Of the representatives of 1296, Daunvers had been appointed sheriff of Anglesey after the previous holder of the office, Sir Roger Puleston, was killed by the insurgents in 1294. Hywel ap Cynwrig may be the man of that name who petitioned to hold the office of *rhaglaw* in Arllechwedd Uchaf free of farm in 1305, claiming to have held it in that way as the result of a gift from the former prince, Llywelyn ap Gruffudd.[54] Even more interestingly, Tudur ap Goronwy is to be identified as the man of that name who had appeared as a witness to a charter issued by the rebel leader Madog ap Llywelyn in the previous year. Accompanied by his brother Goronwy, Tudur was then designated as Madog's steward.[55] It was an appropriate appointment, for

Tudur was a member of the administrative aristocracy of Gwynedd, a grandson of Ednyfed Fychan, steward to Llywelyn ab Iorwerth and Dafydd ap Llywelyn, and a son of Goronwy ab Ednyfed, steward to Llywelyn ap Gruffudd. Tudur was a prominent figure in Gwynedd, and would be closely associated with the rebuilding of the Dominican friary of Bangor, where he was buried in 1311.[56] His support for Madog ap Llywelyn appears to have been overlooked by a king anxious to secure the cooperation of leading figures in the upper strata of society in Gwynedd.

There are frequent indications of the readiness of Edward I's son, both as prince of Wales and as king, to adopt a similar attitude towards grievances on the part of Welsh communities. The Kennington petitions of 1305 represent a particularly good example. Over one hundred and fifty petitions are recorded from communities, from Welsh individuals, from English burgesses, from the bishop of Bangor and from monastic bodies.[57] The great majority emanated from the counties of north Wales though some come from neighbouring communities or individuals bringing forward complaints about the activities of officials from those counties. Petitions concerned, inter alia, requests for justice, for posts in the royal lands, for favours, for the redress of grievances and oppressions, and for enforcement of laws and for flexibility in the application of laws. The diversity of groups and individuals who put their petitions forward is impressive: they include both important ecclesiastical bodies and members of the ministerial elite, as well as much less privileged persons. The responses from the prince and his council were mixed, but their most striking feature is the evident care with which the petitions were considered.

A rather later counterpart to the Kennington petitions, which had focused entirely on north Wales, can be found in the southern principality lands of Gwynionydd, Caerwedros and Mabwynion in the county of Cardigan, from which petitions were received by Edward II in December 1309.[58] The men of these commotes complained of a long-running attempt to secure redress of grievances. They had originally complained that the bailiffs of those parts were taking 2s. of each pound of amercements due to the king; that the constables of the king's castles took their goods without payment or made insufficient payment; that royal officials were making accusations that individuals were not faithful to the king, and that in such cases there should be

an inquisition of the country to decide on the validity of the accusa-
tion. All in all the community felt 'much saddened in heart' by the
harshness of the lordship inflicted on them. In response to their initial
petition Edward had ordered the justiciar of Wales, Roger Mortimer,
to do justice according to the laws and customs of Wales, so that the
petitioners should not have to have recourse to the king again for lack
of justice. That order had been made in April 1309. But the petitioners had been unable to secure a response from Mortimer, and so were
forced to approach the king again. This time the order came to make
hasty accomplishment of right to the community, by writs of the great
seal, according to the law and usage of those parts. It is a measure
both of Mortimer's reluctance to act, and the king's determination
that he should do so, that Edward wrote again to Mortimer in May
1310 to demand that he should act, in a matter on which he had 'still
done nothing, as is shown to us on the part of the aforesaid Welsh'.[59]
It is probably at this period that Mortimer was also told by the king
to attend to complaints from the men of north Wales that they were
being subjected to judicial practices that were not consistent with those
used in the time of the princes. Yet another enquiry was set up in 1315
into oppressive acts by royal officials in Wales.[60]

It is thus no surprise that in 1316, at the time of the revolt of
Llywelyn Bren in Glamorgan, Edward II acceded to petitions presented in the parliament at Lincoln, from the king's lieges of west
and south Wales 'for the removal of grievances inflicted on them by
his ministers, touching the observance of customs and the redress of
such grievances'. These last included

> the custom of amobrage, exemption from the caption of the goods
> of freemen, the custom called blodwite, suits between Welshmen
> and Welshmen touching contracts or trespasses, and between
> Welshmen and Englishmen and other foreigners, the custom
> called *Westua* [i.e. *Gwestfa*, a form of food rent], felonies and tres-
> passes for which they are charged by the king's bailiffs, and the
> punishment of any of his bailiffs or ministers acting contrary to
> the above concession.[61]

It seems possible that the men of south and west Wales may have
encouraged the king to assent to their petition by an offer made in

February 1316 to serve against Llywelyn Bren until Easter, as long as that service should not be to the prejudice of them or their heirs.[62]

On the occasion of the same parliament, Edward made a similar concession to petitions presented by the men of north Wales. Some of the issues raised by them were identical to those brought up by the men of the south and west, such as those relating to amobrage or caption of goods, but others were specific to the men of Gwynedd. These involved demands that each freeman having two or more sons should be able to have one of them ordained to the priesthood without seeking the licence of the king or his justices; that for the next three years all free Welshmen should be able to sell or grant their lands, tenements or rents to other free Welshmen, provided that those sales or grants should not be made to prelates, religious, or to the king's ministers or the ministers of others, seculars or ecclesiastics; that the ordinances made at Kennington in the time of Edward I, when the present king was prince of Wales, upon petition being made by the men of the community of north Wales, should be observed in all their articles, and that the justice or in default of him, the chancellor, should remedy any grievances.[63]

The first point that should be made about these various grants and confirmations of rights is that they may be read in two very different ways. First, they reveal that abuses and oppressions had taken place, under both Crown officials and marcher lords and their officers. But secondly, they reveal that there was a readiness on the part of the Crown and the marchers to remedy abuses, even if that remedy was often offered at some considerable cost to the recipients. In other words, these concessions reveal both the fact of oppression and the provision of machinery to remedy it.

It also needs to be stressed that petitions to prince or king were not simply made on a few occasions, such as at Kennington in 1305. Reference to the class of Ancient Petitions in the National Archives reveals a fairly steady flow of petitions during the decades after the Statute of Wales. Analysis of the petitions submitted to the Crown from Wales once again lays bare the problems, hardships and frustrations suffered by the Welsh of the principality lands, but also reveals that neither individuals nor communities were prevented from bringing their grievances forward, and that in many instances they received a positive response. It is even possible to argue that the practice of petitioning reveals 'the remarkable success with which the English Crown integrated the Welsh people into the administrative and judicial framework of the "greater" English state'.[64]

But it is not only in the field of formal governmental processes, of the consideration of petitions and the remedying of grievances, that paradoxes relating to the response of Welsh people to the conditions which obtained after 1284 are to be found. They appear even in the field of cultural and literary expression. The post-conquest decades were ones of considerable activity in the literary field and in that of the writing of history. They saw both the collection of poetry composed by the poets of the princes which was copied into the Hendregadredd manuscript, almost certainly at Strata Florida abbey,[65] and they also saw the translation into Welsh of a Latin chronicle, or a collection of a group of chronicle materials, also, it seems, at Strata Florida.[66] Strata Florida was an abbey that had been particularly associated with the hegemonic princes, and which had suffered at the hands of English forces in the closing years of the thirteenth century.[67] It was perhaps almost inevitable that it should have emerged as a centre for the preservation of the literary culture and the historical record which marked the princes' achievements.

The work that was apparently carried out at Strata Florida around the turn of the century may be interpreted simply as an attempt to save from oblivion the fruits of Welsh poetic output of the Age of the Princes, and also to preserve a record of the achievements and deeds of the princes themselves. But in the case of the writing of *Brut y Tywysogion* we need to establish exactly what was being accomplished. It has been thought that the *Brut*, in both its putative (lost) Latin form and in the translated text which survives, was the work of a compiler at Strata Florida, who wrote up an extended narrative in a graceful literary style from short original Latin annals, reflected in the surviving materials by the texts known as *Annales Cambriae*.[68] In other words it was a conscious effort to develop, in the aftermath of the Edwardian conquest, a fitting memorial of the past glories of the princes, and perhaps an inspiration for the future. But detailed analysis of *Brut y Tywysogion* in recent years has shown that this was not the case, and that the Welsh text actually reflects very full, but lost, original Latin annals.[69] In other words, we have to abandon the notion that the author of *Brut y Tywysogion* or of a putative (lost) 'Latin *Brut*' which lay behind it was consciously producing a literary composition that would stand as a monument to the past glories of the princes. Instead he is better seen as a translator of already full chronicle materials that had been composed very close in time to the events of the Age of the Princes which they record. He is recording the past, not creating it. But as well as these achievements, other literary impulses were already at work.

If we look first at the work that was evidently taking place on the Welsh chronicles around the turn of the century it seems that the trans-lators of the *Brutiau* may have been preserving the memory and the potency of the Age of the Princes, but some were engaged on the copy-ing of the related text, *Brenhinedd y Saesson*, which attempted, with varying degrees of success, to integrate Welsh and English history. One of the main centres engaged in the work of developing *Brenhinedd y Saesson* was Valle Crucis Abbey, and it was quite probably here that a Continuation of the *Brut* was compiled, taking the chronicle to the year 1332.[70] The Continuation was written principally by a scribe who was also responsible for copying a text of *Brenhinedd y Saesson*. It is highly significant that in one of its last entries the Continuation records the death of one Madog ap Llywelyn, 'the best man that ever was in Maelor'.[71] We shall consider Madog's career shortly.

Turning now to the work of the poets, it is impossible not to be struck by the dedication of those, particularly the scribe known only as 'alpha' (α), who gathered the priceless collection of the poems composed in the Age of the Princes which is to be found in the Hendregadredd manuscript. Here was an attempt, comparable to the translating of the *Brutiau*, to preserve the cultural achievement of the twelfth and thirteenth centuries in Wales. But it should not be allowed to obscure the fact that the poets continued to function in the post-conquest period, when we pass from the 'poets of the princes' to the 'poets of the *uchelwyr*'.[72] We can indeed discern something of the situation that allowed the poets to continue to flourish after the conquest if we consider some representative figures drawn from the upper echelons of Welsh society in the half century after 1284.

AN AGE OF OPPORTUNITY? SOME CASE STUDIES

Members of the post-conquest Welsh elite were frequently mem-bers of families already celebrated for membership of a privileged administrative aristocracy. The most obvious cases of men in this category are those of Sir Gruffudd Llwyd and his cousin Sir Rhys ap Gruffudd, both descendants of Ednyfed Fychan, the steward (*distain*) of Llywelyn ab Iorwerth and of Dafydd ap Llywelyn, and of Ednyfed's son Gruffudd, who was steward to Llywelyn ap Gruffudd. Sir Gruffudd Llwyd's father was Rhys ap Gruffudd and Sir Rhys ap Gruffudd's grandfather was Hywel, Rhys ap Gruffudd's brother. Both Rhys ap Gruffudd and Hywel ap Gruffudd were conspicuous opponents of Llywelyn ap Gruffudd in the later years of his principate.[73] It is unsurprising that Sir Gruffudd Llwyd and Sir Rhys ap Gruffudd should have emerged as perhaps the bulwarks of Edward II's rule in north and south Wales respectively, and that both men were the subjects of praise poems

Sir Gruffudd Llwyd possessed significant estates in north Wales and in west Wales. As a young man he had served in the household of Queen Eleanor and was a yeoman of the household of both Edward I and his son, Edward of Caernarvon. Knighted before 1301, he was active in the period 1297–1314 raising troops in north Wales for both Edwards, and at various times between 1301 and 1327 held the office of sheriff in all three counties of the northern principality, twice in both Caernarvonshire and Merioneth and once in Anglesey.[74] He was closely associated with Edward II in some of the greatest crises of his reign: thus he was one of the three magnates of who held confidential meetings with Edward in 1315, when there were grave fears of a Scottish invasion of Wales via Ireland, in order to work out how to avert or overcome any such intervention.[75] A letter of encouragement apparently sent by Gruffudd to Edward Bruce, who had set himself up as king of Ireland and was apparently considering an invasion of Wales, may indicate simple opportunism on Gruffudd's part, or it may suggest that Gruffudd was acting as an agent provocateur.[76] It is quite possible that he had discussed such a move with Morgan ap Maredudd, who seems to have had some experience of such a role, and who had joined him for discussions with Edward at Clipstone in late 1315. His imprisonment in late 1316 or early 1317 for over eighteen months seems to relate not to this exchange of letters, but to his enmity with Roger Mortimer, who was appointed as justice of north Wales in that year.[77]

Again, in the early part of 1322 Sir Gruffudd led forces that fought in support of Edward as the struggle with the baronial opposition led by Thomas of Lancaster reached crisis point. Gruffudd's capture of a string of castles in the northern borderland, Holt, Chirk and Welshpool, was crucial in enabling Edward to emerge victorious.[78] And in the final period of Edward's reign, and life, Gruffudd, like his kinsman Rhys ap Gruffudd, was deeply implicated in plots to overthrow the Mortimer administration and to restore Edward II to power.[79] He was clearly out of favour in the Mortimer-dominated regime of 1327–30. His son Ieuan was apparently implicated in the unsuccessful plot against Mortimer of the earl of Kent in 1330 and Sir Gruffudd was imprisoned, with a group of his associates, in 1327 – once more as a result of Roger Mortimer's suspicion of him.[80] Gruffudd was also the subject of complaints of past oppressions committed by him against English inhabitants of north Wales but he is subsequently, in 1331, found associated with some of those who had supported Mortimer's execution in the previous year. He was still alive in May 1335, when he received licence to enfeoff his son Ieuan with the manor of Llansadwrn in Carmarthenshire, to be held in chief from the king.[81]

No less distinguished, and no less important, was the career of Sir Gruffudd Llwyd's cousin, Sir Rhys ap Gruffudd. It is no exaggeration to suggest that while Gruffudd Llwyd was the dominant force in the politics of the northern principality in the early decades of the fourteenth century, Rhys ap Gruffudd played the equivalent part in the southern principality. Rhys was, as noted above, descended in the male line from Ednyfed Fychan, and he succeeded to his father's lands in Cardiganshire and Carmarthenshire in 1308; his mother was Nest, the daughter of Gwrwared ap Gwilym of Cemais, a member of a family with a record of prominence in marcher and Crown administration.[82] It is thus hardly a surprise that Rhys followed the same path. Frequently employed in raising and leading troops for the king, he was involved in the suppression of the revolt of Llywelyn Bren in 1316.[83] In the great political/military crisis of 1321–2 and its aftermath Rhys was central to the raising of troops for the king in south Wales, and was also given the custody of numerous castles.[84]

In the final turmoil of Edward II's reign, Rhys was very active in attempting to resist the forces of Roger Mortimer and Queen Isabella, as they invaded the realm in 1326, and when resistance appeared hopeless he was one of those sent by the king to negotiate with Isabella.[85]

After Edward II's capture and confinement in Berkeley Castle in 1327, Rhys was involved in an abortive attempt to free the king, and was therefore forced to flee to the Scots.[86] Pardoned in 1328, he was then accused of involvement in the earl of Kent's plot against the government of Roger Mortimer, and was forced to escape abroad once more.[87] But the fall of Mortimer in 1330 allowed Rhys to return to prominence in royal service and for some two decades he continued to raise and lead troops for Edward III and the Black Prince. He died in 1356, having been knighted in 1346.[88] In the course of this long career Rhys ap Gruffudd accumulated large estates, including for example his acquisition by royal grant in 1317 of the manor of Lampeter, to be held freely and for life, augmented in 1318 by the grant of a weekly market there. His lands at the time of his death included estates in six English counties which had come to him by marriage, and very extensive lordships and lands throughout south-west Wales. These latter included several lordships held by Welsh barony, such as Llansadwrn and Llanrhystud, other large territories held 'in the same way as other Welsh tenants called *uchelwyr*' the lordship of the town of Lampeter, the constableship of Dryslwyn, the town and lands of Dryslwyn, the stewardship of Cantref Mawr, the office of *rhaglaw* in two commotes, and the office of forester in the forests of Glyn Cothi and Pennant.[89]

The most salient point to emerge from consideration of the careers of Sir Gruffudd Llwyd and Sir Rhys ap Gruffudd is that their power and influence in Wales were surely on a par with those wielded by the greatest of their ancestors, even by Ednyfed Fychan, in the principates of the Llywelyns. It is quite evident that while Sir Gruffudd Llwyd and Sir Rhys ap Gruffudd were exceptional in terms of the breadth of their influence, they were representative of a large ministerial class with roots in the pre-conquest administration that included several of their kinsmen and which continued to be a crucial factor in the politics of Wales in the half-century after the events of 1282–4.[90]

It is hardly to be wondered at in this age of ambivalence that the poets emphasized the martial virtues of both Sir Gruffudd Llwyd and Sir Rhys ap Gruffudd, their descent and their leadership in wide swathes of Wales, while not focusing on the precise offices that they held or the official missions that they had undertaken.[91] This last point may be particularly significant, suggesting that Welsh magnates who held important posts in the royal, and perhaps the marcher, administration in Wales may have adopted, or been accorded, two very different personae. One of these might reflect their official role and authority. The other might be based on their status within Welsh society as derived from the eminence of their descent and kin connections, their extensive landed interests and the extent to which they were able to fulfil expectations of them as local or regional lords.

While the roots of Sir Gruffudd Llwyd and Sir Rhys ap Gruffudd lay in *pura Wallia*, they had counterparts who belonged to families that had become prominent in the March. Again, a few representative cases must suffice. We have already encountered Madog ap Llywelyn, a prominent freeman of the lordship of Bromfield and Yale.[92] His father, Llywelyn ap Gruffudd, was a member of the extensive and prominent kin-group descended from Tudur Trefor. Madog's mother was Angharad, daughter of Maredudd ap Madog ap Gruffudd, the lord of Iâl in the mid-thirteenth century. Angharad's mother was Catrin, a sister of Llywelyn ap Gruffudd, prince of Wales.[93] Thus Madog ap Llywelyn's ancestry was an illustrious one. His eminence was evidently recognized by the lord of Bromfield and Yale, William de Warenne, earl of Surrey, for in 1308 when Warenne issued a charter granting a knight's fee in Bromfield to John de Wysham, Madog was the only Welsh witness.[94]

When Warenne was forced out of the lordship of Bromfield and Yale in 1318 by Thomas, earl of Lancaster, Madog ap Llywelyn was promptly appointed by Lancaster to the powerful post of receiver of the lordship.[95] But his appointment in February 1322 to escort levies from the lordship to the king at Coventry suggests that Madog was now acting in the royal interest rather than that of the earl of Lancaster; royal supporters such as Rhys ap Gruffudd were certainly involved in the collection and movement of troops – explicitly declared in the commissions to be for service against the Scots and the Contrariants (i.e. the king's baronial opponents).[96] After Lancaster's execution later that year, Warenne was restored to the lordship. The fact that Madog ap Llywelyn had served the man who had ousted him in 1318 does not seem to have caused Warenne to exclude him from his inner circle, for in 1323 Madog and four other Welshmen, including his brother Gruffudd, witnessed a Warenne grant issued at Reigate.[97] It is uncertain whether Madog held office in Bromfield and Yale at this period, but it is clear that he mixed in the company of the Warenne entourage. As late as 1330 Madog witnessed a further Warenne grant, this time at Holt, the caput of the lordship of Bromfield and Yale.[98] And in a most interesting record of December of 1330 he appears, along with four English officials – including John de Wysham, then justice of north Wales – charged with carrying out a commission of Oyer et Terminer consequent on a petition of the community of the land of north Wales to the king and his council, in which they complained of oppressions committed by William de Shaldeford while he acted as deputy to Roger Mortimer, former justice of north Wales.[99]

Madog was thus prominent in baronial politics and administration at a notably high level, while also acting in royal service. He was closely involved with prominent English families such as the Pulestons of Emral.[100] His importance becomes clear at his death. In an entry in the Continuation of *Brut y Tywysogion* he is memorialized as 'the best man that ever was in Maelor', a phrase that suggests a significant closeness between Madog and the abbey of Valle Crucis, where the Continuation was probably composed.[101] It can be argued that Madog was responsible for gathering information that helped the writer of the Continuation, who can be identified as the scribe of the Valle Crucis text of *Brenhinedd y Saesson*, that version of the Welsh chronicle which had attempted to integrate English and Welsh history.[102] Madog himself appears to have been a striking example of Anglo-Welsh integration.

A second memorial to Madog ap Llywelyn is the splendid stone effigy that marked his tomb at Gresford Church. His military effigy carved in stone shows Madog clad as a soldier, whose shield and surcoat bear the design of a lion rampant – the arms of Powys.[103] The effigy suggests a military role for Madog, which is only briefly hinted at in the surviving records of his career, and strongly suggests his regional eminence. It was not, however, a unique eminence. The significant number of military and other effigies of Welsh magnates surviving from the late thirteenth century and the first generation of the fourteenth suggests that such figures constituted a distinct and relatively numerous stratum of society whose members presented themselves in terms of social leadership comprehensible throughout much of western Europe. Signs of the assimilation of Arthurian and 'chivalric' literature into Welsh storytelling (*Y Tair Rhamant*, *Breuddwyd Rhonabwy*), translations from French into Welsh, such as

Ystoria Bown o Hamtwn, and of more workaday texts such as Walter of Henley's *Husbandry*, tend to underscore this development.[104]

Not surprisingly, members of the families of men whom we have noted as significant figures in the opposition to Llywelyn ap Gruffudd made successful careers in royal and marcher administration in the post-conquest era. Perhaps the most prominent of those who had opposed Llywelyn was Hywel ap Meurig. Hywel has already been noticed, as a prominent supporter of the interests of the Crown and of the Mortimer and de Bohun lords.[105] He had died before the death of Llywelyn ap Gruffudd, but in the post-conquest period his sons Philip and Rhys continued the family's prominence. Master Rhys ap Hywel acted as a royal commissioner in Wales under Edward I, before becoming an official of Prince Edward by 1305.[106] In late October 1315, with his brother Philip, he was associated with Master John Walwayn, a de Bohun associate, in a mission to the principality, to organize defence against a Scottish invasion from Ireland, and to discuss certain secret business that the king had entrusted to them.[107] He was prominent in organizing the defence of south Wales in 1315–16, and recruited 2,500 men in the same region for service in Scotland.[108] He had been in the service of Humphrey de Bohun, earl of Hereford, since the early years of the century, and after 1316 he moved into the service of the great marcher lord Roger Mortimer of Wigmore.

Royal, and subsequently marcher, service had brought Rhys many rewards. He had obtained the Shropshire manor of Pontesbury, and the marcher manors of Talgarth and Bronllys, also acquiring several lucrative wardships.[109] He was involved on the baronial side in the fighting in south-east Wales in 1320–1. In 1320 he had been conspicuous in preventing the seizure of Gower into the hands of the king. And in 1321 he was reported to be active against Hugh Despenser in the latter's lordship of Glamorgan, and Despenser was informed that he was 'making fresh alliances and was leading a great rout of people with him'. As a result his lands of Bronllys and Cantref Selyf were seized by royal order.[110] He was imprisoned in Dover Castle in 1322, but was released when Roger Mortimer and Queen Isabella seized power from Edward II in 1326. He took a prominent part in the hunt for the fugitive Edward in November of that year, and was confirmed in possession of estates in Blaenllyfni, Brecon, Usk and Gower, as well as being granted lucrative ecclesiastical offices.[111] He was briefly custodian of the de Bohun lordship and castle of Builth, before serving in 1326–7 as justiciar of south Wales, in which capacity he investigated alleged abuses by royal officials in the southern principality; he also served as justice in the bishopric of Llandaf and acted as the surveyor of royal castles in the south.[112] He seems to have died in 1328.

Rhys's brother Philip ap Hywel was similarly prominent in both royal and marcher service: he appears as Edmund Mortimer's steward in the later thirteenth century, and was also steward of the de Bohun lordship of Brecon.[113] He was closely involved in the issue of charters for both the Mortimer lordship of Maelienydd and the de Bohun lordship of Brecon in 1297, confirming liberties of the Welsh communities there.[114] And in the same year he was commissioned to organize troops raised for royal service in the lordship of Talgarth.[115] In 1301 he appears as the keeper of the Crown lordship and castle of Builth, and sometimes acted as a royal commissioner, raising troops with his brother Rhys, as in 1301, and again in 1310.[116] With his brother Rhys he acted as commissioner to take into the king's hands Humphrey de Bohun's lands and castles in Wales and Herefordshire, in the course of the surrender by, and re-grant to, de Bohun when he married the king's daughter Elizabeth.[117]

Philip appears as keeper of Builth in 1309, in which post he was succeeded in 1310 by Roger Mortimer of Wigmore, but he resumed custody later in the same year, and retained the lordship and castle in his hands until he handed over to John Charlton, lord of Powys, in 1314.[118] The status of the lords associated with the custody of Builth in this period is a good indication of Philip's eminence. The year 1315 saw him commissioned, with William Butler of Wem, to enquire into complaints by the burgesses of Montgomery against market activity at Chirbury. Far more serious was his role in organizing the defence of Wales against an invasion from Ireland in 1315, already noted,[119] while in the following year he was deputed to settle disputes between the garrison and bailiffs of Builth and the men of that land.[120] Philip was evidently a close and trusted confidant of Roger Mortimer of Wigmore during this period, being involved in the arrangements for the descent of Roger's lands.[121] Philip's involvement in the baronial politics of the early 1320s is shown by his pardon, on the testimony of Humphrey de Bohun, earl of Hereford, in 1321.[122] It is made even clearer by his brief imprisonment in 1322 when it was alleged that he had adhered to Humphrey de Bohun and had 'worn his robes for a long time'.[123]

Of lesser, but still considerable importance in royal administration was Ieuan ap Moelwyn, a son of one of the men of the Middle March who can be identified as opposing the rule of Llywelyn ap Gruffudd in that region. Like his father, he can be associated with the lordship of Builth, where he was steward in 1292.[124] By 1303 he had been appointed as steward of Cardiganshire, at an annual fee of £5 and the constableships of Perfedd, Mabwynion, Creuddyn and Caerwedros. In 1304–5 he was given a £10 bonus,

> because it has been found, from the return of the issues of his bailiwick, that a large sum of money has accrued to my Lord during the said two years [when Ieuan had held the office] over and above what used to be returned in the time of other seneschals, and because, beside this, it has been sufficiently testified that the said Ieuan has not unduly burdened the Welshry during that period …[125]

Those last words are an eloquent testimony to the desire of the royal authorities to conciliate Welsh communities.

Another figure from the March who was of great eminence, and much greater mystery, was Sir Morgan ap Maredudd. Morgan's career was one of the most complex and bewildering of all those who rose high in the service of the Crown in the post-conquest period. A member of the old ruling house of Gwynllwg, he was disinherited of his lands in Machen, Llebenydd and Edlogan by Gilbert de Clare, earl of Gloucester, and was dispossessed of the commote of Hirfryn in Cantref Bychan by Llywelyn ap Gruffudd shortly after the death of his father, Maredudd ap Gruffudd, in 1270.[126] After apparently fruitless attempts to win back his lands by legal process Morgan ap Maredudd appears in the entourage of Dafydd ap Gruffudd in the final stages of his war against Edward I in 1283.[127] Astonishingly, Morgan seems not to have suffered as a result of his adherence to Dafydd. There is no record that he was even imprisoned, as were so many of those who had defied Edward I in that war. Instead, he appears in October 1294 as the leader of rebel forces in Glamorgan against Earl Gilbert of Gloucester. After considerable initial success, which saw the insurgents in control of much of Glamorgan, Morgan surrendered to the king by early June 1295, claiming that his rising was simply a movement against the earl

of Gloucester.[128] This explanation of his motives seems to have satisfied Edward, who proceeded to take the lordship of Glamorgan into
his own hands. Once again, Morgan had displayed an astonishing
capacity for survival.

Even more remarkable is the fact that he was deeply implicated in the treasonous designs of Thomas Turberville later in 1295.
Turberville had served Edward I in the Welsh wars of 1277 and 1282,
had accompanied the king to Gascony in 1286, but had been captured
in early April 1295 by the French in a royal expedition to that prov-
ince. It seems that Turberville was released after he had agreed to
return to England and to instigate risings against Edward I.[129] The key
proof of Turberville's treachery was a letter that he addressed to the
provost of Paris and in which he claimed, inter alia, that he had been
assured by Morgan that if the Scots rose against the king of England,
the Welsh would do likewise. Turberville also wrote that he had not
dared to hand over to Morgan 'the thing that you know about'. There
is very strong evidence that this 'thing' was a letter from the king of
France to Morgan, instructing him to rise, with the Welsh, against
the king of England.[130] Now, Turberville was convicted of treason,
and condemned to be drawn, hanged and to be left hanging as long
as anything remained of him.[131] But there is no record of any trial or
punishment of Morgan ap Maredudd. It must be accepted as a possibility that Morgan, not for the first time, had played a double game,
apparently acting as an opponent of Edward I, while also combining
the roles of agent provocateur and informer.

By 1297 Morgan ap Maredudd was engaged in another enterprise
that involved an element of duplicity. He had undertaken, on behalf
of the king, a mission involving the lordship of Brecon. It is almost
certainly this assignment which is the subject of a record that Morgan
was sent to Wales, between mid-July and 20 August 1297, 'on certain
secret business of the king, by the special order of the king himself'.[132]
But he reported to Edward that before his arrival the lord of Brecon,
Humphrey de Bohun, had ordered that his castles in the lordship
should be well stocked, and that the men of the lordship should know
that he stood against the king. In addition, he had made arrangements,
through his steward – who, interestingly, was Philip ap Hywel – to
confirm all of the ancient liberties of the men of Brecon. At this point
Morgan had arrived in the adjacent territory of Morgannwg, and had

sent messengers into Brecon. The next day he had spoken to those men of Brecon whom he knew best, and had asked whether any of the men of Brecon would oppose the earl. But they said that they were all at one with their lord.[133] Again, Morgan appears to have been sent to undermine the position of Earl Humphrey in Brecon – though in this instance he seems to have been, at least in part, unsuccessful. Local loyalties, as so often in the March, had prevailed, particularly when exploited by a man of the standing of Philip ap Hywel.

From this point onwards, Morgan appears in record sources as a trusted royal official acting as a commissioner of array, recruiting troops for royal campaigns. He was knighted at the famous feast of the Swans in 1306.[134] At times Morgan appears at the very heart of the royal regime in Wales: thus he was one of three Welsh magnates – the others being Einion Sais, bishop of Bangor, and Sir Gruffudd Llwyd of north Wales, in highly confidential talks with Edward II at Clipstone, near Nottingham, between 30 November and 2 December 1315.[135] The first clear result of those talks was the order to respite certain demands made by royal officials on named key figures of north Wales, while more general and extensive concessions to the communities of the principality lands were made in early February 1316.[136] After his death without male heirs in 1331 Morgan was reported as holding significant lands in north Wales, in Llŷn, while in the south he held a third part of the town of St Clears and a third part of the commotes of Amgoed and Peuliniog in Carmarthenshire.[137] He had, it seems, done much to recover from his disinheritance by the earl of Gloucester – upon whom he had taken revenge – and Llywelyn ap Gruffudd. Morgan was surely amongst those who would have regarded the Edwardian regime with some warmth: it had, it seems, provided him with status – the extraordinarily prestigious position of being one of the Swan Knights – with reward and with excitement.

It seems that in the aftermath of the Edwardian conquest of *pura Wallia* and particularly in the generation after *c.*1300, the great majority of the local offices in the principality lands, and a significant number of more senior posts such as that of sheriff, were in the hands of Welsh officials. The same can be said of the local officers of the majority of marcher lordships. Royal administrators and marcher lords alike had learned the lesson adumbrated in 1244 by the vassals of the earl of Pembroke: 'It is not easy in our part of Wales to control Welshmen except by one of their own race.'[138] The continued eminence of Welsh *uchelwyr* after the Edwardian conquest, which has been indicated by the work of J. Beverley Smith and A. D. Carr, seems to have been reinforced by royal and marcher responses to the risings of 1294–5 and the numerous crises of the reign of Edward II.[139] The Welsh magnates who served both kings and marcher lords in the later thirteenth century and the first three decades of the fourteenth in effect constituted an aristocracy of service, which in many ways filled the gap in Welsh society created by the fall, extinction or decline of the old princely houses. A full study of the rise of that new aristocracy throughout Wales is still to be carried out, though recent work by A. D. Carr has done much to fill this gap in our understanding.

A similar continued prominence of Welsh personnel in the decades after 1284 is apparent in the ecclesiastical sphere, most evidently in the northern dioceses, where Welsh ecclesiastics continued to dominate the diocesan hierarchies. In Bangor, Einion, consecrated in 1267, remained in office until 1307; he was succeeded by Gruffudd ab Iorwerth, who held the post for two years, and was in turn followed by Master Einion Sais, who remained in office until his death in 1328, and whom we have noted as playing an important part in the defence of the principality against invasion in 1315. Einion's successor was Master Matthew of Englefield (i.e. Tegeingl), who was bishop until he died in 1357.[140] At St Asaph, the fiery Anian II remained in his office until 1293, continuing to confront Edward I as he had confronted Llywelyn, when he refused to excommunicate the rebellious Welsh forces, and absented himself from the diocese. He was prevented from returning to St Asaph by the king, until some degree of harmony was restored by the intervention of Archbishop Peckham, and even then Anian had to pay 500 marks to secure the king's goodwill. He also proved a determined litigant in a number of causes, especially involving the bishop of Hereford, against whom he fought an ultimately unsuccessful legal battle over the boundaries of the dioceses in the region of Gorddwr. Anian fully deserved the verdict of the chronicler who declared him 'the best man and the strongest in maintaining his diocese that anyone saw'.[141] His successor was Master Llywelyn ab Ynyr (Llywelyn of Bromfield), who remained as bishop until his death in 1314. Llywelyn was followed by Master Dafydd ap Bleddyn, bishop until 1345.[142]

The story was different in the southern dioceses, for at St David's and Llandaf the bishops appear to have been of English or marcher origin. Archdeacons in the northern dioceses, when they can be identified, were almost uniformly Welsh during the period under review.[143] Even in the diocese of St David's, there was a significant Welsh element amongst the holders of the archdeaconry of Brecon.[144] Where deans and canons can be identified, those of St Asaph and Bangor seem also to have been Welsh in the great majority of cases. The parochial clergy, again where they can be identified, were also overwhelmingly Welsh. Monastic personnel in the principality lands and in some parts of the March also remained in large part Welsh.[145]

AN AGE OF CONTRADICTIONS

The depiction of Wales in the decades after 1284 as a society in which English royal and marcher regimes, buttressed by a privileged English settler class, controlled an oppressed and resentful Welsh population is not without a very significant element of truth, but it is not the whole truth. Even some of the causes célèbres of the period, in which ethnic rifts seem to have been a dominant factor, were of much greater complexity than at first appears.

To take just one example, such complexity marks the situation in Glamorgan in the second and third decades of the century. When Llywelyn Bren, the head of the dynasty of the lords of Senghennydd, rose up in 1316, he was supported by many, but not all, of the Welsh of the Glamorgan uplands.[146] His rising is most satisfactorily interpreted in the context of the turbulence following the death of the last of the Clare lords of Glamorgan at Bannockburn in 1314. A rebellion broke out almost at once, closely coinciding with the appointment of the first of a number of royal custodians of the lordship. At least one of those custodians, Bartholomew de Badlesmere (in office from September 1314 to July 1315), exercised a mollifying influence, calming the situation in the aftermath of the 1314 rising. It was in this period that an effort was made to respond constructively to the ambitions and complaints of Llywelyn Bren and to grievances of the men of Glamorgan. But Badlesmere's successor, Payn de Turberville, was far less accommodating, antagonizing the community with demands for increased revenues, and dismissing Llywelyn Bren from offices that he had held.[147] It is clear that there was a strong element of personal hostility in Llywelyn's rising in early 1316. Some areas of significant English population escaped with little or no damage – as was the case with Cowbridge – while others occupied by both English and Welsh, particularly Llantrisant, were hard hit; but the Coety lands of Payn de Turberville seem to have been singled out for particularly rough treatment.[148]

When it became clear that his rising would not succeed, Llywelyn Bren gave himself up to Humphrey de Bohun and Roger Mortimer of Wigmore, who sent him to London, but who wrote to Edward II urgently praying that the king would make no harsh decision concerning Llywelyn and his estate until they had seen him, which they would do as soon as possible.[149] This was, in effect, a plea for clemency, and it was initially successful. But when Hugh Despenser became lord of Glamorgan in 1318 one of his first actions was to have Llywelyn Bren executed. This action provoked outrage, and that outrage was not confined to the Welsh community. The execution featured in the charges made against Despenser by the marchers in 1321, when even the Welsh magnates who had opposed Llywelyn united with his family and supporters in opposition to Despenser and the king.[150]

Upon Llywelyn's fall, his wife Lleucu was apparently held in London, and then, like her husband, moved to Cardiff. But she was released in the baronial assault on Despenser in 1321, and she and her sons joined the attack on her husband's murderer. After Despenser regained power, Lleucu fled to the lordship of Brecon, where she died in 1349, having been supported by the earls of Hereford.[151] Llywelyn's sons survived to wreak revenge on the king who had supported Despenser: they joined a select force led by Henry of Lancaster and Philip ap Hywel who hunted down the fugitive king.[152] After the fall of Edward II, Llywelyn's sons were granted lands that were part at least of their inheritance, and one of them, Gruffudd ap Llywelyn, went on to become constable of Senghennydd.[153] Once again, the politics of the March have to be interpreted in terms not of simple ethnic conflict, but of loyalties rooted in established lordship and of hatred of the person of Hugh Despenser. In other regions of Wales the dynamic was different, with animosity towards Roger Mortimer of Chirk a significant factor in the adherence of some Welsh magnates to Edward II.

In the years after the Edwardian 'settlement' in the 1280s and 1290s, therefore, life in Wales and the March was hardly tranquil, with revolt breaking out in the south-east, and a regional war flaring periodically in Powys.[154] The wars of Edward I and his son imposed burdens on Welsh society, both in terms of money and manpower. In addition it is clear that parts of Wales suffered seriously in the famine years of the second decade of the fourteenth century, while the struggles between the king and the baronial opposition in 1320–2 and the tumultuous years of the Mortimer supremacy in 1327–30 were significantly focused on Wales, and were damaging for many. And yet even wars offered opportunities for advancement and reward, while the very dangers facing regimes in Wales allowed Welsh magnates to take positions of great importance, to engage in missions that were often of a sensitive, not to say secret, nature, and to become prominent in the efforts of both Crown and marchers to reach out to, and secure the loyalty of, the diverse communities of Wales.

English chroniclers might proclaim that the Welsh were at last becoming anglicized, but theirs was far too simplistic a view. Men like those whose careers have been examined above, and the many more who prospered in the early decades of the fourteenth century and whose lives remain to be more fully explored, might see themselves as men of the court, or as the men of a Mortimer, or a de Bohun, but that did not mean that they had sacrificed their Welshness. They retained immense pride in their lineages, and they were the patrons of Welsh culture who were memorialized in poetry that often employed traditional motifs with which to praise them. Some of them were significant in a local or sub-regional context, like Dafydd ap Cadwaladr of Bacheldre (*fl.* 1322–38), a senior figure in the administration of the lordship of Caus and more generally in the Vale of Montgomery where his family had been prominent for generations. He was lauded by the poet Dafydd Bach ('Sypyn Cyfeiliog') for his descent from Elystan Glodrydd, the shadowy eleventh-century ruler of the lands between Wye and Severn, and for his possession of courts at which his generosity was displayed.[155] There were men of great eminence at a regional, and even national, level like Sir Rhys ap Gruffudd, whose services to the Crown were manifest, but who could still be praised by one poet as a man who brought death to the *Bryneich*, the 'Bernicians' – a centuries-old name for Northumbrians which was used in the poetry of the princes to refer to the English.[156] Such men as Dafydd ap Cadwaladr and Rhys ap Gruffudd enjoyed a dual eminence, of service to English kings and marcher lords on the one hand, and of a socio-political leadership which recalled the 'Age of the Princes' on the other. Meanwhile the spiritual welfare of the communities of the northern half of Wales, and in significant parts of the south, was largely in the hands of Welsh ecclesiastics, and the monastic communities of much of Wales were likewise largely Welsh in composition. In truth, the post-conquest decades offered to the people of Wales a kaleidoscopic blend of oppression, suffering, frustration, advancement, accumulation of honours and power.

ENVOI

This book ends with developments in the early 1330s. It is an unconventional point at which to close an analysis of Wales in the high Middle Ages. The deaths of Llywelyn ap Gruffudd in 1282 and his brother Dafydd in 1283 might seem a more logical and dramatic stopping point, or perhaps the risings of 1294–5. But the early 1330s also have elements of great, if generally unobserved, significance.

The year 1332 saw the close of the continuation of the classic chronicle of medieval Wales, *Brut y Tywysogion*, following the death in 1331 of Madog ap Llywelyn, the man who can be identified as the chronicler's chief informant. This alone marks an important break, for the chronicle record of the subsequent decades is very poor. Other Welsh chronicles had ended in the later thirteenth century – including the *Annales Cambriae* 'B' and 'C' texts, the Glamorgan chronicle found, like the 'B' text, in the Breviate of Domesday which has been convincingly argued to have a strong Neath connection, and the annals, probably of Cardiff origin, in British Library Royal MS 6 B xi. For a full generation the *Brut y Tywysogion* Continuation, almost certainly compiled at Valle Crucis Abbey or a nearby church, stood as the principal surviving chronicle text from Wales.[1] After it ends with the annal for 1332 the voices of Welsh chroniclers are almost silenced.

The early 1330s also saw the death of a number of figures who were highly influential members of that ministerial elite which comes clearly into view in the later twelfth and the thirteenth centuries. This corps of senior administrators, whose influence extended even into ecclesiastical governance, was of crucial significance in the Welsh polities and politics of both the Age of the Princes and the decades after the events of 1282–3.[2] They had served Welsh princes and lords for at least a century before those events, and they had been prominent in marcher politics and administration from the early thirteenth century onwards. They would continue to be a crucial element in both marcher and royal administration for decades after the Edwardian campaigns of conquest in Wales. Many of them had given significant support to the armies of Edward I. By the early 1330s many key members of that ministerial aristocracy were dying: men such as Sir Morgan ap Maredudd who died after an illustrious and mysterious career in 1331. That date seems to be the point at which another critically important figure effectively retired from political life: Sir Gruffudd Llwyd, a descendant of both Ednyfed Fychan, chief minister of both Llywelyn ab Iorwerth and Dafydd ap Llywelyn, and of the Lord Rhys, had been central to royal governance and policy in north Wales for more than a generation before his death in 1335. Another very prominent descendant of Ednyfed Fychan, Goronwy ap Tudur of Anglesey, died in 1331, and as we have seen, that year also saw the death of Madog ap Llywelyn of Bromfield, who had been prominent in the lordship of Bromfield and Yale.[3]

Another magnate who died in 1332, and this time a man outside the ranks of the ministerial elite, was Gruffudd Fychan de la Pole. This son of Gruffudd ap Gwenwynwyn laid claim to the whole lordship of Powys, against his niece Hawise and her husband John Charlton. Gruffudd was never able to secure the lordship, but held substantial parts of it, such as Deuddwr and Mechain, and attracted considerable support from other parts of the lordship and from the magnates of the northern March in the course of a twenty-year struggle.[4]

Men such as these were bound by a web of interconnections: Morgan ap Maredudd and Gruffudd de la Pole were both Swan Knights, knighted along with Edward of Caernarfon in 1306.[5] Morgan ap Maredudd and Sir Gruffudd Llwyd were both intimately involved in royal administration, and had held highly confidential talks with Edward II in 1315.[6] And their lineage often went back to the great figures of the Age of the Princes: through his mother, Angharad, Madog ap Llywelyn of Bromfield was descended from both Llywelyn ab Iorwerth, prince of Gwynedd and Madog ap Maredudd, king of the Powysians.[7] Sir Gruffudd Llwyd was descended from both Ednyfed Fychan, Llywelyn ab Iorwerth's chief minister, and Gruffudd ab Ednyfed, the *distain* of Llywelyn ap Gruffudd of Gwynedd. He was in addition descended from the Lord Rhys of Deheubarth.[8] The Lord Rhys was also the ancestor of Morgan ap Maredudd.[9] Gruffudd de la Pole's ancestry went back, through figures such as Gwenwynwyn and Owain Cyfeiliog of southern Powys, to Bleddyn ap Cynfyn, the renowned ruler of much of Wales in the eleventh century.[10]

Some members of the ministerial elite continued to be of great significance for years after the early 1330s – of whom Sir Rhys ap Gruffudd, cousin of Sir Gruffudd Llwyd and pillar of royal governance in southern Wales, is outstanding.[11] But after the fall of Edward in 1326–7, and the chaotic politics of the years of Mortimer ascendancy (1327–30), Wales ceased to enjoy the centrality in royal politics that it had in the previous generation, when Welsh affairs loomed large in the politics of the kingdom, and when the king was at times heavily reliant on support from the principality lands. The government of Edward III, and that of Richard II, would pay less regard to Wales, and would allow the development of the sort of frustrations and resentments that would encourage the hopes and ambitions of Owain Lawgoch, the exiled descendant of the ruling house of Gwynedd, and ultimately those of Owain Glyn Dŵr, a descendant of the royal house of Powys.[12]

In some senses the early 1330s brought to an end a period that had seen conscious efforts on the parts of both royal and marcher administrations to conciliate the leading figures in Welsh society and to base government upon those figures. Seen in this light, the thirteenth century and the early decades of the fourteenth century were a crucial period in the rise of that Welsh gentry class which would eventually play a major part in the Glyn Dŵr rising and would go on to recover from the trauma of that period and emerge as a central force in Welsh life in the fifteenth and subsequent centuries. In the context of the century and a half before the 1330s the emergence and development of an administrative elite represents a strong element of continuity in the political life of Wales, crossing and in many respects diminishing the significance of the apparent chasm of 1282–3.

The continued prominence of the ministerial elite through the thirteenth and early fourteenth centuries was but one of many continuities between the Age of the Princes and the years after the campaigns of Edward I. The Edwardian wars saw the restoration of an already established situation in the March – a situation marked by the ascendancy of marcher lords who had become increasingly ready to listen to, and to employ the services of, the leading Welsh magnates of their lordships.[13] This was a situation that had been challenged for a few years by Llywelyn ap Gruffudd, and that challenge had contributed in no small measure to his subsequent downfall. In the aftermath of the wars of 1277 and 1282–3 the March began to settle into something that can be regarded as the normality which had developed in the early and mid-thirteenth century. In partial contrast to the March, in *pura Wallia*, there developed forms of government that were more clearly dependent on the policies of English royal administration, though in many ways the rule of the princes had often been significantly dependent on the English Crown.[14]

The quarter-millennium with which this book deals had witnessed many political and socio-political transitions within Wales. These included the development of principalities involving rule over increasing swathes of *pura Wallia*. Even the March, that other great development of these centuries, had been targeted as a part of a future Welsh principality by some at least of the princes. The same period had been characterized by developments in ecclesiastical structure (diocesan formation and definition, parochialization, church rebuilding) and monastic establishment (particularly but not exclusively the spread of the Cistercians), and the appearance of the Mendicant Orders, which had brought almost all parts of Wales into line with other parts of Europe.[15]

In part, it has been suggested, stimulated by the ecclesiastical developments, the whole period also saw a growing complexity of the apparatus of rule – the development of a more monetarized economy, of urban centres under lordly and princely patronage, the rise of the administrative elite and growing complexity of forms of governance, as well as the steady increase in the power of rulers which resulted from the adoption of more developed forms of warfare – castles, cavalry and engines of war. All had tended towards a more powerful and in some respects centralized structure of native governance symbolized by Llywelyn's recognition as prince of Wales by Henry III in 1267. The whole process had somewhat paradoxical consequences. On the one hand the growth in princely power had also involved resentments and resistance, and in the end it was the opponents of princely ascendancy – in the March and in *pura Wallia*, amongst regional rulers and magnates, and amongst significant sections of the official class – who proved more successful than the princes themselves.[16] On the other hand the advances made under the princes paved the way for – and even facilitated – the imposition of royal rule over much of *pura Wallia* by Edward I. The whole process of development of governance, and the social changes that accompanied it, such as the emergence of the powerful and often privileged official class, all serve to emphasize continuity between political life before and after Edward I's wars of conquest. Those wars produced a new Welsh ascendancy – English king in place of Welsh prince – and they gave rise to a new wave of castle-building and urban foundation, with significant numbers of English brought in to some parts of Wales in order to provide a demographic basis for these developments. Some new forms of governance were introduced.[17] But personnel and practices derived from the Age of the Princes acted to balance the undoubted novelties of the period after 1283. Our thinking about how Wales developed in this period has thus to incorporate both the traditional tale of princely accomplishment, disaster at the hands of Edward I and subsequent colonial oppression, and a newer narrative of the contradictions inherent in achievement, widespread rejection of princely rule and significant accommodation to, and profit from, regime change. It was indeed an Age of Ambiguity.

NOTES

INTRODUCTION

1 The career of the Lord Rhys has been examined in two studies: Nerys Ann Jones and Huw Pryce (eds), *Yr Arglwydd Rhys* (Cardiff: University of Wales Press, 1996); Roger Turvey, *The Lord Rhys, Prince of Deheubarth* (Llandysul: Gomer Press, 1997); several of the major figures of the dynasty of Gwynedd have been the subjects of recent biographies, including Roger Turvey, *Llywelyn the Great* (Llandysul: Gomer Press, 2007), and the same author's *Owain Gwynedd: Prince of the Welsh* (Talybont: Y Lolfa, 2013). Much the most important and influential biographical study is J. Beverley Smith, *Llywelyn ap Gruffudd, Prince of Wales* (2nd edn; Cardiff: University of Wales Press, 2014). Powysian figures have recently begun to receive attention: see Sean Davies, *The First Prince of Wales? Bleddyn ap Cynfyn, 1063–75* (Cardiff: University of Wales Press, 2016), and n. 6 below.

2 Rees Davies was scrupulous in accepting that there were usually two (or more) sides to historical issues, a characteristic amply demonstrated in his *Age of Conquest*. J. Beverley Smith has shown a similar sensitivity to the complexities of Welsh politics in the twelfth and thirteenth centuries, while his groundbreaking paper on the politics of the post-conquest decades in the Crown lands is a model of nuanced analysis: see J. Beverley Smith, 'Edward II and the allegiance of Wales', *WHR*, 8 (1976), 139–71, and in particular his discussion (at 140) of the political importance of the more powerful members of the class of substantial freemen, who 'formed what was virtually a new aristocracy in Welsh society'. See further A. D. Carr, 'Lineage, power and land in medieval Flintshire: the descendants of Ithel Fychan', *Flintshire Historical Society Journal*, 36 (2003), 59–81, an important study of a Welsh magnate family in the fourteenth century. Carr makes the important point (at p. 81) that though the period between the Edwardian Conquest and the Glyn Dŵr rising 'is sometimes seen as a time when the Welsh were oppressed by alien officials' the careers of men of the class to which he draws attention 'reflect a world in which king, prince or marcher lord might propose but where local leaders certainly disposed'.

3 For the more general studies see *Aspects of Welsh History: Selected Papers of the Late Glyn Roberts* (Cardiff: University of Wales Press, 1969), nos IX ('Wales on the eve of the Norman Conquest'), X ('The significance of 1284') and XII ('Wales and England: antipathy and sympathy 1282–1485'). The first and second of these were given originally as radio talks, and appeared in A. J. Roderick (ed.), *Wales through the Ages* (Llandybïe: Christopher Davies, 1959), and the third was published in *WHR*, 1 (1963), 375–96.

4 *WHR*, 5 (1971), 308–10, at 310.

5 R. A. Griffiths, *The Principality of Wales in the Later Middle Ages: The Structure and Personnel of Government. I. South Wales, 1277–1536* (Cardiff: University of Wales Press, 1972); A. D. Carr, *The Gentry of North Wales in the Later Middle Ages* (Cardiff: University of Wales Press, 2017).

6 Stephenson, *Medieval Powys*; *idem*, 'Conquerors, courtiers and careerists: the struggle for supremacy in Brycheiniog, 1093–1282', *Brycheiniog*, 44 (2013), 27–51; *idem*, 'New light on a dark deed: the death of Llywelyn ap Gruffudd', *Archaeologia Cambrensis*, 166 (2017), 243–52. For the increasing output of scholars in the twenty-first century, particularly evident and distinguished in fields such as monastic studies and the role of women in Welsh polities, particularly at an elite level, see the select bibliography.

7 Lloyd, *A History*, p. 711.

8 Bartrum, *Welsh Genealogies*, 3, p. 496, Gwynfardd 1, has amongst Gwilym's ancestors in the eleventh century two poets, Gwynfardd Dyfed and his son Cuhelyn Fardd.

9 See below, ch. 3.

10 R. I. Jack, *Medieval Wales* (London: Hodder and Stoughton, 1972), p. 233.

11 J. Beverley Smith and Llinos Beverley Smith, 'Wales: politics, government and law', in S. H. Rigby (ed.), *A Companion to Britain in the Later Middle Ages* (Oxford: Blackwell Publishers, 2003), pp. 309–34, at p. 309.

12 A. D. Carr, *Medieval Wales* (London: Macmillan, 1995), p. 24.

13 Rachel Bromwich (ed.), *Trioedd Ynys Prydein* (3rd edn; Cardiff: University of Wales Press, 2006), pp. 254–5.

14 An excellent introduction to this topic is Euryn R. Roberts, 'Mental geographies and literary convention: the poets of the Welsh princes and the polities and provinces of medieval Wales', *Studia Celtica* (2012), 85–110.

15 Smith and Smith, 'Wales: politics, government and law', p. 311.

16 Smith and Smith, 'Wales: politics, government and law', p. 321.

CHAPTER 1: AN OUTLINE SURVEY
OF WELSH POLITICAL HISTORY

1 Glyn Roberts, 'Wales on the eve of the Norman conquest', in *idem*, *Aspects of Welsh History: Selected Papers of the Late Glyn Roberts* (Cardiff: University of Wales Press, 1969), pp. 275–80, at p. 275.

2 Gruffudd ap Llywelyn's career is discussed by Michael and Sean Davies, *The Last King of Wales: Gruffudd ap Llywelyn c. 1013–1063* (Stroud: The History Press, 2012), and by T. M. Charles-Edwards, *Wales and the Britons, 350–1064* (Oxford: Oxford University Press, 2013), pp. 561–9.

3 *ByT Pen. 20 Trans.*, p. 13. One of the stories about Gruffudd's brutality is recounted in Davies and Davies, *The Last King*, p. 29.

4 There is uncertainty regarding the circumstances, and the date, of Gruffudd's death. Davies and Davies, *The Last King*, pp. 105–20 review much of the evidence, placing his death in 1063; Charles-Edwards, *Wales and the Britons*, pp. 566–7 opts for 1064. Davies, *Age of Conquest*, p. 24 settled for 1063.

5 *ByT Pen. 20 Trans.*, pp. 15–16.

6 T. M. Charles-Edwards, *The Welsh Laws* (Cardiff: University of Wales Press, 1989), p. 82; Stephenson, *Medieval Powys*, pp. 212–13; Sean Davies, *The First Prince of Wales? Bleddyn ap Cynfyn, 1063–75* (Cardiff: University of Wales Press, 2016), pp. 41–7.

7 *ByT Pen. 20 Trans.*, pp. 16–17. For Trahaearn ap Caradog see K. L. Maund, 'Trahaearn ap Caradog: legitimate usurper?', *Welsh History Review*, 13 (1986–7), 468–76.

8 Stephenson, *Medieval Powys*, pp. 29–34.

9 Davies, *The First Prince of Wales?*, pp. 63–8, 76–7.

10 Davies, *Age of Conquest*, pp. 28–35.

11 *ByT Pen. 20 Trans.*, pp. 19–21 tends to play down the part played by Gruffudd ap Cynan in the chaotic warfare of the later 1090s; Gruffudd's twelfth-century biography, Paul Russell (ed.), *Vita Griffini filii Conani* (Cardiff: University of Wales Press, 2005), pp. 75–83, predictably places him closer to centre-stage.

12 Stephenson, *Medieval Powys*, pp. 29–38.

13 Davies, *Age of Conquest*, pp. 37–40.

14 *ByT Pen. 20 Trans.*, pp. 51–2, 60–1, 63–5.

15 Domesday Book, f. 183v (Ralph Mortimer) and f. 186v (Osbern fitz Richard), quoted by Max Lieberman, *The Medieval March of Wales: The Creation and Perception of a Frontier, 1066–1283* (Cambridge: Cambridge University Press, 2010), p. 5, n. 9.

16 Lieberman, *Medieval March*, p. 6. Lieberman's central thesis, that the March of Wales (Marchia Wallie) is to be distinguished from earlier references to a *marcha* or to territory which 'marched' with the land of the Welsh, and that it emerged only as a consequence of the failure of Henry II's onslaught on Wales in 1165, has been subjected to withering criticism by David Crouch (in a review in *EHR*, cxxvi, 519 (April 2011), 404–6), who dismisses the argument as founded on 'a bizarre nominalist assumption'. Some verdicts have been less severe: Daniel Power (in a review in *WHR*, 26, 3 (2013), 514–16, at 515) noted that 'it is plausible that the phrase [*Marchia Wallie*] increased in popularity as this sector of the Welsh border [i.e. the Shropshire–Powys region] stabilized under Henry II'. In this context one might refine the concept of stabilization: the Pipe Roll evidence perhaps suggests that the idea of a distinct border zone in a sensitive region had become more important in the English government's perception of Wales. But we perhaps need to distinguish between the English government's acknowledgement of a March, and the actual development of such a zone.

17 Lieberman, *Medieval March*, p. 7; J. Beverley Smith, 'The Kingdom of Morgannwg and the Norman conquest of Glamorgan', in T. B. Pugh (ed.), *Glamorgan County History, Vol. III: The Middle Ages* (Cardiff: Glamorgan County History Committee, 1971), pp. 1–44, at p. 37.

18 Summarized by Davies, *Age of Conquest*, pp. 285–7.

19 Stephenson, *Medieval Powys*, pp. 154, 174 and n. 86.

20 *WAR*, p. 265.

21 Modern works include K. L. Maund (ed.), *Gruffudd ap Cynan: A Collaborative Biography* (Woodbridge: Boydell Press, 1986); Russell (ed.), *Vita Griffini filii*

Conani; Roger Turvey, *Owain Gwynedd: Prince of the Welsh* (Talybont: Y Lolfa, 2013); Roger Turvey, *Llywelyn the Great* (Llandysul: Gomer Press, 2007); Smith, *Llywelyn ap Gruffudd*. The last of these is a magnificent study.

22 Nerys Ann Jones and Huw Pryce (eds), *Yr Arglwydd Rhys* (Cardiff: University of Wales Press, 1996); Roger Turvey, *The Lord Rhys, Prince of Deheubarth* (Llandysul: Gomer Press, 1997).

23 Stephenson, *Medieval Powys*.

24 *ByT Pen. 20 Trans.*, p. 16 (Bleddyn ap Cynfyn); for Cadwgan ap Bleddyn see n. 8 above.

25 *ByT Pen. 20 Trans.*, p. 19.

26 *AWR*, no. 192. Pryce's caution about accepting the validity of this document should be noted.

27 *ByT Pen. 20 Trans.*, pp. 51–2 (activity of Owain and Cadwaladr in Ceredigion, the deaths of Gruffudd ap Rhys 'the light and excellence and strength of all South Wales', and Madog ab Idnerth); for problems in Powys, Stephenson, *Medieval Powys*, pp. 40, 42.

28 The account of the failure of a joint move by Anglo-Norman forces, Cadwaladr ap Gruffudd and Cynan and Hywel, sons of Owain Gwynedd appears to be the last mention in the chronicles of Venedotian activity in Ceredigion in the middle decades of the twelfth century: *ByT Pen. 20 Trans.*, p. 62. See also J. Beverley Smith, 'Hywel ab Owain a gwleidyddiaeth Gwynedd', in Nerys Ann Jones (ed.), *Hywel ab Owain Gwynedd, Bardd-Dywysog* (Cardiff: University of Wales Press, 2009), pp. 61–87, at pp. 71–2.

29 Stephenson, *Medieval Powys*, pp. 48–50, 65–7; *ByT Pen. 20 Trans.*, pp. 64–5.

30 *AWR*, nos 195–6.

31 Discussed by Stephenson, 'Empires in Wales', 30.

32 *AWR*, nos 26, 28.

33 *ByT Pen. 20 Trans.*, p. 96.

34 For Rhys as 'justice in all Deheubarth', see *ByT Pen. 20 Trans.*, p. 68; for the statement that he 'was acclaimed king of Wales' (*de Gales fu reis clamé*) see Evelyn Mullally (ed.), *The Deeds of the Normans in Ireland* (Dublin: Four Courts Press, 2002), p. 62, l. 279. For the date of composition see Mullally (ed.), *The Deeds of the Normans in Ireland*, pp. 28–31.

35 Stephenson, *Medieval Powys*, p. 68.

36 *ByT Pen. 20 Trans.*, p. 72; Lloyd, *A History*, II, pp. 553, 565.

37 Stephenson, 'Empires in Wales', 31 and n. 26.

38 *ByT Pen. 20 Trans.*, pp. 70–1.

39 Stephenson, 'Empires in Wales', 46.

40 *ByT Pen. 20 Trans.*, pp. 64, 79.

41 Lewis Thorpe (trans.), *Gerald of Wales: The Journey through Wales/The Description of Wales* (Harmondsworth: Penguin Books, 1978), p. 75.

42 Stephenson, 'Empires in Wales', 31; Rhian M. Andrews, 'The nomenclature of kingship in Welsh court poetry, 1100–1300, part II: the rulers', *Studia Celtica*, 45 (2011), 53–82, at 57.

43 Stephenson, *Medieval Powys*, p. 82.

44 Stephenson, *Medieval Powys*, pp. 79, 81–2.

45 Stephenson, *Medieval Powys*, pp. 82–3; For Gwenwynwyn's grants to Strata Marcella see *AWR*, nos 541–5, 548–75, 578.

46 Stephenson, 'Empires in Wales', 38.

47 Davies, *Age of Conquest*, pp. 229–30; Stephenson, *Medieval Powys*, pp. 76–7.

48 Stephenson, *Medieval Powys*, p. 78.

49 Morfydd E. Owen (ed.), 'Gwaith Seisyll Bryffwrch', in *GLIF*, 23.16–18.

50 Stephenson, *Medieval Powys*, pp. 296–8; Turvey, *Llywelyn the Great*, p. 30.

51 *ByT Pen. 20 Trans.*, p. 82; Turvey, *Llywelyn the Great*, p. 47.

52 *ByT Pen. 20 Trans.*, pp. 86–91.

53 *ByT Pen. 20 Trans.*, p. 92.

54 *ByT Pen. 20 Trans.*, p. 95; *AWR*, no. 239.

55 Turvey, *Llywelyn the Great*, pp. 79–88.

56 *ByT Pen. 20 Trans.*, pp. 102–3.

57 *AWR*, pp. 75–6.

58 *AWR*, p. 76.

59 *AWR*, nos 17, 280.

60 David Stephenson, 'In search of a Welsh chronicler: the *Annales Cambriae* B-text for 1204–30', *CMCS*, 72 (2016), 73–85, at 81, n. 43.

61 Stephenson, 'Empires in Wales', 32.

62 Lloyd, *A History*, II, p. 687 and nn. 187–90.

63 Turvey, *Llywelyn the Great*, pp. 133–4. The swearing of an oath of fealty created a looser and lesser obligation than the performance of homage. Fealty in this context may have implied little more than an acceptance of Dafydd as Llywelyn's heir, though the precise terms of the oath are not certain. The performance of homage was a more serious matter, in that it involved a significant and public ceremony of submission to a lord (in this case Dafydd) and an agreement on the part of the subordinate lords to hold their lands from the superior lord (Dafydd) and to perform specific services, often military, to him in return for their lands.

64 *AWR*, no. 312, the Treaty of Woodstock.

65 *ByT Pen. 20 Trans.*, p. 110.

66 Smith, *Llywelyn ap Gruffudd*, pp. 90–138 charts the process in detail and with great clarity.

67 Smith, *Llywelyn ap Gruffudd*, p. 145 discusses the use of the title *princeps Wallie*.

68 The text of the treaty is in *AWR*, no. 363.

69 Stephenson, 'Empires in Wales', 33.

70 Smith, *Llywelyn ap Gruffudd*, p. 364 and n. 91 provides important discussion, modifying earlier estimates, but without full analysis of the penalties for non-payment, for which see David Stephenson, 'A treaty too far? The impact of the treaty of Montgomery on Llywelyn ap Gruffudd's principality', *Mont. Colls*, 106 (2018), 19–32.

71 *AWR*, nos 398–9.

72 Stewards and other officers are discussed by Smith, *Llywelyn ap Gruffudd*, pp. 303–4, 312–15; Stephenson, *Political Power*, pp. 11–25; Stephenson, *Medieval Powys*, 194–6.

73 Stephenson, *Political Power*, pp. 26–39.

74 Smith, *Llywelyn ap Gruffudd*, pp. 194–7; Stephenson, *Political Power*, pp. 40–52.

75 *CACW*, p. 92.

76 A good survey is provided by Richard Avent, *Cestyll Tywysogion Gwynedd/Castles of the Princes of Gwynedd* (Cardiff: HMSO, 1983). For Rhyd y Briw see J. D. C. King, 'Camlais and Sennybridge Castles', *Brycheiniog*, 21 (1984–5), 9–11, and for Bryn Amlwg see L. Alcock, J. D. C. King, W. C. Putnam and C. J. Spurgeon, 'Excavations at Castell Bryn Amlwg', *Montgomeryshire Collections*, 60 (1967–8), 8–27. For Dolforwyn see Lawrence Butler, 'Dolforwyn Castle: prospect and retrospect', in John R. Kenyon and Kieran O'Conor (eds), *The Medieval Castle in Ireland and Wales* (Dublin: Four Courts Press, 2003), pp. 149–62. See also for modern revisions Hugh Brodie, 'Apsidal and D-shaped towers of the princes of Gwynedd', *Archaeologia Cambrensis*, 164 (2015) 231–44; David Stephenson, 'A reconsideration of the siting, function and dating of Ewloe castle', *Archaeologia Cambrensis*, 164 (2015), 245–54.

77 David Stephenson, 'Powis Castle: a reappraisal of its medieval development', *Montgomeryshire Collections*, 95 (2007), 9–21; Chris Caple, *Excavations at Dryslwyn Castle 1980–1995* (Leeds: Society for Medieval Archaeology Monograph Series, 26, 2007).

78 See, for just a few examples, *Patent Rolls, 1216–25* (London: HMSO, 1901), p. 386; *Close Rolls, 1227–31* (London: HMSO, 1902), pp. 588, 594; *Close Rolls, 1231–34* (London: HMSO, 1905), pp. 14, 53, 66, 93; Lloyd, *A History*, II, p. 705.

79 *AWR*, no. 364.

80 *AWR*, no. 394.

81 E. Besly, 'Short-cross and other medieval coins from Llanfaes, Anglesey', *British Numismatic Journal*, 65 (1995), 46–82.

82 J. D. Brand, 'The short-cross coins of Rhuddlan', *British Numismatic Journal*, 34 (1965), 90–8. On the development of trading centres see J. Beverley Smith (ed.), *Medieval Welsh Society: Selected Essays by T. Jones Pierce* (Cardiff: University of Wales Press, 1972), especially pp. 149–50; for early developments at Nefyn see Stephenson, *Political Power*, p. 197, and David Stephenson, 'Nefyn, c. 1200: the plundering of King John's Irish hounds and hawks', *CMCS*, 75 (2018), 39–43.

83 Stephenson, *Medieval Powys*, pp. 199–200.

84 Stephenson, *Medieval Powys*, p. 163.

85 For an eloquent treatment of Gwenllian's fate see Smith, *Llywelyn ap Gruffudd*, pp. 580, 586.

86 A. D. Carr, '"The last and weakest of his line": Dafydd ap Gruffudd, the last prince of Wales', *WHR*, 19 (1998–9), 375–99.

87 For the men of the Middle March see Stephenson, 'Empires in Wales', 49–53, and Stephenson, 'New light on a dark deed', *passim*.

88 See, for examples, Richard W. Kaeuper, *Bankers to the Crown: the Riccardi of Lucca and Edward I* (Princeton: Princeton University Press, 1973).

89 Davies, *Age of Conquest*, pp. 363–5 provides a succinct survey.

90 Davies, *Age of Conquest*, pp. 370–3; see also ch. 5 below.

91 Stephenson, *Medieval Powys*, pp. 159–77.

92 For Llywelyn ab Owain's allegations to Edward I that Rhys ap Maredudd had deprived him of much of his patrimony see *AWR*, no. 83; J. Beverley Smith, 'The

origins of the revolt of Rhys ap Maredudd', *BBCS*, 21 (1965), 151–63 provides a thorough study.

93 Important studies of post-conquest administrative structures are provided by W. H. Waters, *The Edwardian Settlement of North Wales in its Administrative and Legal Aspects, 1284–1343* (Cardiff: University of Wales Press, 1935), the same author's posthumously published *The Edwardian Settlement of West Wales 1277–1343* (Abergele: Richard Gwyn Waters, 2000), and Ralph A. Griffiths, *The Principality of Wales in the Later Middle Ages: The Structure and Personnel of Government. I. South Wales, 1277–1536* (Cardiff: University of Wales Press, 1972).

94 Llinos Beverley Smith, 'The Statute of Wales, 1284', *WHR*, 10 (1980–1), 127–54.

95 See, for example, J. Beverley Smith, 'Dower in thirteenth-century Wales. A grant of the commote of Anhuniog, 1273', *BBCS*, 30 (1982–3), 248–55. An important recent study is Emma Cavell, 'Widows, native law and the long shadow of England in thirteenth-century Wales', *EHR* (forthcoming).

96 The extent of Merioneth is given in A. D. Carr, 'The first extent of Merioneth', in J. Beverley Smith and Llinos Beverley Smith (eds), *History of Merioneth Volume II: The Middle Ages* (Cardiff: University of Wales Press, 2001), pp. 703–16, and that of Anglesey in G. Rex Smith, 'The extent of Anglesey, 1284', *Transactions of the Anglesey Antiquarian Society* (2009), 70–118. For the extent of Bromfield and Yale of 1315 see T. P. Ellis (ed.), *The First Extent of Bromfield and Yale, A.D. 1315* (London: Cymmrodorion Record Series, 1924); for the survey of Dyffryn Clwyd see R. I. Jack (ed.), 'Records of Denbighshire: the lordship of Dyffryn Clwyd in 1324', *Transactions of the Denbighshire Historical Society*, 17 (1968), 7–53; for Chirkland see G. Rex Smith, 'The extent of the lordship of Chirk, 1332', *CMCS*, 63 (2012), 91–100, and for Denbigh see P. Vinogradoff and F. Morgan (eds), *Survey of the Honour of Denbigh, 1334* (London: British Academy, 1914). The extent of the episcopal lands of Bangor is in H. Ellis (ed.), *Registrum vulgariter nuncupatum: The Record of Caernarvon* (London: Record Commission, 1838), pp. 93–115 (the date of the extent established by Stephenson, *Political Power*, pp. 236–7), and that of St David's is in J. W. Willis-Bund (ed.), *The Black Book of St Davids, 1326* (London: Cymmrodorion Record Series, 1902).

97 See Diane Williams and John R. Kenyon (eds), *The Impact of the Edwardian Castles in Wales* (Oxford: Oxbow Books, 2010).

98 A useful introduction is provided by John R. Kenyon, *The Medieval Castles of Wales* (Cardiff: University of Wales Press, 2010).

99 See n. 92 above, and Ralph A. Griffiths, 'The revolt of Rhys ap Maredudd, 1287–8', *WHR*, 3 (1966) 121–43, reprinted in his *Conquerors and Conquered in Medieval Wales* (Stroud: Alan Sutton Publishing, 1994), pp. 67–83.

100 Many of the risings are discussed by Craig Owen Jones, *The Revolt of Madog ap Llywelyn* (Pwllheli: Llygad Gwalch, 2008); Meurig ap Dafydd's background and the rising in Gwent are discussed by David Stephenson, 'The continuation of *Brut y Tywysogyon* in NLW Peniarth MS 20 re-visited', in Ben Guy, Owain Wyn Jones and Georgia Henley (eds), *The Chronicles of Medieval Wales and the March: New Contexts, Studies and Texts* (Turnhout: Brepols, forthcoming).

101 Stephenson, *Political Power*, p. 144 and n. 40.

102 See below, ch. 5.

[103] The revolt is discussed by Craig Owen Jones, *Llywelyn Bren* (Llanrwst: Gwasg Carreg Gwalch, 2006); Ralph A. Griffiths, 'The revolt of Llywelyn Bren, 1316', *Glamorgan Historian*, II (1965), 186–96, reprinted in *Conquerors and Conquered in Medieval Wales*, pp. 84–91, and by J. Beverley Smith, 'The rebellion of Llywelyn Bren', in T. B. Pugh (ed.), *Glamorgan County History, Vol. III: The Middle Ages* (Cardiff: Glamorgan County History Committee, 1971).

[104] See below, ch. 5.

[105] David Stephenson, 'Crisis and continuity in a fourteenth-century Welsh lordship: the struggle for Powys, 1312–32', *CMCS* 66 (2013), 57–78.

[106] See below, ch. 5.

[107] R. R. Davies, 'Colonial Wales', *Past and Present*, 65 (1974), 3–23; David Walker, 'Under the heel: Wales in the fourteenth century', *Medieval Wales* (Cambridge: Cambridge University Press, 1990).

[108] William Chester Jordan, *The Great Famine* (Princeton: Princeton University Press, 1996), pp. 84–5.

[109] J. Beverley Smith, 'Gruffydd Llwyd and the Celtic alliance', *BBCS*, 26 (1974–6), 463–78.

[110] J. Beverley Smith, 'Edward II and the allegiance of Wales', *WHR*, 8 (1976–7), 139–71: this is a quite outstanding study.

CHAPTER 2: THE AGE OF THE PRINCES

[1] See ch. 2 above; for Hywel ab Ieuaf as *rex*, see *AWR*, nos 1–2.

[2] *AWR*, nos 548–9, 551, 565.

[3] For Dafydd ab Owain as *rex*: *AWR*, nos 198–9; as *princeps*: nos 200, 202.

[4] *ByT Pen. 20 Trans.*, p. 63.

[5] Thus *ByT Pen. 20 Trans.*, p. 86 refers to Llywelyn ab Iorwerth, prince of Gwynedd, as making 'a solemn pact with the princes of Wales, namely Gwenwynwyn, Maelgwn ap Rhys' and at p. 87 notes that the pope absolved three princes, namely Llywelyn ab Iorwerth and Gwenwynwyn and Maelgwn ap Rhys from their allegiance to King John.

[6] *ymaruolles holl gymry ygyt ac y rodassant lw ar gadw kywirdeb aduhundeb ygyt.* See *ByT, RBH*, pp. 250–1; *ByT Pen. 20 Trans.*, p. 111; Thomas Jones (ed.), *Brut y Tywysogyon, Peniarth MS. 20* (Cardiff: University of Wales Press, 1941), p. 211.

[7] *AWR*, nos 316 (1250: *amicitia*), 323 (1257: *confederatio, unio, unitas*), 347 (1261: *unitas*). There is discussion by David Stephenson, 'Llywelyn ap Gruffydd and the struggle for the principality of Wales, 1258–1282', *THSC* (1983), 36–47, at 38–40. For important analysis see David Carpenter, 'Confederation not domination: Welsh political culture in the age of Gwynedd imperialism', in R. A. Griffiths and P. R. Schofield (eds), *Wales and the Welsh in the Middle Ages* (Cardiff: University of Wales Press, 2011), pp. 20–8.

[8] There is important discussion of the poets' descriptions of regions and the *cylch Cymru* (the circuit of Wales) by Euryn R. Roberts, 'Mental geographies and literary convention: the poets of the Welsh princes and the polities and provinces of medieval Wales', *Studia Celtica* (2012), 85–110.

[9] *AWR*, nos 193, 196, 235 (Owain Gwynedd and then Llywelyn ab Iorwerth with the

French kings), 328 (Llywelyn ap Gruffudd and other Welsh rulers with Walter Comyn, earl of Menteith and other Scottish lords); for Madog ap Maredudd's relations with Ranulf II of Chester in the 1140s and 1150s and for Gwenwynwyn's relations with Ranulf III of Chester see Stephenson, *Medieval Powys*, pp. 40–1, 87, and for Llywelyn ab Iorwerth and Ranulf III see *AWR*, no. 252.

10 *AWR*, nos 202–3 (Emma of Anjou), 276–281 (Joan), 432–6 (Eleanor de Montfort). For marriages into the families of marcher lords see ch. 3 below.

11 *AWR*, nos 253, 306, 390.

12 T. M. Charles-Edwards, *Wales and the Britons, 350–1064* (Oxford: Oxford University Press, 2013), p. 565: 'The relationship which brought Gruffudd ap Llywelyn to the peak of his power was with Aelfgar.'

13 *AWR*, pp. 87–9. The fact that the princes' seals were in the main single-sided brings them more into line with wider knightly practice than with that of the leading European rulers. Dafydd ap Llywelyn's two-sided seal was equestrian on one side, and on the other showed an enthroned ruler. In addition it seems that the Lord Rhys possessed a double-sided seal; see Nicholas Vincent, 'The seals of King Henry II and his court', in Phillipp R. Schofield (ed.), *Seals and their Context in the Middle Ages* (Oxford: Oxbow, 2015), pp. 7–33, at pp. 23–4.

14 Susan Reynolds, *Kingdoms and Communities in Western Europe, 900–1300* (Oxford: Oxford University Press, 1984), p. 260.

15 *The Latin Texts of the Welsh Laws*, ed. H. D. Emanuel (Cardiff: University of Wales Press, 1970), p. 193 (Latin B).

16 *AWR*, no. 235.

17 *AWR*, p. 74 makes the point that the 'switch from *rex* to *princeps* was almost certainly regarded as articulating an elevation in power'. There are a few signs that by the early thirteenth century *princeps* was already beginning to suffer some devaluation: the adoption of the title 'prince of Meirionnydd' (*AWR*, no. 210 and the note) implied no more than a local ascendancy.

18 *ByT, RBH*, pp. 30–1 (with editorial amendments).

19 *ByT Pen. 20 Trans.*, pp 18–21, 28–31, 35–6, 46.

20 *ByT Pen. 20 Trans.*, p. 45.

21 *ByT Pen. 20 Trans.*, p. 24.

22 David Stephenson, 'Mawl Hywel ap Goronwy: dating and significance', *CMCS*, 59 (2009), 41–9.

23 *ByT Pen. 20 Trans.*, p. 46.

24 Stephenson, *Medieval Powys*, p. 1.

25 For the expansionist urges of Gruffudd's sons see *ByT Pen. 20 Trans.*, pp. 49, 51–2; for Madog ap Maredudd's entry into the land of the Iorweirthion see Stephenson, *Medieval Powys*, pp. 43–4.

26 *ByT Pen. 20 Trans.*, p. 64.

27 See the summary by T. M. Charles-Edwards, *The Welsh Laws* (Cardiff: University of Wales Press, 1989). pp. 40–3.

28 *AWR*, no. 431.

29 The process is well described by Davies, *Age of Conquest*, pp. 182–3. For the date of the creation of the defined diocese of St Asaph see M. J. Pearson, 'The creation and development of the St Asaph cathedral chapter, 1141–1293', *CMCS*, 40

(2000), 35–56; and for the senior personnel of the four dioceses M. J. Pearson, *Fasti Ecclesiae Anglicanae, 1066–1300, Volume 9: The Welsh Cathedrals* (London: Institute of Historical Research, 2003).

30 J. R. Davies, *The Book of Llandaf and the Norman Church in Wales* (Woodbridge: Boydell Press, 2003), especially pp. 46–7. For the confrontation over Ceri in 1176 see H. E. Butler (ed. and trans.), *The Autobiography of Gerald of Wales* (new edn; Woodbridge: Boydell Press, 2005), pp. 46–56; comment in Stephenson, 'Empires in Wales', 46–7.

31 Michael Richter, *Giraldus Cambrensis: The Growth of the Welsh Nation* (Aberystwyth: National Library of Wales, 1972), deals with the efforts of both Bernard and Gerald. Bernard's promotion of the claims of St David's to metropolitan status may represent an early example of opportunistic acculturation.

32 *AWR*, nos 192, 220. Both letters are of suspect authenticity, though they may be based on authentic materials.

33 Roger Turvey, *The Lord Rhys, Prince of Deheubarth* (Llandysul: Gomer Press, 1997), pp. 109–10.

34 Davies, *Age of Conquest*, pp. 185–8.

35 See n. 29 above, and Stephenson, *Medieval Powys*, pp. 40–1.

36 See Frank and Caroline Thorn (eds), *Domesday Book, Shropshire* (Chichester: Phillimore, 1986), note to 4,1,15, quoting Domesday Book 269b.

37 Stephenson, *Medieval Powys*, p. 253.

38 Stephenson, *Medieval Powys*, p. 40.

39 Stephenson, *Medieval Powys*, pp. 51, 54–6.

40 G. C. G. Thomas (ed.), *The Charters of the Abbey of Ystrad Marchell* (Aberystwyth: National Library of Wales, 1997), no. 63.

41 *ByT Pen. 20 Trans.*, p. 101; Stephenson, *Medieval Powys*, pp. 259–60.

42 Pearson, *Fasti*, pp. 5–7, 53–9.

43 See David Stephenson, 'The rulers of Gwynedd and Powys', and Andrew Abram, 'Monastic burial in medieval Wales', in Janet Burton and Karen Stöber (eds), *Monastic Wales: New Approaches* (Cardiff: University of Wales Press, 2013), pp. 89–102 and 103–15.

44 The complexities of the establishment of Pendâr have been clarified by Paul Watkins, 'The problem of Pendar: a lost abbey in medieval Senghennydd and the transformation of the Church in South Wales' (unpublished MPhil thesis, University of Wales Trinity St David, 2015).

45 Originally founded by Bishop Bernard of St David's at Little Trefgarn near Haverfordwest, the house was re-founded under Anglo-Norman patronage at Whitland in the middle of the twelfth century; it then fell under the patronage of the Lord Rhys, as he extended his lands. See Janet Burton and Karen Stöber, *Abbeys and Priories of Medieval Wales* (Cardiff: University of Wales Press, 2015), pp. 218–21.

46 Paul Russell (ed.), *Vita Griffini filii Conani* (Cardiff: University of Wales Press, 2005), p. 87.

47 Malcolm Thurlby, *Romanesque Architecture and Sculpture in Wales* (Almeley: Logaston Press, 2006) provides an excellent survey.

48 For an early example, built by 1115, see *ByT Pen. 20 Trans.*, p. 45.

49 See, for example, Stephenson, *Medieval Powys*, pp. 232–3.

50 The importance of the castle as an 'anchor' to territorial control is perhaps demonstrated by the way in which castles defined the rule of even lords in straitened circumstances: Dafydd ab Owain Gwynedd, though his power was broken by his kinsmen, in 1194, was left holding three castles; Elise ap Madog, though humbled by Llywelyn ab Iorwerth in 1202 was granted seven townships and the castle of Crogen: *ByT Pen. 20 Trans.*, pp. 75, 82.

51 See the case of Llys Rhosyr, in south-western Anglesey: Neil Johnstone, 'The location of the royal courts of thirteenth-century Gwynedd', in Nancy Edwards (ed.), *Landscape and Settlement in Medieval Wales* (Oxford: Oxbow Books, 1997), pp. 55–69, at pp. 65–7.

52 Smith, *Llywelyn ap Gruffudd*, pp. 17–20, 221, 336, 285–6, 295.

53 Stephenson, *Medieval Powys*, pp. 237–8.

54 *AWR*, nos 99, 248.

55 For just a few examples see *ByT Pen. 20 Trans.*, pp. 12 (1022), 13 (1042), 14 (1049), 16 (1073, 1074), 17 (1080), 18 (1091), 19 (1094).

56 *ByT Pen. 20 Trans.*, p. 14.

57 Russell (ed.), *Vita Griffini filii Conani*, p. 71 (§18.18–19).

58 *ByT Pen. 20 Trans.*, p. 26.

59 *ByT Pen. 20 Trans.*, p. 13.

60 *ByT Pen. 20 Trans.*, pp. 28–9. For a discussion of the abduction of Nest and the subsequent historiography see Susan M. Johns, *Gender, Nation and Conquest in the High Middle Ages: Nest of Deheubarth* (Manchester: Manchester University Press, 2013).

61 *ByT Pen. 20 Trans.*, p. 30.

62 *ByT Pen. 20 Trans.*, p. 40.

63 *ByT Pen. 20 Trans.*, p. 49.

64 For rules for the sharing out of booty, see *LTMW*, pp. 10, 14, 17–20, 29, 35.

65 *ByT Pen. 20 Trans.*, pp. 15, 17; the notice of Llywelyn ap Seisyll of Gwynedd under 1022, at p. 12, with its celebration of the peace and prosperity which he brought to his lands, seems to me likely to be retrospective. See Stephenson, *Medieval Powys*, pp. 27–8.

66 *ByT Pen. 20 Trans.*, p. 68.

67 J. Beverley Smith, 'The kingdom of Morgannwg and the Norman conquest of Glamorgan', in T. B. Pugh (ed.), *Glamorgan County History, Vol. III: The Middle Ages* (Cardiff: Glamorgan County History Committee, 1971), p. 34.

68 *ByT Pen. 20 Trans.*, p. 82.

69 *ByT Pen. 20 Trans.*, p. 98.

70 *ByT Pen. 20 Trans.*, p. 107.

71 *AWR*, no. 316.

72 *ByT Pen. 20 Trans.*, p. 76.

73 *ByT Pen. 20 Trans.*, p. 84.

74 *ByT Pen. 20 Trans.*, p. 88.

75 *ByT Pen. 20 Trans.*, p. 112.

76 *ByT Pen. 20 Trans.*, pp. 80 (one reference), 81 (two references), 82 (nine references), 83 (eight references), 84 (four references).

77 *ByT Pen. 20 Trans.*, p. 81.

78 *ByT Pen. 20 Trans.*, p. 83.

79 *ByT Pen. 20 Trans.*, p. 92.

80 *ByT Pen. 20 Trans.*, p. 95.

81 *AWR*, no. 358.

82 *ByT Pen. 20 Trans.*, p. 117.

83 There is an illuminating and succinct discussion of the development of *gwelyau* in T. M. Charles-Edwards, *Early Irish and Welsh Kinship* (Oxford: Oxford University Press, 1993), pp. 226–8, and 252–3.

84 Stephenson, *Medieval Powys*, pp. 196–8 for dating and discussion of *Breintiau Gwŷr Powys*; T. M. Charles-Edwards and Nerys Ann Jones, 'Breintiau Gwŷr Powys: the liberties of the men of Powys', in *WKC*, 191–223; see also the tract *Breintiau Arfon*, of probable thirteenth-century origin, discussed by Morfydd E. Owen, 'Royal propaganda: stories from the law-texts', in *WKC*, 224–54, at 240–5.

85 *ByT Pen. 20 Trans.*, p. 95.

86 *ByT Pen. 20 Trans.*, p. 82.

87 *ByT Pen. 20 Trans.*, p. 92.

88 Stephenson, *Medieval Powys*, pp. 98, 105–6.

89 *ByT Pen. 20 Trans.*, p. 99.

90 *ByT, RHB*, pp. 246–9.

91 See *ByT Pen. 20 Trans.*, p. 50.

92 *ByT Pen. 20 Trans.*, pp. 58, 70, 75 and note to 75.14 at p. 189.

93 *ByT Pen. 20 Trans.*, pp. 103, 105.

94 *ByT Pen. 20 Trans.*, p. 110 for Owain's imprisonment; *AWR*, no. 402 for orders for his release in 1277.

95 *AC*, p. 97; for Maredudd's release and (temporary) reconciliation with Llywelyn, see *AWR*, no. 347.

96 For discussion see Stephenson, *Medieval Powys*, pp. 144–51.

97 See W. L. Warren, *King John* (New Haven: Yale University Press, 1997), pp. 81–3.

98 *CACW*, p. 66; for discussion of the campaign of Anian II of St Asaph against Llywelyn see Stephenson, *Political Power*, pp. 174–81.

99 Peter Lord, *The Visual Culture of Wales: Medieval Vision* (Cardiff: University of Wales Press, 2003), pp. 98, 130–2, 138–9.

100 *Littere Wallie*, p. 137. For context see Emma Cavell, 'Intelligence and intrigue in the March of Wales: noblewomen and the fall of Llywelyn ap Gruffudd, 1274–82', *Historical Research*, 88 (2015), 1–19. See also Robin Chapman Stacey, 'King, queen and *edling* in the laws of court', *WKC*, pp. 53–62.

101 *Littere Wallie*, p. 172.

102 Stephenson, *Political Power*, pp. 11–39; *WKC*, passim. Smith, *Llywelyn ap Gruffudd*, pp. 113–14, 204–5, 303–4, 312–15.

103 Ednyfed Fychan, *distain* to Llywelyn ab Iorwerth and Dafydd ap Llywelyn, married a daughter of the Lord Rhys; Rhys ap Gruffudd ab Ednyfed Fychan married a Lestrange.

104 Leading officials from Gwynedd and Powys are the subjects of the following poems: Ednyfed Fychan (first half of the thirteenth century), *GMB*, poem 18; Gruffudd ab Ednyfed (middle of the thirteenth century), *GDB*, poem 33; Gwên

ap Goronwy (middle of the thirteenth century) *GBF*, poem 18; Goronwy ab Ednyfed (d.1268) *GBF*, poems 21, 45; almost certainly from the official elite were Hywel ap Goronwy and Gruffudd ab Iorwerth, both second half of the thirteenth century, *GBF*, poems 47, 56.

[105] For the poets see Rhian M. Andrews, *Welsh Court Poems* (Cardiff: University of Wales Press, 2007), p. xxviii: 'the poets were at the very centre of government'. For the lawyers see T. M. Charles-Edwards, M. E. Owen and D. B. Walters (eds), *Lawyers and Laymen* (Cardiff: University of Wales Press, 1986); for physicians, see David Stephenson, 'The early physicians of Myddfai in Context' and 'The local physicians of medieval Wales', in Robin Barlow (ed.), *Transactions of the Physicians of Myddfai Society 2011–17* (2018), 61–8, 150–7. The possession of armoured cavalry and of siege engines implies the existence of specialists to maintain such equipment and to use it. See Sean Davies, *Welsh Military Institutions 633–1283* (Cardiff: University of Wales Press, 2004), pp. 210–12.

[106] *ByT Pen. 20 Trans.*, pp. 71, 104, and see n. 95 above. See also ch. 4 below for the Welsh rulers whom the Lord Rhys took to a meeting with Henry II at Gloucester in 1175; this seems to presuppose a gathering at Rhys's court.

[107] *AWR*, no. 328.

[108] *AWR*, nos 603–4.

[109] The insistence of Peryf ap Cedifor that the death of Hywel ab Owain Gwynedd and his foster-brothers was the result of treachery on the part of Cristin and her sons seems to point to this: *GLlF*, 19.18.

[110] Stephenson, *Medieval Powys*, p. 108 and n. 60.

[111] *AWR*, no. 284.

[112] Two papers by Emma Cavell on developments in Powys are particularly relevant: 'Welsh princes, English wives: the politics of Powys Wenwynwyn re-visited', *WHR*, 27 (2014), 214–52; 'Emma d'Audley and the clash of laws in thirteenth-century northern Powys', in Patricia Skinner (ed.), *The Welsh and the Medieval World: Travel, Migration and Exile* (Cardiff: University of Wales Press, 2018), pp. 49–73. See also *AWR*, pp. 24, 33; *ByT Pen. 20 Trans.*, p. 84.

[113] *ByT Pen. 20 Trans.*, p. 108.

[114] *AWR*, no. 276. See in general Louise Wilkinson, 'Joan, wife of Llywelyn the Great', in M. Prestwich, R. H. Britnell and R. Frame (eds), *Thirteenth Century England X* (Woodbridge: Boydell, 2005), pp. 81–94.

[115] *AWR*, no. 280.

[116] *AWR*, nos 433, 435–6.

[117] Lewis Thorpe (trans.), *Gerald of Wales: The Journey through Wales/The Description of Wales* (Harmondsworth: Penguin Books, 1978), p. 203.

[118] For the elders in Powys see Stephenson, *Medieval Powys*, pp. 93, 188–92. For elders and learned men of Gwynedd see *ByT Pen. 20 Trans.*, pp. 92, 107, and *AWR*, no. 345 §10.

[119] For examples of the consent of family members to a ruler's grant see *AWR*, nos 119, 121, 124, 131–8, 142, 143, 146, 152, 154–5, 161, all from Glamorgan; nos 506, 508, 514, 515, 516, 529, all from northern Powys.

[120] *ByT, RBH*, pp. 238–9 has 'chief counsellor'; *ByT Pen. 20 Trans.*, p. 106 has 'eminent counsellor'.

121 Rhian M. Andrews, 'Cerddi bygwth a dadolwch Beirdd y Tywysogion', *Studia Celtica* 41 (2007), 117–36.

122 See the two papers by Rhian M. Andrews, 'Y bardd yn llysgennad, rhan I: Llywarch Brydydd y Moch yn Neheubarth', *Dwned*, 20 (2014), 11–30; 'Y bardd yn llysgennad, rhan II: Bleddyn Fardd yn Neheubarth', *Dwned*, 21 (2015), 49–68.

123 See Rhian M. Andrews and David Stephenson, '*Draig Argoed*: Iorwerth Goch ap Maredudd c. 1110–1171', *CMCS*, 52 (2006), 65–91.

124 *GMB*, poem 25.

125 Aneurin Owen (ed.), *Ancient Laws and Institutes of Wales* (single-vol. edn; London: Record Commission, 1841), p. 105.

126 *Calendar of Inquisitions, Miscellaneous*, I (London: HMSO, 1916), no. 1357.

127 C. T. Martin (ed.), *Registrum Epistolarum Johannis Peckham* (London: Rolls Series, 1882–5), II, pp. 741–2; III, pp. 776–7.

CHAPTER 3: THE OTHER WALES

1 To a greater or lesser degree, this emphasis marks each of the following: R. R. Davies, 'Kings, lords and liberties in the March of Wales', *TRHS*, 5th series, 29 (1979), 41–61; Brock Holden, *Lords of the Central Marches: English Aristocracy and Frontier Society 1087–1265* (Oxford: Oxford University Press, 2008); Max Lieberman, *The Medieval March of Wales: The Creation and Perception of a Frontier, 1066–1283* (Cambridge: Cambridge University Press, 2010). There have been frequent efforts to set the Welsh March in the wider context of frontier societies; see, for example, Max Lieberman, *The March of Wales, 1067–1300: A Borderland of Medieval Britain* (Cardiff: University of Wales Press, 2008), especially chapter 5 and references there cited, but again the emphasis is on the perspectives of the incomers.

2 It should be emphasized that the March always appears as a zone rather than a borderline.

3 Stephenson, *Medieval Powys*, p. 61, n. 19 provides some examples.

4 David Stephenson, 'Llywelyn the Great, the Shropshire March and the building of Montgomery castle', *Shropshire History and Archaeology*, 80 (2005), 52–8.

5 Lieberman, *The March of Wales, 1067–1300*, p. 48; Davies, *Lordship and Society*, pp. 302–18.

6 R. R. Davies, 'Plague and revolt', in Ralph A. Griffiths, Tony Hopkins and Ray Howell (eds), *Gwent County History, Volume 2: The Age of the Marcher Lords, c. 1070–1536* (Cardiff: University of Wales Press, 2008), pp. 217–40, at p. 220; but see also Paul Courtney, 'The Marcher lordships' in the same volume, pp. 47–69, at pp. 60–2.

7 J. Beverley Smith, 'The kingdom of Morgannwg and the Norman Conquest', in T. B. Pugh (ed.), *Glamorgan County History, Vol. III: The Middle Ages* (Cardiff: Glamorgan County History Committee, 1971), pp. 1–43, at p. 37; *ByT Pen. 20 Trans.*, p. 71.

8 *ByT Pen. 20 Trans.*, p. 79.

9 H. E. Butler (ed. and trans.), *The Autobiography of Gerald of Wales* (new edn; Woodbridge: Boydell Press, 2005), p. 82.

10 *ByT Pen. 20 Trans.*, pp. 53–4.

11 David Stephenson, 'Llywelyn Fawr, the Mortimers and Cwm-hir abbey: the politics of monastic re-building', *Transactions of the Radnorshire Society*, 80 (2010), 29–41; J. Beverley Smith, 'The middle march in the thirteenth century', *BBCS*, 24 (1970–2), 77–93; *ByT Pen. 20 Trans.*, p. 112. Uncertainty has persisted into modern historiography, for J. Beverley Smith suggests (*Llywelyn ap Gruffudd*, p. 183) that at the time of the Treaty of Montgomery, Llywelyn held Maelienydd, whereas it has been argued (David Stephenson, 'The chronicler at Cwm-hir abbey, 1257–63: the construction of a Welsh chronicle', in R. A. Griffiths and P. R. Schofield (eds), *Wales and the Welsh in the Middle Ages* (Cardiff: University of Wales Press, 2011), pp. 29–45, at pp. 44–5, n. 54) that it was held by Mortimer.

12 *ByT Pen. 20 Trans.*, p. 90.

13 *ByT Pen. 20 Trans.*, pp. 90–1.

14 *ByT Pen. 20 Trans.*, p. 92.

15 *ByT Pen. 20 Trans.*, p. 96.

16 *ByT Pen. 20 Trans.*, p. 102.

17 *ByT Pen. 20 Trans.*, pp. 102–3.

18 See the analysis by Rhian M. Andrews, 'Y bardd yn llysgennad, rhan I: Llywarch Brydydd y Moch yn Neheubarth', *Dwned*, 20 (2014), 11–30.

19 R. C. Christie (ed.), *Annales Cestrienses* (London: Record Society of Lancashire and Cheshire 14, 1887), pp. 74–5.

20 *ByT Pen. 20 Trans.*, p. 111.

21 Smith, *Llywelyn ap Gruffudd*, p. 160 and n. 80.

22 See the notably perceptive discussion by Smith, *Llywelyn ap Gruffudd*, pp. 145–52.

23 The economic attractions of the March, albeit at a later fourteenth-century stage of development, are discussed by Davies, *Lordship and Society*, pp. 107–29. For an attempt by Llywelyn ab Iorwerth to protect the lands and possessions of religious houses, Ratlinghope, a dependent house of Wigmore, and Leominster Priory, from depredation see *AWR*, nos 234, 238. Llywelyn's concerns for the safety of ecclesiastical property did not, it seems, restrain his own conduct in his forays through the March in the spring of 1231, when it was reported by the Tewkesbury chronicler that 'he did not spare the churches' from the destruction and pillaging which he inflicted. See H. R. Luard (ed.), *Annales de Theokesberia*, in *Annales Monastici*, I (Rolls Series: London, 1864), p. 79.

24 Lewis Thorpe (trans.), *Gerald of Wales: The Journey through Wales/The Description of Wales* (Harmondsworth: Penguin Books, 1978), pp. 93 (Brycheiniog), 150–1 (Manorbier and Dyfed).

25 Davies, *Lordship and Society*, p. 115.

26 Luard (ed.), *Annales de Margan*, in *Annales Monastici*, I, pp. 34–6.

27 *ByT Pen. 20 Trans.*, p. 96.

28 Luard (ed.), *Annales de Margan*, p. 39; *Annales de Theokesberia*, p. 80.

29 See above, ch. 2, n. 64.

30 Thomas Jones (ed.), '"Cronica de Wallia"' and other documents from Exeter Cathedral Library MS 3514', *BBCS*, 12 (1946–8), 27–44, and in a separate print, indexed and paginated 1–24. References are to the separate print, here p. 5.

31 *ByT Pen. 20 Trans.*, p. 81 and note to 81.18 at p. 193.

32 *GLlLl*, 25.15–24.

33 *GLlLl*, poem 26.

34 Peredur I. Lynch (ed.), 'Gwaith Llygad Gŵr', in *GBF*, 24.139–40.

35 *GBF*, 28.11–12.

36 Thus Llywelyn's agreement with Gruffudd ap Gwenwynwyn of southern Powys provided that any territories from the Camlad down towards Shrewsbury annexed by Gruffudd should remain with him and his heirs, while territory annexed above the Camlad should remain with Llywelyn and his heirs. The Treaty of Montgomery of 1267 notes some of the marcher territories that Llywelyn had conquered, and which were to remain in his possession: Brecon, Gwerthrynion and Builth. See *AWR*, nos 358 and 363.

37 See above, ch. 2.

38 Thorpe (trans.), *Gerald of Wales*, p. 149.

39 Bartrum, *Welsh Genealogies*, 3, pp. 446–7 (Gruffudd ap Cynan 4 and 5). The complexities of the relationships between marcher magnates and Welsh rulers have been illuminatingly discussed, for the lordship of Gower, by Daniel Power, 'The Briouze family in the thirteenth and early fourteenth centuries: inheritance strategies, lordship and identity', *Journal of Medieval History*, 41, 3 (2015), 341–61.

40 See ch. 2 above.

41 Bartrum, *Welsh Genealogies*, 4, p. 783 (Rhys ap Tewdwr 8).

42 Bartrum, *Welsh Genealogies*, 4, p. 786 (Rhys ap Tewdwr 11).

43 Bartrum, *Welsh Genealogies*, 4, p. 781 (Rhys ap Tewdwr 6).

44 Bartrum, *Welsh Genealogies*, 4, p. 778 (Rhys ap Tewdwr 3). See also Jones (ed.), *Cronica de Wallia*, pp. 15–16.

45 Bartrum, *Welsh Genealogies*, 3, p. 545 (Iestyn 4).

46 Stephenson, *Medieval Powys*, pp. 138–9, 154–5.

47 Davies, *Lordship and Society*, pp. 245–8 provides a succinct summary.

48 Alan Harding (ed.), *The Roll of the Shropshire Eyre of 1256* (London: Selden Society 1981), p. 137.

49 See ch. 1 above, n. 19.

50 The marriage of Gerald and Nest is discussed by Susan M. Johns, *Gender, Nation and Conquest in the High Middle Ages: Nest of Deheubarth* (Manchester: Manchester University Press, 2013). Perceptive comment on the consequences of the union is provided by Huw Pryce, 'Giraldus and the Geraldines', in Peter Crooks and Seán Duffy (eds), *The Geraldines and Medieval Ireland* (Dublin: Four Courts Press, 2016), pp. 53–68, at p. 63. The participation of a son of 'the king of Wales' in the expedition to Leinster in 1167 and his death in the subsequent fighting is recorded in the Annals of the Four Masters, and is noticed by Seán Duffy, *Ireland in the Middle Ages* (Dublin: Gill and Macmillan, 1997), p. 62. For Cynan ap Hywel see *AC*, p. 76; *CACW*, p. 48; Maredudd ap Rhys's alliance with Gilbert Marshal is established by J. Beverley Smith, 'The "Cronica de Wallia" and the dynasty of Dinefwr; a textual and historical study', *BBCS*, 20 (1963), 261–82, at 266–70.

51 *Calendar of Various Chancery Rolls, 1277–1326 (Welsh Rolls)* (London: HMSO, 1912), p. 285, records Rhys's gift to Margaret, daughter of John Lestrange, of Tregarnedd when he married her.

[52] See the article by Emma Cavell, 'Emma d'Audley and the clash of laws in thirteenth-century northern Powys', in Patricia Skinner (ed.), *The Welsh and the Medieval World: Travel, Migration and Exile* (Cardiff: University of Wales Press, 2018), pp. 49–73.

[53] See ch. 1 above.

[54] David Stephenson, 'Ystrad Yw, 1208: a haven for Arwystli exiles?', *Brycheiniog*, 38 (2006), 49–54.

[55] Rachel Swallow, 'Gateways to power: the castles of Ranulf III of Chester and Llywelyn the Great of Gwynedd', *Archaeological Journal*, 171 (2014), 291–314. See also Craig Jones, 'How to make an entrance: an overlooked aspect of native Welsh masonry castle design', *Journal of the Mortimer History Society*, I (2017), 73–89.

[56] P. G. Barton, 'Gruffudd ap Gwenwynwyn's Trefnant market charter, 1279–82', *Montgomeryshire Collections*, 90 (2002), 69–86.

[57] See above, chapter 2 and n. 45.

[58] Janet Burton and Karen Stöber, *Abbeys and Priories of Medieval Wales* (Cardiff: University of Wales Press, 2015), pp. 187–93.

[59] B. G. Charles, 'An early charter of the abbey of Cwmhir', *Transactions of the Radnorshire Society*, 40 (1970), 68–74.

[60] *AWR*, no. 114 and the note.

[61] P. M. Remfry, *A Political History of Abbey Cwmhir* (Malvern: SCS Publishing, 1994), pp. 8–12.

[62] Davies, *Age of Conquest*, p. 424; Stephenson, *Medieval Powys*, p. 116.

[63] E. J. Hathaway, P. T. Ricketts, C. A. Robson and A. D. Wilshere (eds), *Fouke le Fitz Waryn* (Oxford: Basil Blackwell for Anglo-Norman Text Society, 1973). For the date see David Stephenson, '*Fouke le Fitz Waryn* and Llywelyn ap Gruffudd's claim to Whittington', *Shropshire History and Archaeology*, 77 (2002), 26–31.

[64] Hathaway, Ricketts, Robson and Wilshere (eds), *Fouke le Fitz Waryn*, 20.20–1, 35.5.

[65] *Calendar of Inquisitions, Miscellaneous*, I (London: HMSO, 1916), no. 2078, p. 557.

[66] The inquisition to which reference is made in the previous note was held on Wednesday after St Lucia, that is, on 17 December 1253, and the record of the inquisition records the arrival of the raiders in Rhys ap Gruffudd's lands in October, and notes that 'they have been harboured there ever since'.

[67] University of Kansas, Kenneth Spencer Research Library, MS 191. 8. For the likely date see MS 191.12, dated 1276, to which Philip ap Goronwy is one of the witnesses.

[68] He is discussed by David Stephenson, 'Conquerors, courtiers and careerists: the struggle for supremacy in Brycheiniog, 1093–1282', *Brycheiniog*, 44 (2013), 27–51, at 40, 47.

[69] Stephenson, 'Conquerors, courtiers and careerists', 40.

[70] See below in the present chapter.

[71] *Calendar of Liberate Rolls, 1260–67* (London: HMSO, 1961), p. 11.

[72] *ByT Pen. 20 Trans.*, p. 112.

[73] The charter in which he appears as a witness is edited and discussed by Stephenson, 'Conquerors, courtiers and careerists', 43, 50–1.

74 *CACW*, p. 49.

75 *WAR*, p. 118.

76 *Littere Wallie*, pp. 32, 41–2, 44.

77 Wages in August 1277 for the force led by Hywel ap Meurig are found in London, The National Archives E 101/3/11, on a membrane pencil-marked '3'.

78 See, for example, *WAR*, p. 259.

79 N. Denholm-Young, *History and Heraldry, 1254–1310* (Oxford: Oxford University Press, 1965), pp. 90–4.

80 See ch. 5 below.

81 See Stephenson, 'Empires in Wales', 49–53, and ch. 4 below.

82 Anon., *Baronia de Kemeys* (London: Cambrian Archaeological Association, n.d.), pp. 53–4; cf. pp. 50–1.

83 Thomas Parry (ed.), *Gwaith Dafydd ap Gwilym* (Cardiff: University of Wales Press, 1952), p. xxv; *CACW*, p. 48.

84 *CChR*, I, p. 347; *CPR, 1247–58*, p. 126; *ByT Pen. 20 Trans.*, p. 109.

85 *Close Rolls 1256–59*, pp. 466–7; *Littere Wallie*, pp. 30–1. Gwilym ap Gwrwared's letter records that he had been entrusted with the custody of the castle of Cardigan, whereas Nicholas Fitz Martin's records that the custody of the town and castle of Carmarthen had been committed to him. Both letters were issued in London, Gwilym's on 13 May, and Nicholas's on 12 May.

86 *CPR, 1266–72*, p. 114.

87 Smith, *Llywelyn ap Gruffudd*, pp. 551–2; David Stephenson, 'New light on a dark deed: the death of Llywelyn ap Gruffudd, prince of Wales', *Archaeologia Cambrensis*, 166 (2017), 243–52.

88 See ch. 4 below.

89 *AWR*, no. 377.

CHAPTER 4: THE LIMITS TO PRINCELY POWER

1 *ByT Pen. 20 Trans.*, p. 63 records that when Henry pitched his tents on the Berwyn mountains, 'there came upon them a mighty tempest of wind and bad weather and rains, and lack of food'.

2 Lewis Thorpe (trans.), *Gerald of Wales: The Journey through Wales/The Description of Wales* (Harmondsworth: Penguin Books, 1978), pp. 96, 178, 182, 185, 194.

3 Thorpe (trans.), *Gerald of Wales*, pp. 224–7; H. E. Butler (ed. and trans.), *The Autobiography of Gerald of Wales* (new edn; Woodbridge: Boydell Press, 2005), p. 249.

4 For just a few examples see *Calendar of Various Chancery Rolls, 1277–1326* (*Welsh Rolls*) (London: HMSO, 1912), pp. 182, 184–5, 254, 293, 318–19, 326.

5 It is instructive to study the map of *cantrefi* and *cymydau* in M. Richards, *Welsh Administrative and Territorial Units* (Cardiff: University of Wales Press, 1969), p. 229.

6 *ByT Pen. 20 Trans.*, pp. 37, 85, notes that Owain ap Cadwgan, under pressure from Henry I in 1114, 'gathered his men and all their chattels along with them, and moved into the mountains of Eryri; for that was the wildest and safest place to which to retreat' and records how Llywelyn ab Iorwerth, when attacked by

King John in 1211, 'had Perfeddwlad and Anglesey and all their chattels moved to the wilderness of Eryri'.

7 See ch. 2 above.

8 Lloyd, *A History*, II, p. 537.

9 For the use of forces from Ireland in attacks on Wales see *ByT Pen. 20 Trans.*, pp. 99 (1223, led by William Marshal), 107 (1245, organized by Henry III). For Irish contributions to Edward I's attack on Llywelyn, and subsequently Dafydd, see Seán Duffy, *Ireland in the Middle Ages* (Dublin: Gill and Macmillan, 1997), p. 130. Ironically, the prospect in 1315 of a 'Celtic alliance' and an intervention in Wales by Scottish forces operating from Ireland brought great concern to the government of Edward II, but it came too late to be of help to the aspirations of any Welsh ruler, for the native principalities were by then a thing of the past. For the Celtic alliance of 1315 see ch. 5 below.

10 Examples from Gwynedd include Cadwaladr ap Gruffudd (d.1172), maintained in Shropshire by Henry II during his exile from Gwynedd between 1152 and 1157. Dafydd ab Owain (d.1203) was given shelter in England after 1198; and it was from England that Senana, wife of Gruffudd ap Llywelyn (d.1244) orchestrated efforts to secure his release and re-instatement in his lands. For these see *AWR*, pp. 23 and 25, and no. 284.

11 Stephenson, *Medieval Powys*.

12 See ch. 1 above.

13 See ch. 3 above.

14 He made several attempts to secure such recognition, and was prepared to pay handsomely for it: 1,500 marks for a seven-year truce in 1257 and maintenance in possession of Gwynedd, an unspecified sum in 1258, 16,000 marks over eighty years and restoration of territories, for a permanent settlement, and 30,000 marks for a settlement in 1265 and 1267; see *AWR*, nos 327, 330, 338, 361, 363.

15 See ch. 1 above. There are pertinent comments in Rhys Jones, 'Changing ideologies of medieval state formation: the growing exploitation of land in Gwynedd c.1100–c.1400', *Journal of Historical Geography*, 26 (2000), 505–16.

16 See Thomas Jones Pierce, 'The growth of commutation in Gwynedd in the thirteenth century', in J. Beverley Smith (ed.), *Medieval Welsh Society: Selected Essays by T. Jones Pierce* (Cardiff: University of Wales Press, 1972), pp. 103–25; Stephenson, *Medieval Powys*, pp. 205, 225, 237.

17 David Stephenson, 'Jewish presence in, and absence from, Wales in the twelfth and thirteenth centuries', *Jewish Historical Studies*, 43 (2011), 7–20.

18 Stephenson, *Political Power*, pp. 95–135.

19 Stephenson, *Political Power*, pp. 194–5. See below, in the present chapter, and Llinos Beverley Smith, 'The *gravamina* of the community of Gwynedd against Llywelyn ap Gruffudd', *BBCS*, 31 (1984–5), 158–76.

20 For examples relating to the diocese of Bangor see Stephenson, *Political Power*, p. 180.

21 See ch. 1 above.

22 See A. W. Wade-Evans (ed. and trans.), *Vitae Sanctorum Britanniae et Genealogiae*, new edn by Scott Lloyd (Cardiff: Welsh Academic Press, 2013), pp. 16–22, and 337–63.

23 Stephenson, *Medieval Powys*, pp. 66–7.

24 Stephenson, *Medieval Powys*, pp. 1, n. 3, 249, n. 3; for the distribution of Cadog dedications see E. G. Bowen, *The Settlements of the Celtic Saints in Wales* (Cardiff: University of Wales Press, 1954), p. 42.

25 See, for examples of such formulae, *AWR*, nos 154–5, 161, 164–5, 167 (all grants by Lleision ap Morgan (d.1214 × 1217) of Glamorgan); 213, 225–7, 229, 231, 250, 258, 272, (all grants of Llywelyn ab Iorwerth (d.1240) of Gwynedd); 541–2, 545, 548–9, 551–6, 563–5, 569, 575 (all grants of Gwenwynwyn (d.1216) of southern Powys).

26 See Stephenson, *Political Power*, pp. 175–8 for the dispute between Llywelyn ap Gruffudd and Bishop Anian II of St Asaph regarding Llywelyn's alleged encroachments on or usurpation of many of the financial rights enjoyed by the bishop throughout the episcopal lands.

27 The extent is given in H. Ellis (ed.), *Registrum vulgariter nuncupatum: The Record of Caernarvon* (London: Record Commission, 1838), pp. 93–115; for the rents and services due to the prince see Stephenson, *Political Power*, p. xxxv.

28 A. W. Haddan and W. Stubbs (eds), *Councils and Ecclesiastical Documents relating to Great Britain and Ireland*, vol. I (Oxford: Clarendon Press, 1869), p. 499.

29 Stephenson, *Political Power*, pp. 171–81 for clashes with the bishops, and pp. 182–3 and n. 78 for those with Basingwerk.

30 *Littere Wallie*, p. 25.

31 Stephenson, *Medieval Powys*, pp. 137–8, and n. 34.

32 *ByT Pen. 20 Trans.*, pp. 64–5.

33 *ByT Pen. 20 Trans.*, p. 80.

34 Stephenson, *Medieval Powys*, pp. 85–91.

35 *ByT Pen. 20 Trans.*, pp. 91–2.

36 The evidence is assembled and discussed by J. Beverley Smith, 'The "Cronica de Wallia" and the dynasty of Dinefwr', *BBCS*, 20 (1963), 261–82, 266–70.

37 *AWR*, no. 347.

38 Llywelyn was still promising to pay it in 1277: *AWR*, no. 398.

39 That the lord of Bromfield (northern Powys) had ambitions to acquire parts of southern Powys is suggested by Stephenson, *Medieval Powys*, p. 126.

40 Stephenson, *Medieval Powys*, p. 93; *WAR*, p. 15.

41 Stephenson, *Medieval Powys*, pp. 126, 130, 143.

42 The partition of northern Powys is considered by Stephenson, *Medieval Powys*, p. 159, and the events of 1274 at pp. 144–51.

43 *AWR*, no. 603.

44 Stephenson, *Medieval Powys*, especially chapters 4, 7 and 8. For the dynasty of Maredudd ap Rhys and Rhys ap Maredudd, two papers by J. Beverley Smith are crucial: 'The "Cronica de Wallia" and the dynasty of Dinefwr', 261–82, and 'The origins of the revolt of Rhys ap Maredudd', *BBCS*, 21 (1965), 151–63.

45 *AWR*, no. 316.

46 *AWR*, no. 347.

47 *AWR*, no. 92.

48 Smith, 'The "Cronica de Wallia" and the dynasty of Dinefwr', 272.

49 *CACW*, p. 48. Maredudd ab Owain was to emerge as a supporter of Llywelyn ap Gruffudd in his quest to secure a principality of Wales. But even in Maredudd's

case we can perhaps glimpse tension between attachment to a 'national' cause and commitment to regional ascendancy: in his obituary notice under the year 1265 the *Brut* – which shows clearly a close connection to Maredudd's line in this period – noted that he was 'counsellor of all Wales', but preceded that by describing him as 'defender of all Deheubarth'. *ByT Pen. 20 Trans.*, p. 114. It is tempting to suppose that the former role was an aid to the attainment of the latter.

[50] Smith, 'The origins of the revolt of Rhys ap Maredudd', 156–62.

[51] *GLlLl*, 23.131–4.

[52] *ByT Pen. 20 Trans.*, pp. 79, 81 and note to 81.18 at p. 193.

[53] *AWR*, no. 603.

[54] *AWR*, no. 604.

[55] Stephenson, *Medieval Powys*, pp. 45–6.

[56] *ByT Pen. 20 Trans.*, pp. 53, 56–8.

[57] *ByT Pen. 20 Trans.*, p. 60.

[58] *AWR*, no. 197; Stephenson, *Political Power*, pp. 148–51.

[59] *ByT Pen. 20 Trans.*, p. 65; Una Rees (ed.), *The Cartulary of Haughmond Abbey* (Cardiff: University of Wales Press, 1985), no. 804; Geoffrey Barraclough (ed.), *The Charters of the Anglo-Norman Earls of Chester, c.1071–1237* (n.p.: Record Society of Lancashire and Cheshire, 1988), nos 64, 84. For Cadwaladr's burial in a double vault with Owain see Thorpe (trans.), *Gerald of Wales*, p. 190.

[60] *ByT Pen. 20 Trans.*, p. 74.

[61] *ByT Pen. 20 Trans.*, p. 75.

[62] *ByT Pen. 20 Trans.*, p. 75.

[63] Smith, *Llywelyn ap Gruffudd*, pp. 31–2.

[64] R. C. Christie (ed.), *Annales Cestrienses* (London: Record Society of Lancashire and Cheshire 14, 1887), pp. 82–3; Smith, *Llywelyn ap Gruffudd*, p. 374.

[65] *WAR*, pp. 238–9.

[66] For the case against the notion of partibility of the Welsh realms see J. Beverley Smith, 'Dynastic Succession in Medieval Wales', *BBCS*, 33 (1986), 199–232, and the same author's 'The succession to Welsh princely inheritance: the evidence reconsidered', in R. R. Davies (ed.), *The British Isles 1100–1500: Comparisons, Contrasts and Connections* (Edinburgh: John Donald, 1988), pp. 64–81. For the comments of Llyfr Iorwerth see *LTMW*, p. 7.

[67] That was certainly the eventual division of lands between the brothers. See *ByT Pen. 20 Trans.*, p. 70; *AWR*, pp. 15–16, and no. 103; Butler (ed. and trans.), *Autobiography of Gerald of Wales*, pp. 46–54.

[68] Stephenson, *Medieval Powys*, p. 44.

[69] *ByT Pen. 20 Trans.*, p. 62.

[70] See ch. 1 above.

[71] *ByT Pen. 20 Trans.*, pp. 58, 64, 66.

[72] Stephenson, *Medieval Powys*, pp. 67–8.

[73] *ByT Pen. 20 Trans.*, pp. 70–1.

[74] Thorpe (trans.), *Gerald of Wales*, p. 75; *ByT Pen. 20 Trans.*, p. 76.

[75] *Pipe Roll 21 Henry II* (London: Pipe Roll Society, 1897), pp. 88–9.

[76] For the initial payment see the previous note; the fact that no more was paid is established by Lloyd, *A History*, II, p. 546, n. 51.

[77] Butler (ed. and trans.), *Autobiography of Gerald of Wales*, pp. 54–6.

[78] Butler (ed. and trans.), *Autobiography of Gerald of Wales*, p. 49.

[79] For discussion see F. G. Cowley, *The Monastic Order in South Wales, 1066–1349* (Cardiff: University of Wales Press, 1977), pp. 25–6.

[80] *ByT Pen. 20 Trans.*, p. 72.

[81] Stephenson, 'Empires in Wales', 48 and n. 108.

[82] W. Stubbs (ed.), *Gesta Regis Henrici Secundi Benedicti Abbatis*, 2 vols (London: Rolls Series, 1867), I, p. 162.

[83] J. C. Dickinson and P. T. Ricketts (eds), 'The Anglo-Norman chronicle of Wigmore Abbey', *Transactions of the Woolhope Naturalists' Field Club*, 39 (1969), 413–46, at 436.

[84] *AWR*, no. 113.

[85] See *AWR*, p. 252, following P. M. Remfry, *A Political History of Abbey Cwmhir* (Malvern: SCS Publishing, 1994), pp. 8–12.

[86] *ByT Pen. 20 Trans.*, p. 85.

[87] *ByT Pen. 20 Trans.*, p. 87.

[88] *ByT Pen. 20 Trans.*, pp. 83–8, 91–2; supplemented by the B-text entries in *AC*, p. 66.

[89] *ByT Pen. 20 Trans.*, p. 92.

[90] *ByT Pen. 20 Trans.*, p. 95.

[91] *ByT Pen. 20 Trans.*, p. 97.

[92] *AWR*, no. 248. The whole episode of Llywelyn's intervention in Ystrad Tywi is considered by Rhian M. Andrews, 'Y bardd yn llysgennad, rhan I: Llywarch Brydydd y Moch yn Neheubarth', *Dwned*, 20 (2014), 11–30.

[93] *AWR*, no. 248.

[94] *GLlLl*, 26.13–14, 57–64. See further *ByT Pen. 20 Trans.*, pp. 97–8.

[95] *GLlLl*, 26.77.

[96] *Rotuli Litterarum Clausarum*, i, p. 459; *AWR*, no. 52.

[97] *Rotuli Litterarum Clausarum*, i, p. 459: '*Mandatum est Reso Crek*' ('Rhys Gryg is ordered').

[98] *GLlLl*, 26.119.

[99] *ByT Pen. 20 Trans.*, p. 101.

[100] Smith, 'The "Cronica de Wallia" and the dynasty of Dinefwr', 265. For the 1222 settlement see *ByT Pen. 20 Trans.*, p. 99: 'after him [Rhys Ieuanc ap Gruffudd] Owain his only brother, succeeded to his patrimony, but he received only a portion of his brother's patrimony; and the other portion Llywelyn gave to Maelgwn ap Rhys'.

[101] *AWR*, no. 54; *Patent Rolls 1216–25*, p. 481.

[102] *ByT Pen. 20 Trans.*, p. 102.

[103] *AWR*, no. 266.

[104] *ByT Pen. 20 Trans.*, p. 103.

[105] Roger Wendover reported that in mid-January *comes Marescallus et princeps Norwallie Leolinus, collectis omnibus viribus quas habere poterant ... villam vero Salopesberi igne combusserunt* (the Earl Marshal and Llywelyn prince of north Wales gathered all the forces which they could muster [and] burned the town of Shrewsbury): see H. G. Hewlett (ed.), *The Flowers of History of Roger Wendover* (London: Rolls Series vol. iii, 1889), pp. 71–2. See also *AWR*, no. 269 and the note.

[106] *ByT Pen. 20 Trans.*, p. 103.

[107] *GLlLl*, 26.8, 145; Morfydd E. Owen (ed.), *Gwaith y Prydydd Bychan*, in *GBF*, 3.4–5, 16, 23.

[108] A. W. Wade-Evans (ed.), *Medieval Welsh Law* (Oxford: Clarendon Press, 1909), pp. 3–4. For the context see Huw Pryce, 'The context and purpose of the earliest Welsh lawbooks', *CMCS*, 39 (2000), 39–63.

[109] See ch. 3 above.

[110] See ch. 3 above.

[111] The lordship of Abergavenny had been held by Eva de Cantilupe; on her death in 1255 the lordship was taken into royal custody, and administered by officials of Edward, son of the king. See *CPR, 1247–58*, pp. 421, 586, which show Abergavenny being administered with the Three Castles.

[112] See A. J. Roderick and William Rees (eds), 'The lordships of Abergavenny, Grosmont, Skenfrith and White Castle: Accounts of the ministers for the year 1256–1257, Part 2', in H. J. Randall and W. Rees (eds), *A Breviate of Glamorgan and Other Papers* (n.p.: South Wales and Monmouth Record Society Publications no. 3, 1954), pp. 41, 45.

[113] The March territories specifically conceded were the lordships of Brecon, Gwerthrynion and Builth: see *AWR*, no. 363; Elfael was not named in the treaty, but Llywelyn was in possession of that region.

[114] *Littere Wallie*, pp. 40–1.

[115] For the wages-roll which records Einion ap Madog as a troop-leader under Hywel ap Meurig in 1277 see ch. 3 above, and n. 77; for Einion as a surety for John, son of Hywel ap Meurig see *Littere Wallie*, pp. 41–2; for the 1278 deed in which Einion received a 120-year lease of lands in Builth see *WAR*, p. 299.

[116] See ch. 3 above, and n. 77.

[117] *Littere Wallie*, pp. 41–2.

[118] *CPR, 1258–66*, pp. 45, 65, 69.

[119] Kenneth Spencer Research Library, Special Collections, University of Kansas MS191:15. This and the other charters in the sequence can be viewed online at *http://vm136.lib.berkeley.edu/BANC/digitalscriptorium/browse_location.html* (accessed 28 July 2018).

[120] See the above note.

[121] Stephenson, 'Empires in Wales', 50 and n. 123.

[122] See n. 119 above.

[123] *WAR*, p. 299.

[124] *Littere Wallie*, p. 184.

[125] *WAR*, pp. 299–300.

[126] David Stephenson, 'Conquerors, courtiers and careerists: the struggle for supremacy in Brycheiniog, 1093–1282', *Brycheiniog*, 44 (2013), 27–51, 43, 50–1.

[127] *Littere Wallie*, pp. 24–5, 26, 30, 35–6.

[128] F. Jones, 'The subsidy of 1292', *BBCS*, 13 (1948–50), 210–30, at 225.

[129] *Littere Wallie*, pp. 40–1.

[130] For Llywelyn ap Madog's role in 1277 see ch. 3 above, and n. 77. For Moelwyn, *maer* of Builth, see n. 119 above and *Littere Wallie*, pp. 40–1; for Ieuan ap Moelwyn see R. A. Griffiths, *The Principality of Wales in the Later Middle Ages:*

The Structure and Personnel of Government. I. South Wales, 1277–1536 (Cardiff: University of Wales Press, 1972), pp. 283–4, and ch. 5 below.

131 *Littere Wallie*, pp. 33–4; Einion's letters of the same date, at p. 28, reveal that he had to surrender a hostage to the prince. For his castle see Stephenson, 'Conquerors, courtiers and careerists', 38 and n. 75.

132 For Meurig's provision of sureties see *Littere Wallie*, p. 126; for his military service in 1277 see ch. 3 above, and n. 77.

133 See David Stephenson, 'New light on a dark deed: the death of Llywelyn ap Gruffudd', *Archaeologia Cambrensis*, 166 (2017), 243–52.

134 R. R. Davies, 'The identity of "Wales" in the thirteenth century', in R. R. Davies and Geraint J. Jenkins (eds), *From Medieval to Modern Wales* (Cardiff: University of Wales Press, 2004), pp. 45–63; the quotation is at p. 60; for the equation, implicit in that comment, of Gwynedd with Wales see pp. 58–9 and 61.

135 For the residence of Hywel's son Philip at Hergest in 1290, when he entertained Bishop Swinfield there, see John Webb (ed.), *A Roll of the Household Expenses of Richard de Swinfield, Bishop of Hereford, 1289–90* (London: Camden Society, 1854), p. 88; timbers at Hergest court have been dendrochronologically dated to 1267, suggesting that the house was built by Hywel ap Meurig. I am grateful to Laurence Banks for discussion of this point.

136 See ch. 1 above.

137 The cases of the sons of Gruffudd ab Ednyfed, *distain* to Llywelyn ap Gruffudd in the early part of that prince's career, and himself a son of the principal minister of Llywelyn ab Iorwerth and Dafydd ap Llywelyn, are relevant; they are noticed by Smith, *Llywelyn ap Gruffudd*, pp. 430–3 and 553. For Llywelyn's loss of support amongst the poets see the hints provided by Peredur I. Lynch, 'Court poetry, power and politics', in *WKC*, pp. 167–90, especially at pp. 189–90, culminating in the suggestion that it 'is conceivable … that the poets were a disillusioned element in Gwynedd by 1277'.

CHAPTER 5: NEW ASCENDANCIES

1 Smith, *Llywelyn ap Gruffudd*, p. 332 and n. 215.

2 N. Denholm-Young, 'The tournament in the thirteenth century', in R. W. Hunt, W. A. Pantin and R. W. Southern (eds), *Studies in Medieval History presented to F. M. Powicke* (Oxford: Clarendon Press,1948), pp. 240–68, at pp. 265–6.

3 The Waverley annalist noted that 'thus the glory of Wales was transferred to the English': H. R. Luard (ed.), *Annales Monasterii de Waverleia*, in *Annales Monastici*, II (London: Rolls Series, 1865), p. 401.

4 For recent discussion see Diane Williams and John R. Kenyon (eds), *The Impact of the Edwardian Castles in Wales* (Oxford: Oxbow Books, 2010).

5 See ch. 1 above.

6 Ivor Bowen (ed.), *The Statutes of Wales* (London: Fisher Unwin, 1908), p. 3.

7 Stephenson, *Medieval Wales*, pp. 169–77.

8 Max Lieberman, 'Striving for marcher liberties: the Corbets of Caus in the thirteenth century', in M. Prestwich (ed.), *Liberties and Identities in the Medieval British Isles* (Woodbridge: Boydell Press, 2008), pp. 141–54.

9 See, for example, Davies, *Lordship and Society*, p. 238.

10 See Stephenson, *Medieval Powys*, pp. 138–40, 153–4.

11 As early as 1275 Edward had made it clear that even in the March of Wales 'the king who is sovereign lord shall do right therein to all such as will complain': Davies, *Lordship and Society*, p. 252; for more general comment see pp. 27–8.

12 J. E. Morris, *The Welsh Wars of Edward I* (Oxford: Clarendon Press, 1901), p. 202 notes that Earl Gilbert had treated the king 'as if he were a brother potentate'.

13 Michael Altschul, 'The Lordship of Glamorgan and Morgannwg, 1217–1317', in T. B. Pugh (ed.), *Glamorgan County History, Vol. III: The Middle Ages* (Cardiff: Glamorgan County History Committee, 1971), pp. 45–86, at p. 57.

14 *Calendar of Various Chancery Rolls, 1277–1326* (London: HMSO, 1912), p. 338.

15 *Calendar of Various Chancery Rolls, 1277–1326*, p. 336.

16 Altschul, 'The Lordship of Glamorgan and Morgannwg, 1217–1317', p. 59.

17 *Calendar of Various Chancery Rolls, 1277–1326*, p. 335.

18 See, for example, *CPR, 1292–1301*, pp. 439, 464.

19 Ralph A. Griffiths, 'The Revolt of Rhys ap Maredudd, 1287–8', *WHR*, 3 (1966), 121–43, at 138–9.

20 The risings in Gwynedd, west Wales, Brycheiniog and Glamorgan are well known but that in Gwent, led by Meurig ap Dafydd, has passed virtually unnoticed: see ch. 1 above. It seems possible that the attack on Abergavenny Castle, which has been attributed to Morgan ap Maredudd, may well have been undertaken by Meurig ap Dafydd, who had connections with Abergavenny lordship. The Worcester Annals, while reporting a siege, and the heavy casualties suffered by the besiegers when it was broken by Humphrey de Bohun, do not name Morgan as the attacker of Abergavenny: H. R. Luard (ed.), *Annales Prioratus de Wigornia*, in *Annales Monastici*, IV (London: Rolls Series, 1869), p. 519.

21 See n. 129 in the present chapter below for French involvement.

22 See R. R. Davies, 'Colonial Wales', *Past and Present*, 65 (1974), 3–23, at 13.

23 Diane M. Korngiebel, 'Forty acres and a mule: the mechanics of English settlement in north-east Wales after the Edwardian conquest', *Haskins Society Journal*, 14 (2003), 91–104, at 99–100.

24 Quoted by Davies, 'Colonial Wales', 11.

25 See A. D. Carr, *Medieval Anglesey* (2nd edn; Llangefni: Anglesey Antiquarian Society, 2011).

26 E. A. Lewis, *The Mediaeval Boroughs of Snowdonia* (London: H. Sotheran for the Guild of Graduates of the University of Wales, 1912), p. 58.

27 See ch. 1 above.

28 Davies, 'Colonial Wales', 17.

29 Merioneth: Gruffudd ap Dafydd, 1300–1; Ieuan ap Hywel, 1306–9; Gruffudd ap Rhys (i.e. Sir Gruffudd Llwyd), 1314–17, 1321–8; Gruffudd ap Gwilym de la Pole, 1330–1; a total of some 14 years. Anglesey: Gruffudd ap Rhys (i.e. Sir Gruffudd Llwyd), 1305–6; Gruffudd ab Owain, 1306–8; Madog Llwyd, 1308–12; Einion ab Ieuan, 1216–27; a total of some eighteen years. Caernarfonshire: Gruffudd ap Rhys (i.e. Sir Gruffudd Llwyd), 1302–5, 1308–9. See for these appointments W. H. Waters, *The Edwardian Settlement of North Wales in its Administrative and Legal Aspects, 1284–1343* (Cardiff: University of Wales Press, 1935), pp. 171–3.

30 The outstanding example is Sir Gruffudd Llwyd, a grandson of Gruffudd ab Ednyfed, *distain* of Llywelyn ap Gruffudd, and a great-grandson of Ednyfed Fychan, *distain* of Llywelyn ab Iorwerth and Dafydd ap Llywelyn. Through Gwenllian, wife of Ednyfed Fychan, Sir Gruffudd Llwyd was also descended from the Lord Rhys.

31 See Ralph A. Griffiths, *The Principality of Wales in the Later Middle Ages: The Structure and Personnel of Government. I. South Wales, 1277–1536* (Cardiff: University of Wales Press, 1972), pp. 97–8 (Rhys ap Hywel), 99–102 (Rhys ap Gruffudd), 103 (Philip de Clanvow).

32 Griffiths, *Principality of Wales*, pp. 194–5.

33 *CAP*, pp. 75–6.

34 H. Ellis (ed.), *Registrum vulgariter nuncupatum: The Record of Caernarvon* (London: Record Commission, 1838), pp. 131–2. Amongst several oppressive ordinances alleged to exist 'amongst the records of North Wales' are regulations that no Welshman should carry offensive or defensive arms to any towns, fairs, churches or assemblies, on pain of confiscation of the arms and a year's imprisonment, and that no Welshman was to acquire lands or tenements in the English mercantile towns or in their liberties, or even to reside there. The list of restrictions is worth further detailed study.

35 TNA, SC6/1227/3. The case of Einion the Physician is examined in some detail by David Stephenson, 'The local physicians of medieval Wales', in Robin Barlow (ed.), *Transactions of the Physicians of Myddfai Society, 2011–2017* (The Physicians of Myddfai Society, 2018), pp. 150–7, at p. 154.

36 See M. F. Stevens, *Urban Assimilation in Post-Conquest Wales: Ethnicity, Gender and Economy in Ruthin, 1282–1348* (Cardiff: University of Wales Press, 2010), pp. 258–9.

37 Stevens, *Urban Assimilation*, pp. 112–14, 259.

38 R. Morgan, 'A Powys lay subsidy roll, 1293', *Montgomeryshire Collections*, 71 (1983), 91–112.

39 A. Chapman, *Welsh Soldiers in the Later Middle Ages, 1282–1422* (Woodbridge: Boydell Press, 2015), pp. 228–9.

40 William Chester Jordan, *The Great Famine* (Princeton: Princeton University Press, 1996), pp. 84–5; Keith Williams-Jones (ed.), *The Merioneth Lay Subsidy Roll, 1292–3* (Cardiff: University of Wales Press, 1976), p. cxxxiv, and references there cited. See also Rhys W. Hays, *The History of the Abbey of Aberconway, 1186–1537* (Cardiff: University of Wales Press, 1963), p. 92.

41 *Calendar of Chancery Warrants, 1244–1326* (London: HMSO, 1927), p. 473.

42 *Merioneth Lay Subsidy Roll*, p. cxxxiv and n. 3; *CCR, 1318–23*, p. 19.

43 *Merioneth Lay Subsidy Roll*, p. cxxxv.

44 See below in the present chapter, esp. n. 52 and associated text.

45 For Maelienydd see *CPR, 1292–1301*, p. 290.

46 *CPR, 1292–1301*, p. 293. See further for events in Brecon lordship below in the present chapter, esp. nn. 132–3 and associated text. For the Glamorgan grants see *CCR, 1296–1302*, pp. 34, 39, 114–15.

47 Davies, *Lordship and Society*, p. 464, n. 22.

48 T. Salt, 'Ancient Documents relating to the Honour, Forest and Borough of

Clun', *Transactions of the Shropshire Archaeological and Natural History Society*, 11 (1887–8), 244–72.

49 Summarized by Davies, *Lordship and Society*, p. 463, n. 22.

50 See, for example, Llinos Beverley Smith, 'The Arundel charters to the lordship of Chirk in the fourteenth century', *BBCS*, 23 (1969), 153–66.

51 See n. 45 above.

52 *CPR, 1292–1301*, p. 165.

53 *CPR, 1292–1301*, p. 223.

54 For Daunvers see Waters, *The Edwardian Settlement*, p. 172; for Hywel ap Cynwrig see *Record of Caernarvon*, p. 219.

55 See G. Rex Smith, 'The Penmachno letter patent and the Welsh uprising of 1294–95', *CMCS*, 58 (2009), 49–67, transcribed and translated at pp. 56–8.

56 Glyn Roberts, *Aspects of Welsh History: Selected Papers of the Late Glyn Roberts* (Cardiff: University of Wales Press, 1969), pp. 187–8.

57 *Record of Caernarvon*, pp. 212–25.

58 *Calendar of Chancery Warrants*, pp. 306–7.

59 J. Beverley Smith, 'Edward II and the allegiance of Wales', *WHR*, 8 (1976–7), 139–71, at 145 and n. 30.

60 See the above note.

61 *CPR, 1313–17*, p. 433.

62 *CPR, 1313–17*, p. 433.

63 *CPR, 1313–17*, p. 434.

64 G. Dodd, 'Petitions from the king's dominions: Wales, Ireland and Gascony, c. 1290–1350', in P. Crooks, D. Green and W. M. Ormrod (eds), *The Plantagenet Empire* (Donnington: Shaun Tyas, 2016), pp. 187–215, at p. 196.

65 For a thorough, and cautious, assessment see Daniel Huws, *Medieval Welsh Manuscripts* (Cardiff: University of Wales Press and National Library of Wales, 2000), pp. 193–226: 'The Hendregadredd Manuscript'.

66 A good starting point for analysis of *Brut y Tywysogion* is Huws, *Medieval Welsh Manuscripts*, pp. 53–4, 76. See also the important discussion by O. W. Jones, 'Historical Writing in Medieval Wales' (unpublished PhD thesis, Bangor University, 2013), chapters 1 and 4.

67 See David H. Williams, *The Welsh Cistercians* (Leominster: Gracewing, 2001), p. 37.

68 See, for example, J. Beverley Smith, 'Castell Gwyddgrug', *BBCS*, 26 (1974–6), 74–7.

69 David Stephenson, 'Welsh chronicles' accounts of the mid-twelfth century', *CMCS*, 56 (2008), 45–57.

70 David Stephenson, 'The Continuation of Brut y Tywysogion in NLW Peniarth MS 20 re-visited', in Ben Guy, Owain Wyn Jones and Georgia Henley (eds), *The Chronicles of Medieval Wales and the March: New Contexts, Studies and Texts* (Turnhout: Brepols, forthcoming).

71 *ByT Pen 20 Trans.*, p. 126.

72 The series of editions of the work of *Beirdd yr Uchelwyr*, a project of the Centre for Advanced Welsh and Celtic Studies, Aberystwyth has produced editions of the work of over eighty later medieval Welsh poets.

73 See Stephenson, *Political Power*, p. 105.

74 For an excellent survey of his career see J. Beverley Smith, 'Gruffudd Llwyd, Sir' in *ODNB*.

75 Smith, 'Edward II and the allegiance of Wales', 150; with Sir Gruffudd Llwyd were Anian, bishop of Bangor and Sir Morgan ap Maredudd.

76 The letters are given cautious consideration by Smith, 'Edward II and the allegiance of Wales', 155–6, who suggests that they may indicate either treacherous intent on the part of Sir Gruffudd, or 'an ill-judged response ... to the return of Mortimer [to the office of Justiciar]'. It must be questioned, however, whether Sir Morgan ap Maredudd's involvement with Sir Gruffudd at the Clipstone meeting with Edward II may not raise the possibility that a deeper game was being played.

77 Note the conclusion of Smith, 'Edward II and the allegiance of Wales', 157, that 'there is much to suggest that the alignment of the Welsh was determined less by their attitude to the crown than by their loyalty or aversion to the family of Mortimer'.

78 Seymour Phillips, *Edward II* (New Haven: Yale University Press, 2010). pp. 403–4.

79 Smith, 'Edward II and the allegiance of Wales', 166–7.

80 Sir Gruffudd and twelve others suspected of plotting against the Mortimer administration were released in October 1327: see *CCR, 1327–30*, p. 182; the group included Madog Llwyd, who might be the sheriff of Anglesey of 1308–12, and Cynwrig ap Gruffudd, who would be sheriff of Anglesey in the early 1330s. See Walters, *Edwardian Settlement*, p. 172.

81 *CPR, 1334–8*, p. 106.

82 Her grandfather was Gwilym ap Gwrwared, noticed in ch. 3 above.

83 *CPR, 1313–17*, p. 433.

84 *CCR, 1318–23*, pp. 421, 464, 507, 521; *Calendar of Fine Rolls, 1319–27* (London: HMSO, 1912), p. 98.

85 Smith, 'Edward II and the allegiance of Wales', 165.

86 *CPR, 1327–30*, pp. 238, 242, 256, 272–3; see Smith, 'Edward II and the allegiance of Wales', 167, n. 155, and 169.

87 *CCR, 1330–3*, p. 51.

88 D. L. Evans, 'The later Middle Ages (1282–1536)', in J. E. Lloyd (ed.), *A History of Carmarthenshire*, vol. I (London: Carmarthenshire Society, 1935), p. 249.

89 *Calendar of Inquisitions Post Mortem*, X, 1352–61 (London: HMSO, 1921), no. 324.

90 Roberts, *Aspects of Welsh History*, pp. 186–90.

91 The comment by Evans, 'The later Middle Ages', p. 250, that 'Sir Rhys ap Gruffydd does not figure largely in the Welsh poetry of the century; references to him are few, and are mainly to his martial activities' remains pertinent.

92 See n. 71 above in the present chapter.

93 Bartrum, *Welsh Genealogies*, I, p. 31, Bleddyn ap Cynfyn 4, and III, p. 447, Gruffudd ap Cynan 5.

94 *CPR, 1307–13*, p. 405; Diane M. Korngiebel, 'English colonial ethnic discrimination in the lordship of Dyffryn Clwyd: segregation and integration 1282–c.1340', *WHR*, 23 (2006), 1–24 at 9–10.

[95] Michael Rogers, 'The Welsh Marcher Lordship of Bromfield and Yale, 1282–1485' (unpublished PhD thesis, University College of Wales, Aberystwyth, 1992), 64.

[96] *CCR, 1319–23*, p. 521.

[97] Rogers, 'The Welsh Marcher Lordship of Bromfield and Yale', 327.

[98] Rogers, 'The Welsh Marcher Lordship of Bromfield and Yale', 327

[99] *CPR, 1330–34*, p. 61.

[100] According to C. A. Gresham, *Medieval Stone Carving in North Wales* (Cardiff: University of Wales Press, 1968), p. 186, Madog's son married a Puleston, and a Puleston was a member of the commission of 1330.

[101] Jones, 'Historical Writing in Medieval Wales', 58 and chapter 2.

[102] The suggestion is made by Stephenson, 'The Continuation of Brut y Tywysogion in NLW Peniarth MS 20 re-visited'.

[103] Gresham, *Medieval Stone Carving in North Wales*, pp. 184–6.

[104] For an excellent translation of the 'chivalric' tales see *The Mabinogion*, trans. Sioned Davies (Oxford: Oxford University Press, 2007). Professor Davies also provides a very interesting introduction. She argues that the description of *Peredur son of Efrog*, *Geraint son of Erbin*, and *The Lady of the Well* as 'the Three Romances' (*Y Tair Rhamant*) is unhelpful (p. xi). But she discusses the three tales together, and uses them as the basis for the suggestion (p. xxiv) that 'Wales accepted certain themes prevalent in the romance tradition, such as the education of the knight, and moderation between love and military prowess, however other features were rejected as being too foreign, culminating in three hybrid texts, typical of a post-colonial world.' For the other works mentioned see Erich Poppe and Regine Reck (eds), *Selections from Ystorya Bown o Hamtwn* (Cardiff: University of Wales Press, 2009), for which the editors accept a date in the second half of the thirteenth century, and *Welsh Walter of Henley*, ed. Alexander Falileyev (Dublin: Institute of Advanced Studies, 2006), which may have a fourteenth-century origin. There was certainly a readership, and an audience, for books amongst the leaders of Welsh society: amongst the possessions of Llywelyn Bren, the lordly rebel of 1316, was a *Roman de la Rose* and six other books, three in Welsh: J. Beverley Smith, 'The rebellion of Llywelyn Bren', in Pugh (ed.), *Glamorgan County History, Vol. III*, pp. 72–86, at p. 85.

[105] See ch. 3 above.

[106] *Record of Caernarvon*, p. 214.

[107] Smith, 'Edward II and the allegiance of Wales', 149 and n. 48.

[108] *CCR, 1313–18*, p. 253; Griffiths, *Principality of Wales*, p. 87.

[109] Natalie Fryde, *List of Welsh Entries in the Memoranda Rolls* (Cardiff: University of Wales Press, 1974), p. 54; *CChR, 1300–26*, p. 125; *Calendar of Inquisitions Post Mortem*, V (*Edward II*), p. 107.

[110] *Calendar of Fine Rolls, 1319–27*, pp. 91–2.

[111] Griffiths, *Principality of Wales*, p. 98.

[112] *Calendar of Fine Rolls, 1327–37*, p. 19; *CPR, 1327–30*, pp. 72–3, 273.

[113] Davies, *Lordship and Society*, pp. 205, 291.

[114] *CPR, 1292–1301*, pp. 290–1 and see below in the present chapter.

[115] *CCR, 1296–1302*, p. 44.

116 *CChR, 1300–26*, p. 6; *CPR, 1292–1301*, p. 598; *CPR, 1307–13*, p. 80.

117 *CCR, 1296–1302*, p. 603.

118 *Calendar of Fine Rolls, 1307–19*, pp. 46, 58, 76, 188. Philip appears as bailiff of Builth in 1315: Fryde, *List of Welsh Entries in the Memoranda Rolls*, p. 35.

119 *CCR, 1313–18*, p. 253.

120 *CCR, 1313–18*, p. 270.

121 *CCR, 1330–33*, pp. 345, 350, 461.

122 *CPR, 1321–24*, p. 18.

123 *CCR, 1318–23*, pp. 458, 582.

124 See Francis Jones, 'The subsidy of 1292', *BBCS*, 13 (1948–50), 210–30, at 221.

125 Ieuan was succeeded as steward of Cardiganshire by no less a person than Sir Rhys ap Gruffudd, who held the office 'in the same way as Ieuan ap Moelwyn held it': *CCR, 1313–18*, p. 408.

126 *Calendar of Inquisitions Post Mortem*, II (*Edward I*), p. 164, no. 289.

127 *Littere Wallie*, pp. 75, 133.

128 *CACW*, p. 20.

129 The case is examined by J. G. Edwards, 'The treason of Thomas Turberville', in R. W. Hunt, W. A. Pantin and R. W. Southern (eds), *Studies in Medieval History presented to F. M. Powicke* (Oxford: Clarendon Press, 1948), pp. 296–309.

130 Edwards, 'Treason', pp. 298, 302.

131 Edwards, 'Treason', p. 308.

132 Smith, 'Edward II and the allegiance of Wales', 142, n. 16.

133 *CACW*, p. 101, where the letter is misdated to 1321–2. The incident is discussed by Davies, *Lordship and Society*, pp. 268–9, who reaches the conclusion that Morgan was acting as an agent provocateur.

134 Constance Bullock-Davies, *Menestrellorum Multitudo* (Cardiff: University of Wales Press, 1978), p. 186.

135 Smith, 'Edward II and the allegiance of Wales', 150.

136 *CCR, 1313–18*, p. 256; *CPR, 1313–17*, pp. 433–4. The concessions to the men of north Wales included freedom for three years to alienate lands, thereby removing a prohibition that had been maintained since the 1280s.

137 *Calendar of Inquisitions post Mortem*, VIII (*Edward III*), p. 247, no. 329.

138 *CACW*, p. 48.

139 See Smith, 'Edward II and the allegiance of Wales', 139–43. See also A. D. Carr, 'Lineage, power and land in medieval Flintshire: the descendants of Ithel Fychan', *Flintshire Historical Society Journal*, 36 (2003), 59–81, at 81 notes that 'the period between the Edwardian conquest and the outbreak of the Glyn Dŵr [rising] is sometimes seen as a time when the Welsh were oppressed by alien officials … this belief over-simplifies a complex social and cultural milieu'.

140 For the succession to the episcopate in Bangor diocese see B. Jones, *Fasti Ecclesiae Anglicanae 1300–1541 Volume 11, The Welsh Dioceses* (London: Institute of Historical Research, 1965), pp. 3–5.

141 For Anian II of St Asaph and his successor, Llywelyn of Bromfield see M. J. Pearson, *Fasti Ecclesiae Anglicanae 1066–1300, Volume 9: The Welsh Cathedrals* (London: Institute of Historical Research, 2003), p. 36 and for a study of the

former, T. Jones Pierce, 'Einion ap Ynyr bishop of St Asaph', *Flintshire Historical Society Publications*, 17 (1957), 16–33. For the chronicler's obituary see *ByT Pen. 20 Trans.*, p. 121 (1292).

142 Jones, *Fasti*, pp. 37–9.

143 See Jones, *Fasti*, pp. 8–11, 43–4 and Pearson, *Fasti*, pp. 5–8, 38–9.

144 Jones, *Fasti*, p. 61 and Pearson, *Fasti*, p. 56.

145 See, for example, the identifications of Cistercian abbots made by Williams, *The Welsh Cistercians*, pp. 295–8.

146 See Smith, 'Rebellion of Llywelyn Bren', p. 82 for the names of some of the Welsh who did not join the rising. The list is headed by Morgan ap Maredudd.

147 Smith, 'Rebellion of Llywelyn Bren', p. 75.

148 Craig Owen Jones, *Llywelyn Bren* (Llanrwst: Gwasg Carreg Gwalch, 2006), p. 47.

149 *CACW*, p. 68.

150 *CCR, 1323–7*, p. 582; *CCR, 1321–4*, p. 77; *Calendar of Fine Rolls, 1319–27*, pp. 100, 189; Smith, 'Edward II and the allegiance of Wales', 158.

151 Smith, 'Rebellion of Llywelyn Bren', p. 86.

152 Roy Martin Haines, *King Edward II* (Montreal and Kingston: McGill-Queen's University Press, 2003), p. 184.

153 *CCR, 1323–7*, p. 622; *CCR, 1327–30*, p. 121; *CPR, 1327–30*, p. 66.

154 David Stephenson, 'Crisis and continuity in a fourteenth-century Welsh lordship: the struggle for Powys, 1312–32', *CMCS*, 66 (2013), 57–78.

155 See R. Iestyn Daniel (ed.), *Gwaith Dafydd Bach ap Madog Wladaidd 'Sypyn Cyfeiliog' a Llywelyn ab y Moel* (Aberystwyth: Centre for Advanced Welsh and Celtic Studies, 1998), pp. 13–14; there is important editorial comment at pp. 41–3.

156 Ann Parry Owen (ed.), *Gwaith Llywelyn Brydydd Hoddnant, Dafydd ap Gwilym, Hillyn ac Eraill* (Aberystwyth: Centre for Advanced Welsh and Celtic Studies, 1996), p. 134 (9.12).

ENVOI

1 David Stephenson, 'The Continuation of *Brut y Tywysogyon* in NLW Peniarth MS 20 re-visited', in Ben Guy, Owain Wyn Jones and Georgia Henley (eds), *The Chronicles of Medieval Wales and the March: New Contexts, Studies and Texts* (Turnhout: Brepols, forthcoming).

2 The rise of such a powerful official class was of course not unique to Wales. Thus Alice Taylor has discussed the way in which Scottish kings were able to consolidate their authority by granting lands and offices to local magnates, who in turn were able to use such offices and royal favour to buttress their own power: Alice Taylor, *The Shape of the State in Medieval Scotland, 1124–1290* (Oxford: Oxford University Press, 2016).

3 *ByT Pen. 20 Trans.*, p. 126, and see ch. 5 above.

4 See David Stephenson, 'Crisis and continuity in a fourteenth-century Welsh lordship: the struggle for Powys, 1312–32', *CMCS*, 66 (2013), 57–78.

5 See ch. 5 above, and Constance Bullock-Davies, *Menestrellorum Multitudo* (Cardiff: University of Wales Press, 1979), pp. 184–7.

6 See ch. 5 above.

[7] See ch. 5 above.

[8] Bartrum, *Welsh Genealogies*, 3, Rhys ap Tewdwr 4.

[9] Bartrum, *Welsh Genealogies*, 1, Bleddyn ap Cynfyn 30.

[10] See ch. 1 above.

[11] See A. D. Carr, *Owen of Wales: the End of the House of Gwynedd* (Cardiff: University of Wales Press, 1991), especially chapter VI.

[12] R. R. Davies, *The Revolt of Owain Glyn Dŵr* (Oxford: Oxford University Press, 1995), especially chapters 2 and 3.

[13] See chs 3 and 5 above.

[14] See Stephenson, 'Empires in Wales', 37–8 for examples.

[15] See ch. 2 above, and for the mendicants see Janet Burton and Karen Stöber, *Abbeys and Priories of Medieval Wales* (Cardiff: University of Wales Press, 2015), pp. 15–18, 41–2, 61, 68–9, 75–6, 106, 114–15, 172–3.

[16] See chs 4 and 5 above.

[17] See ch. 5 above.

SELECT BIBLIOGRAPHY

The following is not intended to be a comprehensive survey of writing on the subject. It is confined to listing essential major works, particularly editions of primary sources, and also those secondary studies produced in recent decades that are likely to have a significant influence on future work on, and thinking about, the subject.

1. EDITIONS AND DISCUSSIONS OF PRIMARY SOURCES

a) Chronicles. The editions of the Welsh vernacular chronicles *Brut y Tywysogion* and *Brenhinedd y Saesson*, and the Welsh Latin chronicle *Cronica de Wallia* (more correctly *Cronicon de Wallia*) produced by Thomas Jones are the basis for all subsequent study. To these must be added the splendid editions of the Latin texts known as *Annales Cambriae*, supplied by Henry Gough-Cooper. These, together with full bibliographies of editions and secondary scholarship can be found on the website of the *Welsh Chronicles Research Group*, located at *croniclau.bangor.ac.uk* (accessed 3 January 2018).

b) Biography. Paul Russell (ed.), *Vita Griffini filii Conani* (Cardiff: University of Wales Press, 2005) is not a chronicle, but rather a (unique) near-contemporary biography of a Welsh ruler. The life of Gruffudd ap Cynan exists in a thirteenth-century Welsh version. It was known that this was derived from an original Latin text, which was thought to be lost, until Paul Russell succeeded, in a brilliant piece of scholarship, in re-constructing it from a sixteenth-century copy.

c) Charters, letters, etc. Huw Pryce (ed., with the assistance of Charles Insley), *The Acts of Welsh Rulers, 1120–1283* (Cardiff: University of Wales Press, 2005) is a work of the highest scholarship, and contains an introductory section that probes many aspects of political, administrative and diplomatic history of the period. It deals only with the *acta* of rulers, so that it is still necessary to turn to other collections of material to find charters and letters of individual freemen or those issued in the name of Welsh communities. Some such material is to be found in the great collection of materials relating to Glamorgan: G. T. Clark (ed.), *Cartae et alia munimenta quae ad dominium de Glamorgancia pertinent*, 6 vols (2nd edn, Cardiff: n.p., 1910), in G. C. G. Thomas (ed.), *Charters of the abbey of Ystrad Marchell* (Aberystwyth, 1997), and in such volumes as J. G. Edwards (ed.), *A Calendar of Ancient Correspondence concerning Wales* (Cardiff: University of Wales Press, 1935), and William Rees (ed.), *A Calendar of Ancient Petitions relating to Wales* (Cardiff: University of Wales Press, 1975). But many documents are still unpublished, or scattered through volumes of the transactions of county societies. The collection of the charters issued by those who were not rulers but were persons of influence constitutes a challenging task for future scholars.

d) Law texts. The single most effective introduction to native Welsh law (Cyfraith Hywel or Hywel's Law) is Dafydd Jenkins (ed. and trans.), *The Law of Hywel Dda. Law texts from Medieval* Wales (Llandysul: Gomer Press, 1986). This contains not only a text of Welsh law, but extensive notes and a bibliography. But the most helpful source of information about Welsh law is now the website of *Seminar Cyfraith Hywel*, located at *cyfraith-hywel.cymru.ac.uk* (accessed 12 December 2017). This is a real treasury of texts, commentaries and bibliographic information.

e) Poetry. The court poems of the Age of the Princes have been edited with great skill in the series of volumes published in seven volumes under the auspices of the Centre for Advanced Welsh and Celtic Studies, Aberystwyth: *Cyfres Beirdd y Tywysogion* (Cardiff: University of Wales Press, 1991–6). For the post-conquest period another, and much longer series of editions, *Cyfres Beirdd yr Uchelwyr*, provide sound texts and valuable introductions and notes to the poetry composed for the *uchelwyr*, the 'gentry'. The careful integration into the political history of the post-conquest generations of the poetry produced for the *uchelwyr* promises to add much to our knowledge. A very useful introduction to the poetry of the princes is provided by Rhian M. Andrews, *Welsh Court Poems* (Cardiff: University of Wales Press, 2007).

f) Prose literature. A very good introduction to the Mabinogion is provided by Sioned Davies (trans.), *The Mabinogion* (Oxford: Oxford University

Press, 2007). This volume contains an effective introduction and a useful bibliography of editions and critical studies. Erich Poppe and Regine Reck (eds), *Selections from Ystorya Bown o Hamtwn* (Cardiff: University of Wales Press, 2009) is a useful introduction to that text, which was probably translated into Welsh in the second half of the thirteenth century. Alexander Falileyev (ed.), *Welsh Walter of Henley* (Dublin: Institute for Advanced Studies, 2006), contains not only a very well-edited text, but also an important introduction.

g) Genealogical materials. These are important and numerous, but often survive in manuscripts that are much later in date than the period covered by this book. The genealogical texts are also often problematic, often betraying the inventiveness of the pedigree-compilers. The work of making sense of the huge amount of genealogical material relating to medieval Wales was done by Peter Bartrum, amongst whose publications the eight volumes of *Welsh Genealogies A.D. 300–1400* (Cardiff: University of Wales Press, 1974) was a landmark. The work of Bartrum, with revisions and additions, is now available online, as a result of a project developed in the Department of Welsh in Aberystwyth University. It is located at *cadair. aber.ac.uk/dspace/handle/2160/4026* (accessed 14 November 2017).

SECONDARY LITERATURE
General surveys

Two works are of outstanding importance:

J. E. Lloyd, *A History of Wales from the Earliest Times to the Edwardian Conquest*, 2 vols with continuous pagination (3rd edn; London, 1939). The first volume is now so outdated as to be unreliable, but the second volume, covering the period from the arrival of the Normans to 1282 remains an essential work of reference. For a penetrating study of Lloyd's contribution, see Huw Pryce, *J. E. Lloyd and the Creation of Welsh History* (Cardiff: University of Wales Press, 2011).

R. R. Davies, *The Age of Conquest: Wales 1063–1415* (Oxford: Oxford University Press, 2000). (Originally published as *Conquest, Coexistence and Change: Wales 1063–1415* (Oxford: Oxford University Press, 1987)). This contains less chronological narrative and more analysis than Lloyd's work, and includes a very comprehensive bibliography.

Amongst shorter survey volumes the following are well worth consulting:

A. D. Carr, *Medieval Wales* (London: Macmillan, 1995), dealing with the period from the arrival of the Normans to the reign of Henry VII.

David Walker, *Medieval Wales* (Cambridge: Cambridge University Press, 1990), covering developments from the post-Roman period to the late fifteenth century.

There has in addition been a significant amount of published work focused on specific topics. Only the more significant work published since 2000 is included here. For previously published work the bibliography in Davies, *Age of Conquest* should be consulted. Where articles in journals have subsequently been substantially incorporated in books by the same author, only the books have been included.

Political and governmental history

Carpenter, D. A., 'Dafydd ap Llywelyn's submission to King Henry III in October 1241: a new perspective', *WHR*, 23 (2007), 1–12.

——, 'Confederation not domination: Welsh political culture in the age of Gwynedd imperialism', in R. A. Griffiths and P. R. Schofield (eds), *Wales and the Welsh in the Middle Ages* (Cardiff: University of Wales Press, 2011), pp. 20–8.

Hurlock, Kathryn, 'Counselling the prince: advice and counsel in thirteenth-century Welsh society', *History*, 94 (2009), 20–35.

Insley, Charles, 'From Rex Wallie to Princeps Wallie: charters and state formation in thirteenth century Wales', in J. R. Maddicott and D. M. Palliser (eds), *The Medieval state. Essays presented to James Campbell* (London: The Hambledon Press, 2000), pp. 179–96.

——, 'The wilderness years of Llywelyn the Great', in Michael Prestwich, Richard Britnell and Robin Frame (eds), *Thirteenth Century England XI* (Woodbridge: Boydell Press, 2003), pp. 163–73.

——, 'Kings, lords, charters, and the political culture of twelfth-century Wales', *Anglo-Norman Studies*, 30 (Woodbridge: Boydell Press, 2008), pp. 133–53.

Pryce, Huw, 'Negotiating Anglo-Welsh relations: Llywelyn the Great and Henry III', in B. K. U. Weiler with I. W. Rowlands (eds), *England and Europe in the Reign of Henry III* (Aldershot: Ashgate Publishing, 2002), pp. 13–29.

——, 'Welsh rulers and European change, *c*.1100–1282', in Huw Pryce and John Watts (eds), *Power and Identity in the Middle Ages: Essays in Memory of Rees Davies* (Oxford: Oxford University Press, 2007), pp. 37–51.

——, 'Anglo-Welsh agreements, 1201–77', in R. A. Griffiths and P. R. Schofield (eds), *Wales and the Welsh in the Middle Ages* (Cardiff: University of Wales Press, 2011), pp. 1–19.

Stephenson, David, *Political Power in Medieval Gwynedd: Governance and the Welsh Princes* (Cardiff: University of Wales Press, 2014). This volume was originally published as *The Governance of Gwynedd* in 1984; the present version includes a new introductory section dealing with relevant studies in the subject since it first appeared.

——, 'Empires in Wales: from Gruffudd ap Llywelyn to Llywelyn ap Gruffudd', *WHR*, 28 (2016), 26–54.

——, 'New light on a dark deed: the death of Llywelyn ap Gruffudd, prince of Wales', *Archaeologia Cambrensis*, 166 (2017), 243–52.

Problems of Welsh 'identity'

Davies, R. R., 'The identity of "Wales" in the thirteenth century', in R. R. Davies and Geraint J. Jenkins (eds), *From Medieval to Modern Wales* (Cardiff: University of Wales Press, 2004), pp. 45–63.

Pryce, Huw, 'British or Welsh? National identity in twelfth-century Wales', *EHR*, 116 (2001), 777–801.

Roberts, Euryn R., 'Mental geographies and literary convention: the poets of the Welsh princes and the polities and provinces of medieval Wales', *Studia Celtica*, 46 (2012), 85–110.

The poets of the princes and the politics of the twelfth and thirteenth centuries

Andrews, Rhian M., 'The nomenclature of kingship in Welsh court poetry, 1100–1300. Part I: the terms', *Studia Celtica*, 44 (2010), 79–109.

——, 'The nomenclature of kingship in Welsh court poetry, 1100–1300. Part II: the rulers', *Studia Celtica*, 45 (2011), 53–82.

——, 'Y bardd yn llysgennad, rhan I: Llywarch Brydydd y Moch yn Neheubarth', *Dwned*, 20 (2014), 11–30.

——, 'Y bardd yn llysgennad, rhan II: Bleddyn Fardd yn Neheubarth', *Dwned*, 21 (2015), 49–68.

Studies of regional polities

Carr, A. D., *Medieval Anglesey* (2nd edn; Llangefni: Anglesey Antiquarian Society, 2011).

Stephenson, David, 'Conquerors, courtiers and careerists: the struggle for supremacy in Brycheiniog, 1093–1282', *Brycheiniog*, 44 (2013), 27–51.

——, *Medieval Powys: Kingdom, Principality and Lordships, 1132–1293* (Woodbridge: Boydell and Brewer, 2016).

In addition, some recent county history volumes dealing with the medieval period are important:

Griffiths, Ralph A., Tony Hopkins and Ray Howell (eds), *The Gwent County History, Volume 2: The Age of the Marcher Lords, c.1070–1536* (Cardiff: University of Wales Press, 2008).

Smith, J. Beverley and Llinos Beverley Smith (eds), *History of Merioneth Volume II: The Middle Ages* (Cardiff: University of Wales Press, 2001).

Walker, R. F. (ed.), *Pembrokeshire County History Volume II: Medieval Pembrokeshire* (Haverfordwest: Pembrokeshire Historical Society, 2002).

The March

The standard discussion of the development of the March in the late thirteenth and fourteenth centuries is still R. R. Davies, *Lordship and Society in the March of Wales 1282–1400* (Oxford: Oxford University Press, 1978). More recent work has focused on the twelfth and thirteenth centuries, especially the following:

Holden, Brock, *Lords of the Central Marches: English Aristocracy and Frontier Society 1087–1265* (Oxford: Oxford University Press, 2008).

Lieberman, Max, *The March of Wales 1067–1300* (Cardiff: University of Wales Press, 2008).

——, *The Medieval March of Wales. The Creation and Perception of a Frontier, 1066–1283* (Cambridge: Cambridge University Press, 2010).

Power, Daniel, 'The Briouze family in the thirteenth and early fourteenth centuries: inheritance strategies, lordship and identity', *Journal of Medieval History*, 41, 3 (2015), 341–61.

Suppe, Frederick, 'Interpreter families and Anglo-Welsh relations in the Shropshire–Powys Marches in the twelfth century', *Anglo-Norman Studies*, 30 (Woodbridge: Boydell Press, 2008) pp. 196–212.

The emergence of the gentry

Carr, A. D., *The Gentry of North Wales in the Later Middle Ages* (Cardiff: University of Wales Press, 2017).

Ecclesiastical and monastic history

Davies, J. R., *The Book of Llandaf and the Norman Church in Wales* (Woodbridge: Boydell Press, 2003).

Petts, David, *The Early Medieval Church in Wales* (Stroud: The History Press, 2009).

Thurlby, Malcolm, *Romanesque Architecture and Sculpture in Wales* (Almeley: Logaston Press, 2006).

In the field of monastic studies, David H. Williams, *The Welsh Cistercians* (Leominster: Gracewing, 2001) remains very valuable as a summary of the very significant contribution of the author to Cistercian studies. More recently, monastic studies in Wales have been driven forward by the Monastic Wales project. There is much useful material on the project's very substantial website, at *www.monasticwales.org* (accessed 7 August 2017). The project has also given rise to some important books, notably the following:

Burton, Janet and Karen Stöber (eds), *Monastic Wales: New Approaches* (Cardiff: University of Wales Press, 2013).

—— and ——, *Abbeys and Priories of Medieval Wales* (Cardiff: University of Wales Press, 2015).

On a topic that cuts across the boundaries of religious, political and cultural history, the following work is important:

Hurlock, Kathryn, *Wales and the Crusades c.1095–1291* (Cardiff: University of Wales Press, 2011).

Biographical studies

One biography stands out. J. Beverley Smith, *Llywelyn ap Gruffudd, Prince of Wales* (2nd edn; Cardiff: University of Wales Press, 2014). Originally published in 1998, this edition contains an updated bibliography.

There are several recent biographies of Welsh rulers, which are aimed at a general audience, but are well researched and securely based on both the original sources and on the secondary literature. These include:

Davies, Michael and Sean Davies, *The Last King of Wales: Gruffudd ap Llywelyn c. 1013–1063* (Stroud: History Press, 2012).

Davies, Sean, *The First Prince of Wales? Bleddyn ap Cynfyn, 1063–75* (Cardiff: University of Wales Press, 2016).

Turvey, Roger, *The Lord Rhys* (Llandysul: Gomer Press, 1997).

——, *Llywelyn the Great* (Llandysul: Gomer Press, 2007).

——, *Owain Gwynedd: Prince of the Welsh* (Talybont: Y Lolfa, 2013).

Accessible and sound studies of some of the rebel leaders of 1294–5 and 1316, and of the risings which they led, are provided by

Jones, Craig Owen, *Llywelyn Bren* (Llanrwst: Gwasg Carreg Gwalch, 2006).

——, *The Revolt of Madog ap Llywelyn* (Pwllheli: Llygad Gwalch, 2008).

Military history and castle studies

Brodie, Hugh, 'Apsidal and D-shaped towers of the princes of Gwynedd', *Archaeologia Cambrensis*, 164 (2015), 231–43.

Chapman, Adam, *Welsh Soldiers in the Later Middle Ages, 1282–1422* (Woodbridge: Boydell Press, 2015).

Davies, Sean, *War and Society in Medieval Wales, 633–1283: Welsh Military Institutions* (Cardiff: University of Wales Press, 2014).

Williams, Diane M. and John R. Kenyon (eds), *The Impact of the Edwardian Castles in Wales* (Oxford: Oxbow Books, 2010).

The role of women

Cavell, Emma, 'Welsh princes, English wives: the politics of Powys Wenwynwyn revisited', *WHR*, 27 (2014), 214–52.

——, 'Intelligence and intrigue in the March of Wales: noblewomen and the fall of Llywelyn ap Gruffudd, 1274–82', *Historical Research*, 88 (2015), 1–19.

——, 'Emma d'Audley and the clash of laws in thirteenth-century northern Powys', in Patricia Skinner (ed.), *The Welsh and the Medieval World: Travel, Migration and Exile* (Cardiff: University of Wales Press, 2018), pp. 49–73.

——, 'Widows, native law and the long shadow of England in thirteenth-century Wales', *EHR* (forthcoming).

Johns, Susan M., *Gender, Nation and Conquest in the High Middle Ages: Nest of Deheubarth* (Manchester: Manchester University Press, 2013).

Richards, Gwenyth, *Welsh Noblewomen in the Thirteenth Century: A Historical Study of Medieval Welsh Law and Gender Roles* (Lampeter: Edwin Mellen Press, 2009).

Wilkinson, Louise J., 'Joan, wife of Llywelyn the Great', in Michael Prestwich, Richard Britnell and Robin Frame (eds), *Thirteenth Century England*, X (Woodbridge: Boydell Press, 2005), pp. 81–93.

Sigillography

Schofield, P. R. and E. A. New (eds, with S. M. Johns and J. A. McEwan), *Seals and Society: Medieval Wales, the Welsh Marches and their Border Region* (Cardiff: University of Wales Press, 2016). See also the review article by David Stephenson, 'Seals in Medieval Wales', *Archaeologia Cambrensis*, 166 (2017), 223–31.

A brief but useful study is David H. Williams, *Images of Welsh History: Seals of the National Library of Wales* (Aberystwyth: National Library of Wales, 2007).

Urban history

Dyer, Christopher, 'Modern perspectives on medieval Welsh towns', in R. A. Griffiths and P. R. Schofield (eds), *Wales and the Welsh in the Middle Ages* (Cardiff: University of Wales Press, 2011), pp. 163–79.

Fulton, Helen (ed.), *Urban Culture in Medieval Wales* (Cardiff: University of Wales Press, 2012).

Stevens, Matthew Frank, *Urban Assimilation in Post-conquest Wales: Ethnicity, Gender and Economy in Ruthin, 1282–1348* (Cardiff: University of Wales Press, 2010). This is a careful and thought-provoking study, sharply focused, but with wide implications.

The visual arts

Lord, Peter, *The Visual Culture of Wales: Medieval Vision* (Cardiff: University of Wales Press, 2003) provides an excellent and wide-ranging introduction.

INDEX